Who's Afraid of James Joyce?

THE FLORIDA JAMES JOYCE SERIES

UNIVERSITY PRESS OF FLORIDA

Florida A&M University, Tallahassee
Florida Atlantic University, Boca Raton
Florida Gulf Coast University, Ft. Myers
Florida International University, Miami
Florida State University, Tallahassee
New College of Florida, Sarasota
University of Central Florida, Orlando
University of Florida, Gainesville
University of North Florida, Jacksonville
University of South Florida, Tampa
University of West Florida, Pensacola

WHO'S AFRAID OF JAMES JOYCE?

Karen R. Lawrence

FOREWORD BY SEBASTIAN D. G. KNOWLES, SERIES EDITOR

University Press of Florida
Gainesville · Tallahassee · Tampa · Boca Raton
Pensacola · Orlando · Miami · Jacksonville · Ft. Myers · Sarasota

Copyright 2010 by Karen R. Lawrence
All rights reserved
Printed in the United States of America on acid-free paper. This book is printed on Glatfelter Natures Book, a paper certified under the standards of the Forestry Stewardship Council (FSC). It is a recycled stock that contains 30 percent post-consumer waste and is acid-free.

First cloth printing, 2010
First paperback printing, 2012

Library of Congress Cataloging-in-Publication Data
Lawrence, Karen, 1949–
Who's afraid of James Joyce? / Karen R. Lawrence ; foreword by Sebastian D. G. Knowles, series editor.
p. cm.—(The Florida James Joyce series)
Includes bibliographical references and index.
ISBN 978-0-8130-3477-5 (cloth: alk. paper)
ISBN 978-0-8130-4168-1 (pbk.)
1. Joyce, James, 1882–1941—Criticism and interpretation. I. Title.
PR6019.O9Z6935 2010
823'.912—dc22
2009051042

The University Press of Florida is the scholarly publishing agency for the State University System of Florida, comprising Florida A&M University, Florida Atlantic University, Florida Gulf Coast University, Florida International University, Florida State University, New College of Florida, University of Central Florida, University of Florida, University of North Florida, University of South Florida, and University of West Florida.

University Press of Florida
15 Northwest 15th Street
Gainesville, FL 32611-2079
http://www.upf.com

Contents

Foreword   vii
Acknowledgments   ix
List of Abbreviations   xi
Living with Joyce: Grand Passion and Small Pleasures   1

Part I. Retracing *The Odyssey of Style*   13

1. The Narrative Norm   15
2. "Wandering Rocks" and "Sirens": The Breakdown of Narrative   27
3. "Eumaeus": The Way of All Language   42
4. "Ithaca": The Order of Things   53

Part II. Compromising Letters: Joyce, Women, and Feminism   69

5. Joyce and Feminism   71
6. Women Building the Foundation   90

Part III. Bloom in Circulation: Navigating Identifications   97

7. "Eumaeus" Redux   99
8. Legal Fiction or Pulp Fiction in "Lestrygonians"   119
9. "Twenty Pockets Arent Enough For Their Lies": Pocketed Objects as Props of Bloom's Masculinity in *Ulysses*   132
10. Bloom in Circulation: Who's He When He's Not at Home?   140

Part IV. Close Encounters: Hospitality and the Other   151

11. Close Encounters   153
12. Joyce in Transit   168

Part V. Return to Dublin   181

13. Reopening "A Painful Case"   183
    Karen R. Lawrence and Paul K. Saint-Amour

Notes   203
Bibliography   223
Index   235

Foreword

How daring is "Telemachus"? Karen Lawrence rightly scoffs at the "risks" that the narrator takes in the first episode, comparing the adverbial intrusions to "a clown walking a tightrope only one foot above the ground." But as *Ulysses* progresses Joyce is provoked to more and more elaborate circus acts, leading to the double high-wire display in "Ithaca," where questioner and answerer pass the trapeze from one hand to the other, high among the stars. If *Ulysses* is a three-ring circus, and it has long been recognized as such, then Karen Lawrence must be our ringmaster. Watching Karen Lawrence put the narrator through his paces in the sawdust of "Circe" and "Eumaeus," one feels the same delight of an audience watching a lion dancing in the ring: the only thing missing is ice cream (from Rabaiotti's, perhaps).

Lawrence's term for the ponderous stylistics of "Telemachus" is "adverbial mania": an excellent coinage in a book full of *mots* and *phrases justes*. Lawrence calls the figuration of women in Joyce's life and work a "skirtscreen," another wonderfully felicitous phrase extracted from *Finnegans Wake*'s "squirtscreened." In Lawrence's convincing formulation, "Penelope" represents the problem of female representation by the male pen, "a staging of alterity that reveals itself as masquerade." Always and everywhere, Karen Lawrence has her ear to the ground of Joyce's text, hearing echoes that we can only guess at. When Mrs Sinico exclaims, "What a pity there is such a poor house tonight!," the reader could be forgiven for thinking it a stray remark that happens to catch her neighbor's sympathy: in "Reopening 'A Painful Case,'" Karen Lawrence and Paul Saint-Amour show us that Mrs Sinico's statement is the opening salvo in a carefully calculated assault on Mr Duffy's defenses.

"The drama of the writing usurps the dramatic act," the telling trumps the tale: so it is for Lawrence's Joyce, and in Lawrence Joyce has found his perfect reader, for in matters of style she is very nearly unmatched. Many of her readings achieve an ideal state of syntactic equilibrium, a Johnsonian balance. Take, for example, the discussion of Bloom's purchased kidney in "Calypso": "The sensuous symmetry between the gland sliding into his pocket and his own coins sliding quickly into the till conveys the tactile, even sexual, pleasure that Bloom derives from his role in commodity culture, in the rituals of buying and selling." In the space of one short sentence, "sensuous symmetry" is placed in alliterative parallel with "commodity culture," the gland slides into Bloom's pocket in syntactic parallel with the coin sliding quickly into the till (with a slight stretto in the metallic slide), and "tactile" is given a second accent with "even sexual," a double climax that allows a double fall into "the rituals of buying and selling." And all in honor of Joyce's own symmetries: "They lay, were read quickly and quickly slid, disc by disc, into the till." One is left with the inescapable impression that Karen Lawrence, like Joyce, is incapable of writing a dull or unmusical line.

There are other delights in *Who's Afraid of James Joyce?* The narrative of "Eveline," set against the author's own indecision at a crucial stage in her career, had this reader on the edge of his seat. "Women Building the Foundation" is a review of the progress of feminist studies of Joyce by one who was there, while "Joyce and Feminism" is a sharp and sophisticated rebuttal to Gilbert and Gubar's "refusal to be Mollified" by the special pleadings on behalf of feminist Joyceans. This is a fine set of essays, moving steadily from gender and sexuality to empathy and hospitality, radiating outward into a full engagement with Joyce's work. In a triumphant return to the work and the author that launched her spectacular career, Karen Lawrence gives us a masterly balancing act: a peek behind the curtain of Joyce's theatrical effects, and a rich defense of the humanity of Joyce.

Sebastian D. G. Knowles
Series Editor

Acknowledgments

I am grateful to the publishers or periodicals listed below for permission to reprint the following essays:

Chapters 1–4 were previously published as part of Karen Lawrence, *The Odyssey of Style in "Ulysses"* (Princeton: Princeton University Press, 1981).

"Joyce and Feminism" was previously published in *The Cambridge Companion to James Joyce*, ed. Derek Attridge (Cambridge: Cambridge University Press, 1990: 237–58).

"Women Building the Foundation" was first published as "Building on the Foundation: Women in the IJJF," by Karen Lawrence, in *Joyce Studies Annual* Volume 2001, pp. 163–71. Copyright 2001 by the University of Texas Press. All rights reserved.

"Eumaeus Redux" was first published as "'Beggaring Description': Politics and Style in Joyce's 'Eumaeus,'" in *Modern Fiction Studies* 38.2 (Summer 1992): 355–76.

"Legal Fiction or Pulp Fiction in 'Lestrygonians'" was previously published in *Ulysses En-Gendered Perspectives: Eighteen New Critical Essays on the Episodes*, ed. Kimberly Devlin and Marilyn Reizbaum (Columbia: University of South Carolina Press, 1999: 100–110).

"'Twenty Pockets Arent Enough For Their Lies'" was previously published as "'Twenty Pockets Arent Enough For Their Lies': Pocketed Objects as Props of Bloom's Masculinity in *Ulysses*," in *Masculinities in Joyce: Postcolonial Constructions. European Joyce Studies*, 10, eds. Christine Van Boheemen-Saaf and Colleen Lamos: 163–76.

"Bloom in Circulation: Who's He When He's Not at Home?" was first published in *Joyce on the Threshold*, eds. Anne Fogerty and Timothy Martin (Gainesville: University Press of Florida, 2005: 15–27).

"Close Encounters" was first published in the *James Joyce Quarterly*, vol. 41, 1–2, Fall 2003–Winter 2004: 127–42.

"Joyce in Transit" is a revised version of the Introduction: "Metempsychotic Joyce" and chapter "In Transit: From James Joyce to Brigid Brophy" in *Transcultural Joyce*, ed. Karen R. Lawrence (Cambridge: Cambridge University Press, 1998).

"Reopening 'A Painful Case,'" co-authored with Paul K. Saint-Amour, has not been published previously.

Abbreviations

D	*Dubliners*
FW	*Finnegans Wake*
GJ	*Giacomo Joyce*
JJ	*James Joyce* by Richard Ellmann
JJII	*James Joyce* by Richard Ellmann, revised edition
Letters	*Letters of James Joyce (Volume I, II, or III)*
P	*A Portrait of the Artist as a Young Man*
SH	*Stephen Hero*
SL	*Selected Letters of James Joyce*
U	*Ulysses*

Living with Joyce

Grand Passion and Small Pleasures

At the International James Joyce Symposium in Dublin in 2004, I participated on a panel called "Living with Joyce," chaired by Derek Attridge. He had assembled a group of inveterate Joyceans that included academics who had been teaching, writing about, and studying Joyce for many years; some in the group, I am happy to say, were even older than I. At least one person on the panel was actually related to Joyce—Kenneth Monaghan, Joyce's nephew, who directed the James Joyce Centre in Dublin.

Although I had read *A Portrait of the Artist as a Young Man* in high school, I consider that I have "lived with Joyce" for about thirty-five years, ever since I was exposed to *Ulysses* as an undergraduate in a course in college. I remember being bowled over by the originality and richness of the novel when we finally came to it at the end of a course on epic literature that included the *Odyssey*, the *Aeneid*, the *Inferno*, and *Don Quixote*. As we read *Ulysses*, the framework of the epic gave us something to hold on to, a useful tool for confronting the novel's bewildering barrage of detail so difficult to organize through the normal reading process. One of two survey requirements for English majors at Yale, the course was divided into lectures and sections—two lectures a week taught by specialists of each text and a smaller section taught by a different professor. The talks were riveting; each professor gave a masterful performance that built on the context provided by his or her (mostly his) predecessors in the study of the genre of the epic. I came to understand that all of the speakers were untenured assistant professors, at a time when no one was getting tenure from within at Yale. These brilliant and charismatic teachers belted out their lectures to the rafters. The students were captivated.

The serious study of Joyce occurred for me in graduate school, when I decided to write my thesis on a topic that I had mulled over since my undergraduate days. As brilliant as the lecturers had been, what had struck me as I thought about their approaches to *Ulysses* was a certain conspiracy of silence about one aspect of the text. Strangely enough, not one lecturer focused on the way the narrative changed radically as the book proceeded. Instead, reading the book as an epic poem meant adopting what I came to see as an aerial view, a reading, that is, from 30,000 feet. This view regarded the book's 700 pages steadily and whole. It was a view that knitted together the details, symbols, and allusions into a great symbolic poem "present" all at once in the reader's consciousness, from the first page to the novel's end. The silence over the bizarrely changing styles in the narrative bewildered me. I began to learn something about critical fashions. What we see is partly a product of how we have been taught to read by professors and critics and on what we have learned to focus. At the time I studied Joyce, structural and symbolic approaches, so appropriate for the reading of poetry, were being applied to fiction as well. The *Odyssey of Style in "Ulysses,"* four chapters of which comprise part I of this volume, grew out of my dissertation, itself a response to this silence about narrative style and its effect on the reading process.

The Odyssey of Style focuses on the way the narrative of *Ulysses* changes, develops, and transforms itself, as the drama of the writing competes with the drama of the characters. As the reader encounters *Ulysses*, a series of stylistic masks replace what I call "the narrative norm" established in the early chapters of the novel, that narrative voice that begins to build the fictional world we inhabit. With the writing of *Ulysses*, the idea of style changes from style as the identifiable "signature" of the writer (a Jamesian sentence, a Hemingwayesque narrator) to style as what Roland Barthes called "a citational" process, a body of formulae, a memory, a cultural and not an expressive inheritance.[1] With the entrance of the journalistic headings of "Aeolus" in the seventh chapter, the Victorian ladies' magazine prose of "Nausicaa," and the clichés of "Eumaeus," to name some examples, style goes "public." The "subliterary" intrudes on the more literary language of the narrative; language is flooded by its prior quotidian uses.

This "flooding" is one example of the way the text of *Ulysses* expands to include what initially seemed to be outside its borders. Another way in which the book opens its borders unexpectedly is the "replay" of the first three chapters of the novel, dominated by Stephen Dedalus's consciousness during the first three hours of the Dublin day. Suddenly, in the fourth chapter, these hours are replayed in a new key with the appearance of Leopold Bloom. About the writing of novels, Henry James once said: "Really, universally, relations stop nowhere, and the exquisite problem of the artist is eternally but to draw, by a geometry of his own, the circle within which they shall happily *appear* to do so."[2] In *Ulysses*, Joyce draws and redraws the boundaries of the novel before our eyes. In *The Odyssey of Style*, I read *Ulysses* as a book that demonstrates both an ambition for epic inclusiveness and the recognition that all formal closure is arbitrary. Repeated beginnings, proliferating detail and relationships, citational language, and multiple styles—all expose the artist's sleight of hand in drawing the boundaries of the novel.

My "grand passion" for Joyce is linked to this sense of Joyce's capacious imagination, the broadest and deepest I have ever encountered, with the possible exception of Shakespeare's. In *Ulysses*, Stephen Dedalus thinks of a phrase that Dante uses to refer to Aristotle, "the master of those that know." That is how I think of Joyce. As I was writing my dissertation on *Ulysses*, this perception became almost all-consuming. It seemed to me that every idea or notion that I would have on a given day, and everything that happened to me, was somehow anticipated in Joyce's work. In a strange way, he seemed to predict or know everything. This might be explained away as the typical over-investment that occurs when one is a graduate student and the dissertation topic takes over one's life. Perhaps it is a kind of transference, a casting of Joyce into some godlike parental role, like an analyst. Joyce, more than many other writers, lends himself to this kind of projection. James McMichael, in a very good book called *"Ulysses" and Justice*, named this authoritative narrative quality "Jamesy," an Archimedean point of all-knowingness.[3] This projection doesn't preclude our endlessly reinventing what "James Joyce" or "Jamesy" is, including a consciousness that even knows what it doesn't know. Joyce's texts acknowledge their own limitations, exposing their own blindnesses. On some level they "know" they cannot be all inclusive, can never truly circumscribe "reality." Both timeless and "dated" historical fictions, they are self-deconstructive artifacts.

Regarding his intention in writing *Ulysses*, Joyce told his friend Frank Budgen: "I want . . . to give a picture of Dublin so complete that if the city one day suddenly disappeared from the earth it could be reconstructed out of my book."[4] This famous pronouncement gestures toward the accuracy of historical realism as well as the inclusiveness of epic in its stated desire to provide a picture of a time and place both so accurate and full that the representation itself could replace the "original." Joyce encouraged us to think of *Ulysses* as an enormously elaborated "photograph" of the Dublin of June 16th, 1904. In his book *Camera Lucida: Reflections on Photography*, Roland Barthes speaks of the photograph as "a certain but fugitive testimony."[5] "In Photography," he writes, "I can never deny that *the thing has been there*. There is a superimposition here: of reality and the past" (76). Interestingly, Joyce made his statement to Budgen in 1918, when the unique referent of his "photograph" had, in fact, already vanished fourteen years earlier, "dating" his fiction in more ways than one. And, if in tracing the activities of the Dublin day, the novel commemorates history, the day itself has been "bent" to honor Joyce's fiction. For *Ulysses* presents so powerful a representation of June 16, 1904, that the day has come to be known as "Bloomsday" in homage to Joyce's fictional character. Celebrating Bloomsday has become a ritual in many cities all over the world, in ceremonies in which *Ulysses* is interpreted and staged and read in its entirety.

It is this day that is celebrated at all the International James Joyce Symposia that have occurred biannually since 1967, when the first international Joyce conference was held in Dublin. Indeed, the "Living with Joyce" panel took place at the symposium billed as the 100th anniversary of Bloomsday, that is, the centenary not of the writer's birth (far more typical), but of the creation of his fictional character.

Many of the essays in this collection started life as presentations at these international events. As such, they not only represent my own critical trajectory, but also give a sense of the changing critical and theoretical preoccupations in Joyce studies. This work is in my own idiom, particular to my own interests, passions, and modes of inquiry. It is fueled, though, by rereading Joyce with the help of other readers, and fueled as well by two sources of energy: my rereading of Joyce "with" other theoretical and literary texts and my teaching of Joyce over thirty years. From the first symposium I attended in Zurich in 1979, where I presented my work for the first time on a panel on narrative in *Ulysses*, to the 2004 centenary of Bloomsday in Dublin and the retrospective occasion that "Living with Joyce" provided, my work on Joyce has reflected and, hopefully, contributed to changing critical conceptions of his work. At these occasions I had the pleasure and honor of hearing important work from scholars and theorists around the world who offered new lenses not only on Joyce, but also on literature and interpretation more generally. Feminist, psychoanalytic, Marxist, and post-structuralist theories, particularly deconstruction, offered new ways of thinking about Joyce. However, it is important to point out that Joyce's texts have offered such fertile objects for these critical lenses *because* he anticipated these theories in his fiction. Joyce has proven hospitable to "theory" because it was already within the geometry of his texts. Indeed, Jacques Derrida recognized Joyce as precursor in calling his work only a footnote to *Finnegans Wake*.

As the following essays suggest, Joyce's work has proven hospitable to feminist, Marxist, and psychoanalytic interpretations, as well as to deconstruction and cultural studies, because his texts thematize and formally enact a kind of hospitality to various "others" and other realms of experience. His fiction focuses on processes of identification, incorporation, and interpellation in the construction of both the subjectivity of the characters and the texts themselves. Searching for his father's initials carved in a schoolroom desk when he visits his father's hometown, Stephen Dedalus in *A Portrait of the Artist as a Young Man* discovers instead the word "foetus" shockingly carved where the initials "SD" (Simon Dedalus) were expected. In *A Portrait*, *Ulysses*, and *Finnegans Wake*, signs of the mother's body erupt as fatherhood is revealed as a legal "fiction" and not a biological inheritance. Patriarchal signature cannot completely write over the sign of the mother. Masculinity, as well as fatherhood, is revealed as a construction, not a natural quality. Performing his masculinity with the aid of multiple props, Bloom forges his subjectivity and person in identification with others on a spectrum of gender and class—from the meat-eaters in the Burton (whose brute cannibalism he rejects) to the cabbies in the cabman's shelter (whom he both "hails" and eyes with wariness) to the various females, including Molly, with whom he identifies and from whom he defends himself. Indeed, *Finnegans Wake* refers to itself as a letter "selfpenned to one's other" (*FW* 489.33–34).

The organization of *Who's Afraid of James Joyce?* reflects the trajectory of my own thinking and teaching of Joyce as well as the opening of Joyce's work to powerful theoretical currents in literary studies. Language and form remain enduring concerns, but the progression of essays reveals an increasing attention to the social and cultural contexts of language and its "hospitality" to excluded others. In *The Odyssey of Style* I wrote of the way *Ulysses* progressively incorporates what has been banished from it. The metaphor of hospitality operates implicitly throughout the collection in its focus on the opening of the self, and the text, to the other. In the essay

"Close Encounters" in part IV, the metaphor of hospitality functions explicitly and provides the operating principle for acts of inclusion and exclusion, both formally and thematically in Joyce's and other modernist texts.

Part II of the volume focuses on Woman as "other," in its examination of the "compromising letters" Joyce writes to and about women in his fiction and personal letters. Addressing the harsh judgment of some corners of feminist criticism which reject more positive "feminologist re-Joyceings,"[6] the essay looks at the way Joyce associates women with writing practices that disrupt patriarchal authority even as the male pen attempts to "lasso" the feminine libido in writing (*FW* 123.05–10). The language of Joyce's texts unmasks male anxieties of women's power. Touching on *Dubliners*, *A Portrait*, *Ulysses*, and *Finnegans Wake*, as well as some of Joyce's letters, the essay "Compromising Letters" traces the circulation of desire as well as the mechanisms of defense in Joyce's writing. The final essay in this section addresses the issue of hospitality to women in a more institutional context: the International James Joyce Foundation, through my own experience beginning at the Zurich symposium of 1979.

Part III, "Bloom in Circulation: Navigating Identifications," begins with "'Eumaeus' Redux," a second examination of the "Eumaeus" chapter of *Ulysses* that produced a different, though not incompatible, reading from the one in *The Odyssey of Style*. Presented as a plenary talk at the International James Joyce Symposium in Monaco in 1990, the essay takes as its starting point the "received ideas" in "Eumaeus" discussed in *The Odyssey of Style*, but discovers in this second look at the language of the chapter a tissue of economic metaphors that encode class consciousness, colonial exploitation, and violence. Tracing the perambulations of "Mr Bloom" and Stephen in the vicinity of the cabman's shelter, the narrative reveals both Bloom's sympathy with the down-and-out denizens of the area and his attempt to bolster his own respectability. The three remaining essays in this section extend this focus on the construction of Bloom's subjectivity through both his fluid identifications with various "others" and his self-protective consolidations of his masculinity. "Legal Fiction or Pulp Fiction in 'Lestrygonians'" focuses on orality and its relation to the psychoanalytic concept of identification. Drawing on Julia Kristeva's influential work on Joyce's use of the symbol of the Eucharist, the essay juxtaposes Bloom's repulsion from the cannibalistic male-eating rituals he witnesses in the Burton Restaurant ("men, men, men" [*U* 8.653]) with the erotic memory of communion with Molly as they exchanged the seedcake on Howth Hill. Moments of carnivorous and vegetarian assimilation, present and remembered, constitute Bloom's consciousness.

"Twenty Pockets," delivered at the International James Joyce Symposium in Rome in 1998, "picks" Bloom's pockets: it analyzes the way the male suit helps Bloom consolidate his bourgeois masculine image of self-possession and restraint, allowing him to compartmentalize his desires in the various pockets of his attire. Again in ritualized performances, Bloom hoards, exchanges, fondles and protects objects of desire in the repositories of privacy provided by the pockets of his suit as he circulates through Dublin streets. Finally, "Bloom in Circulation: Who's He When He's Not at Home?"—based on a talk delivered at the Dublin symposium of 2000—continues exploration of *Ulysses* as a novel of walking, in which Bloom, traveling homebody and wily commuter, navigates the familiar, yet dangerous, city terrain. Neither quite European flaneur nor subversive subaltern, Bloom uses his Odyssean *metis* to chart a tactical course through city streets and novel pages.

At the Trieste symposium in 2002, I delivered a talk called "Confessions of Xenos: Hospitality and the Foreign in *Dubliners*." Rituals of identification and interchange discussed in earlier work were rethought in terms of rituals of hospitality described in the work of Derrida: an address to the "other" that goes beyond the kind of hospitality—the civilized welcoming of guests in Greek culture—that so fascinated Joyce in much of his work. In certain stories from *Dubliners* that I had taught for years, I returned to the theme of openness to the "other," now through the lens of hospitality. "Close Encounters," the essay that forms the bulk of part IV of the collection, steps back to look at Joycean hospitality and its implications for questions of inclusion and exclusion in modernist texts. Linking formal boundary drawings in these texts with socially symbolic identifications and exclusions, the essay explores the interpenetration of the living and the dead in "The Sisters" and "The Dead." In the final essay in this section, "Joyce in Transit," I consider the way Joyce himself haunts the imaginations of writers who come after him, crossing geographic and temporal borders, and the way they are both hospitable and inhospitable to this daunting precursor. Brigid Brophy, a writer who is half-Irish and half-English, is a "compalien" of Joyce, identifying him as her Irish, modernist precursor, father of linguistic experiment and gender bending, yet whose overbearing power must be resisted as well. "Pardon me, ma'am," the narrative voice says to its self-created "interlocutor," "your mollibloomers is shewin."[7] At times, she closes her ears: "Old

Father Finnergan Go-and-don'tsinagain . . . I can't hear you, ex-father. I've switched me deaf-aid off" (*In Transit* 228). Comically, punningly, Brophy turns a deaf-ear to the Other.

In a very different register, the final essay in the collection, co-authored with Paul Saint-Amour, explores the difficulty of closing the "case" on hospitality between Mrs Sinico and Mr Duffy in "A Painful Case." The thematics of hospitality in the story are historically charged by Dublin's status as an occupied city. As it explores gestures of welcome and rejection represented in the story, the essay also regards gestures of appeal to its reader. The dynamic of address to the ear of the Other (the one Brophy satirically refuses) extends to the reader of this story, which reminds us that hospitality to the Other is never an open-and-shut case.

The trajectory of these essays coincides with my own rethinking of Joyce's texts in light of different theoretical possibilities and approaches. But the essays also bear the imprint of another important process: the rereading and rethinking that goes with the territory of teaching Joyce over the years. "Living with Joyce" means not only fueling a "grand passion" for the epic reach of his imagination, it means supporting the "small pleasures" that come with attention trained and retrained on the concrete details, as well as the grand schemes, of his texts. It means having one's attention repaid in sudden small "epiphanies," those bursting manifestations of meaning that Joyce spoke of often. Teaching "A Painful Case" in a freshman seminar provided such a moment—the sudden manifestation of a small detail never noticed on similar occasions. In teaching the story I had taught many times before, I noticed that there was only one line of direct discourse in the entire story, a comment made by Mrs Sinico to Mr Duffy. At a concert where they sit side by side in the audience, she offers the comment, "—What a pity there is such a poor house to-night! It's so hard on people to have to sing to empty benches" ("A Painful Case" 109). Every word of this locution is perfect for conveying, in Mrs Sinico's own voice, the way that her attention—passionate, respectful, and empathetic—bathes Mr Duffy in a compassion he both welcomes and fears. "A Painful Case" is all about hearing, or not hearing, the voice of the Other, and Mrs Sinico's direct dialogue, an exclamation that in turn recognizes the importance of being heard, so starkly contrasts Mr Duffy's self-distancing techniques. This single example of direct discourse in the story appears in a sea of narrative mediation and indirection, narration epitomized by Mr Duffy's odd autobiographical habit of thinking about himself in the third person. Direct discourse depends upon the use of first and second person (I and you), but in the story, and in Mr Duffy's consciousness (which come together often), these two "persons" are drowned out by his third-personing of himself, through his odd autobiographical habit. Indeed, at one point we see this self-alienation at work when, in the midst of an intimate meeting with Mrs Sinico, Mr Duffy hears "the strange impersonal voice which he recognized as his own, insisting on the soul's incurable loneliness. We cannot give ourselves, it said: we are our own" (111).

It is worth charting the double loop of mediation that occurs here: Mr Duffy's voice is rendered not as indirectly representing what was said, but what was HEARD by the speaker himself. This self-hearing is, of course, an extension of his "odd autobiographical habit." That much is obvious. But less obvious is the way that this self-distancing, this self-dramatizing insistence on loneliness, is the lesser of two evils. For at least in this instance, Mr Duffy hears his own voice as someone else's, because he is also hearing it as if in Mrs Sinico's place. Paradoxically, as he voices his pessimistic pronouncement strategically to ward off the intimacy Mrs. Sinico impulsively seeks, he remains in the realm of imagining what he sounds like to another person. He still occupies the realm of dialogue. In contrast, the story ends with the words, "He listened again: perfectly silent. He felt that he was alone" (117). What I realized in teaching the story again was that there is something lonelier than hearing one's voice and having it sound like a stranger's. Losing Mrs Sinico means that Mr Duffy has lost even the sound of his own voice from the place of another. He cannot hear himself speak. In this moment, what he hears—to quote a line from the "Ithaca" chapter of *Ulysses*—is "the apathy of the stars" (*U* 604.2226).

My second example of the way that teaching and rereading Joyce repays our attention with meaningful aperçus about life, as well as art, draws on my experience teaching "Eveline," also from *Dubliners*. Again, I had read the story countless times before, but this time around something new happened: I suddenly understood the story in a completely different way, from the inside out. Like Leopold Bloom, who says he consults the works of Shakespeare for some practical information about life, I felt that I understood something about my own life through Eveline's story and vice versa—I understood her story in a visceral way.

My perception occurred when I had to make an important decision—like Eveline—though, admittedly, in a very different context. I had been teaching at the University of Utah for almost twenty years in the position I had held since finishing graduate school; I had begun my career as an assistant professor and was promoted through the ranks to professor of English. In 1997, I was offered a position at the University of California, Irvine, as dean of Humanities. I had taken extra time to consider this rather momentous move from Utah, where my husband and two sons would continue to live for six months before joining me. On a particular day, I was scheduled to call the Executive Vice Chancellor of UC Irvine, the person negotiating with me and trying to recruit me. The time had come for me to give my final answer. The class I was teaching, a Joyce class, was not scheduled until the afternoon, and I had the morning at home to make my decision. My family had been consulted thoroughly and everyone was willing to move, with varied degrees of enthusiasm. At this point, the decision was entirely mine. Everyone had given up on my seesawing conversation. The kids had gone to school, my husband had gone to work, everyone not knowing what I was going to do because I myself had not fully decided.

At 10:00 A.M., I picked up the phone to call to say I was coming. But I hung up before the call was completed. How could I commute for six months and leave my family at a time when everyone needed me? I weighed further the pros and the cons, the benefits and the dangers of change after twenty years, of leaving great friends and a city that had been surprisingly welcoming. I picked up the phone to call to say that I couldn't accept the position. I hung up. I felt paralyzed, truly paralyzed. I had led the Executive Vice Chancellor to believe that I would probably accept the job.

"She had consented to go away, to leave her home. Was that wise? She tried to weigh each side of the question." There I was on page 2 of "Eveline." After reading the story many times, I suddenly felt I understood how it felt to be paralyzed, to be a deer caught in the headlights, to be immobilized by the weight of the phone call. "Her time was running out but she continued to sit by the window, leaning her head against the window curtain." I finally picked up the phone, not knowing what I was going to say, heard the Vice Chancellor's voice, and accepted the job.

That afternoon I taught my class on *Ulysses*. The class had read "Eveline" earlier in the quarter. I told them about my sense of understanding "Eveline" in a new way and I recounted my scene of indecision. At the end of my story I revealed my decision by saying that I had decided to go to "Buenos Ayres." There was an audible gasp in the room. I had not meant to be particularly dramatic about my decision, but my almost uncanny experience prompted me to relate my decision via the story.

With some stories in *Dubliners*, it is too easy to feel that the lives of the characters are stunted, narrow, so different from our own educated and promising lives. Joyce knew something about both the specific and stultifying conditions in Ireland at the turn of the century—the pressures on a young woman to marry, to care for her family, to avoid poverty, to be devout. Yet there's something translatable in his stories, transposable in their wisdom, that accompanies what I think is Joyce's firm conviction of the significance of ordinary lives, including my own.

When I teach Joyce, I want to present his work both to the first-time reader and the aficionado in ways that demonstrate his comedy, his profundity, his deep originality, and his deep derivativeness. The essays in this collection are meant to convey a sense of the large and the small, Joyce's grand vision and idiosyncratic detail. One last small pleasure of living with Joyce over twenty years: as you get older, you can sometimes make discoveries in Joyce's texts that you have made before but haven't remembered. This forgetting ensures that you will never run out of fresh perceptions.

Again, in 2007, I have taken on a new position, as president of Sarah Lawrence College, though this time around I did not feel like Eveline in making my decision. Although my time to devote to teaching is limited as president, I have already offered a Sarah Lawrence seminar called "Who's Afraid of James Joyce?" My students—curious, intelligent, eager—were not afraid. In these essays, as in my classes, I hope to make Joyce more fascinating and less daunting, both more understandable and more complex.

I

Retracing *The Odyssey of Style*

1

The Narrative Norm

The first three chapters of *Ulysses* pay homage to both the personal tradition Joyce had created in his previous works of fiction and to the traditional novel. In its dominant narrative voice and interest in the character of the artist, the "Telemachiad" resembles *A Portrait of the Artist as a Young Man* in particular, and even the reader of *Ulysses* who fails to recognize this continuity will experience a sense of security from the presence of this narrative voice. The staples of the novel—third-person narration, dialogue, and dramatization of a scene—also promise narrative security to the reader who begins *Ulysses*: they act as signposts promising him familiar terrain on the subsequent pages. No matter what we may know about the structural apparatus and levels of allegory in the work after reading Joyce's note sheets, letters, and tips to Stuart Gilbert, what we experience when beginning *Ulysses* is a novel that promises a story, a narrator, and a plot. "Stately, plump Buck Mulligan came from the stairhead" (*U* 1.1) is a plausible beginning for any novel. *Ulysses* begins like a narrative with confidence in the adequacy of the novel form.

It is important to underscore the initial narrative promises to the reader made in the novel not only because they will be broken later on, but also because they provide an interesting contrast to the change in Joyce's basic conceptions of plot and significance in fiction, a change that must have antedated, at least in part, the beginning of the novel. *Ulysses* offers, in a sense, a "rewriting" of *Dubliners*: it presents another portrait of Dublin designed to reveal the soul of the city and its citizens. But in arriving at the basic conception of *Ulysses*—the condensing of the wanderings of Odysseus to one day in the life of certain Dublin citizens—Joyce radically altered his conception of what a portrait of Dublin should be.

In the initial conception of *Ulysses*, Joyce departed from the aesthetic of economy and scrupulous choice that had directed the writing of *Dubliners* in favor of an aesthetic of comprehensiveness and minute representation.

This aesthetic is implied in Joyce's statement to Budgen about his desire to give so complete a picture of Dublin in *Ulysses* that if the city were to disappear it could be reconstructed from the book.[1] Although the "story" of *Ulysses* takes place during one day only, this day is infinitely expansible by being infinitely divisible—the rendering of the complete "details" of life almost obscure the sense of story. Unlike *Dubliners*, which promises to end the narrative as soon as the "soul" of a character is revealed, *Ulysses* offers no clear principle of completeness. The frustration critics felt at what they thought of as Joyce's infidelity to the minimal requirements of a story is reflected in Edmund Wilson's comment in *Axel's Castle*: "It is almost as if he had elaborated [the story] so much and worked over it so long that he had forgotten . . . the drama which he had originally intended to stage."[2]

Ulysses also offers no clear principle of emphasis or proportion. In the stories of *Dubliners*, the right "trivial" incident in the life of a character epiphanizes the meaning of the life; in *Ulysses*, no one particular incident in a life is considered to be of supreme importance. Because the characters carry within them the same problems, desires, and past, no matter when we see them, no day is essentially different from any other. If *Dubliners* focuses on a particularly significant day in the lives of its characters, *Ulysses* focuses on any day in Dublin's diary, and the day happens to be June 16, 1904. It is as if an entry in the diary of Dublin, rather than in a personal diary such as the one that ends *A Portrait*, was blown up in a great, Brobdingnagian gesture; in the world of *Ulysses*, as in Brobdingnag, a molehill can indeed become a mountain. The slight rise in the plot that the theory of epiphany suggests is almost completely eliminated in the narrative of *Ulysses*. What is important here is not the transition between a "short story" and the long story of development told in a traditional novel but the transition from fiction interested in plot to fiction in which plot becomes synonymous with digression.

The stream of consciousness technique in the "Telemachiad" does alert the reader to some of these changes in overall conception. In using this technique increasingly until it almost dominates the narrative in chapter 3 ("Proteus"), Joyce offered his third-person narrator less and less to do. The retrospective narrative voice of a conventional novel is replaced almost entirely, so that "plot" changes from a form of narrative memory to a rendering of "the very process in which meaning is apprehended in life."[3]

But in the first three chapters of the novel (even in "Proteus"), the third-person narrator exists and serves some important narrative functions.

The dominant narrative voice in the "Telemachiad" provides the narrative norm for the novel (and continues in subsequent chapters), and it is the voice that, for a long time, was ignored in critical discussions of *Ulysses*. Although some critics have described the quality of this voice,[4] many passed over this narrative norm on the way to discussions of narrative distortions that occur primarily in the latter half of the book.[5] But the primary reason for this omission is the importance that decades of critics have placed on the stream of consciousness technique in the early chapters: in focusing on the "innovativeness" of this technique, they have tended to underestimate the importance of the narrative norm.

The narrative conventions established in the early chapters of *Ulysses* include the presence of an identifiable and relatively consistent style of narration that persists in the first eleven chapters of the book and the tendency of the narrative to borrow the pace and diction of the characters' language. In other words, the conventions include both the continued presence of a particular style and the adaptability of style to character. Critics who focus on the stream of consciousness emphasize the importance of the character's mind and treat the third-person narration as an adjunct of character.[6] This is only partly correct, since it fails to acknowledge the recognizable, idiosyncratic narrative voice that does exist.

For example, the following sentences, the first from "Telemachus," the second from "Proteus," display the characteristic Joycean qualities seen in *A Portrait* and now heightened in *Ulysses*: "Two shafts of soft daylight fell across the flagged floor from the high barbicans: and at the meeting of their rays a cloud of coalsmoke and fumes of fried grease floated, turning" (*U* 1.315–17); and "The cry brought him skulking back to his master and a blunt bootless kick sent him unscathed across a spit of sand, crouched in flight" (*U* 3.354–55). The denotative style in *A Portrait* is evident here, with greater syntactic dislocation and more unusual diction. The extreme concern with the sounds of words—that is, the alliteration ("flagged floor," "blunt bootless," "spit of sand") and what Anthony Burgess has called the "clotted" effect of the double and triple consonants[7]—and the strange placement of the modifying adverb ("fried grease floated, turning") produce a sentence that, as Burgess says, reveals "a distinctive approach to what might be termed literary engineering."[8] This is prose that is competently, indeed masterfully crafted, precisely and poetically written.

Especially in the "Telemachiad," this literate, formal, poetic language is associated with the character of Stephen Dedalus. In the first three chapters, we perceive the world largely through the eyes of an aspiring artist, and, as in *A Portrait*, the linguistic "sympathy" between character and narrative voice blurs the distinctions between them. "Wood-shadows floated silently by through the morning peace from the stairhead seaward where he gazed" (*U* 8.242–43) is a narrative statement that "borrows" Stephen's lyricism. Throughout the chapter, the narration will often present Stephen's poetic and melancholy perceptions of things in language appropriate to his sensibility.

But despite the close connection between the style and the mind of Stephen in the "Telemachiad," the style exists independently in subsequent chapters, as is evident from the following examples:

> The caretaker hung his thumbs in the loops of his gold watch chain and spoke in a discreet tone to their vacant smiles. (*U* 6.719–21)
> It passed statelily up the staircase, steered by an umbrella, a solemn beardframed face. (*U* 7.45–46)
> The young woman with slow care detached from her light skirt a clinging twig. (*U* 10.440–41)
> Miss Douce's brave eyes, unregarded, turned from the crossblind, smitten by sunlight. (*U* 11.460–61)

In the first eleven chapters of *Ulysses*, this narrative style establishes the empirical world of the novel; it provides stability and continuity. The persistence of this type of narrative sentence provides a sign of the original narrative authority amidst the increasingly bizarre narrative developments of the later chapters, until it disappears in "Cyclops." (It reappears briefly in "Nausicaa," for reasons I will discuss later.) It is a style that orients the reader and offers him a certain security by establishing the sense of the solidity of external reality.

It seems to me that this type of narrative sentence, along with the other staples of the narrative mode of the early chapters—interior monologue, free indirect discourse, and dialogue—functions as the "rock of Ithaca," "the initial style" to which Joyce alluded in a letter to Harriet Weaver in 1919: "I understand that you may begin to regard the various styles of the episodes with dismay and prefer the initial style much as the wanderer did who longed for the rock of Ithaca."[9] This is the nonparodic style that establishes the decorum of the novel. When it disappears later on in the text, we realize that it too was a choice among many possibilities, a mode of presentation. But, in its seeming fidelity to the details of both the thoughts and actions of the characters, it provides us with a sense of the real world of the novel. With all its precision and fastidiousness, it functions for us as a narrative norm.[10]

However, while the decorum of the novel is established, the presence of another narrative strand in the first chapter slyly questions the assumptions about language upon which the normative style is based. The effect of this narrative strand is subtle, nothing like the radical disruptions of narrative stability in the later chapters. And yet this narrative fluctuation in the first chapter of the book serves as a warning to the reader of the strange narrative distortions to come. The following passage illustrates the intertwining of the narrative strands in the first chapter:

> He [Mulligan] shaved evenly and with care, in silence, seriously. Stephen, an elbow rested on the jagged granite, leaned his palm against his brow and gazed at the fraying edge of his shiny black coatsleeve. Pain, that was not yet the pain of love, fretted his heart. (*U* 1.99–102)

The second sentence is an example of the denotative narrative norm. The past participle "rested," surprising the reader prepared to encounter the present participle "resting," is a characteristic kind of dislocation. The third sentence, "Pain, that was not yet the pain of love, fretted his heart," is a clear example of free indirect discourse. But the first sentence is puzzling—the number of adverbs and adverbial phrases surprises us. There is a naive quality to this writing that separates parts of speech as if they were about to be diagrammed.

In fact, the first chapter of *Ulysses* provides numerous examples of this naive narrative quality. This strand of the narration reveals itself in the repeated use of certain formulaic narrative constructions of which no student of creative writing, however inexperienced, would be proud. The proliferation of the following phrases in the early pages of the novel suggests that something strange is taking place in the narrative: "he said sternly," "he cried briskly," "he said gaily" (*U* 1.19, 1.28, 1.34); and "He laid the brush aside and, laughing with delight, cried," "Stephen said quietly," "he said frankly," "Stephen said with energy and growing fear," "he cried thickly" (*U* 1.44, 1.47, 1.60, 1.66). What kind of narrative world is created by these descriptions and what purpose could Joyce have had in using this type of prose in the beginning of the novel?

Joyce called the technique of this chapter "narrative young," and this description, while it probably refers to Stephen to some extent, also applies to the quality of narration: it is appropriate to the self-conscious, naive literary style exemplified above. Unlike the naiveté of the narrator in stories like "Clay" in *Dubliners*, stories in which through free indirect discourse the narrator ostensibly accepts his protagonist's assessment of the world, the naiveté of the narrative in "Telemachus" is literary as well as psychological. We notice an innocence concerning the very act of telling a story, an innocence that is a quality of the narrative itself rather than a property of a particular character.

What we are provided with in the early pages of *Ulysses*, disturbing the basically serious and authoritative narrative voice that creates a world we can believe in, is a different narrative strand that parodies the process of creation. Prose like "he cried thickly" and "he said contentedly" is the unsophisticated prose of fourth-rate fiction; a novel that begins this way parodies its own ability to tell a story. Even in the first chapter of the novel, Joyce begins to turn novelistic convention into novelistic cliché, and it is here that the reader glimpses language beginning to quote itself, its characteristic activity in the latter half of the book. While making use of the conventional tools of the novel, Joyce uses one strand of the narrative to upset the stability created by these conventions and to point to their inadequacy. As the normative style asserts its ability to capture reality in language, this narrative voice advertises its own incompetence. The world in which Buck Mulligan wears a "tolerant smile" and laughs "with delight" or in which Stephen says something "with energy and growing fear" is about as far from Henry James's world of "delicate adjustments" and "exquisite chemistry"[11] as a novelist can get. The sentences of this naive narrative point to the falsification and oversimplification that language wreaks on emotions by organizing them in discrete grammatical parts.

This narrative strand in chapter 1 provides the first example of narrative performance and stylistic bravado in *Ulysses*, different from that in later chapters like "Cyclops" and "Ithaca," but stylistic exhibition nonetheless. There is a comic excess of labor in evidence in the narration: the narrator seems to wrestle with the discrete parts of speech available to him only to pin down the most commonplace of descriptions. The subtle nuances captured in sentences of the "initial style" elude the narrator's grasp. The excess of labor here is the antithesis of the coolness of scrupulous meanness in *Dubliners*—the production of meaning seems to be a Herculean task.[12] But there is an air of safety that surrounds the "risks" the narrator seems to take. He is like a clown walking a tightrope only one foot above the ground. What is suppressed here is not so much a narrator as a grin.

It is possible to explain this adverbial mania in "Telemachus" in relation to the characters described. Hugh Kenner, for example, has discussed the presence of these adverbs in regard to the role-playing of Stephen and Buck Mulligan.[13] While the thematic connection between the adverbial style and the role-playing of the characters makes sense, it limits the significance of the strange verbal tic by giving it so exclusively a character-based explanation. The adverbial style tells us something about the kinds of utterances we find in certain types of narratives, as well as something about the characters in this one. The presence of the naive literary style suggests that the text as well as the character is trying on a costume. In chapter 1, we get a brief glimpse of the kind of narrative mimicry that dominates the later chapters of the book—the mimicry of a type of text rather than a particular character. What I find most interesting about the naive narrative strand in chapter 1 is the beginning of an interest in language apart from character, language that calls attention to its own clichéd nature without providing the vehicle for the ironic exposure of a character. Instead of parodying the linguistic idiosyncrasies of a type of character, the narrator dons a stylistic mask of innocence to parody the very enterprise of telling a story. Parody is cut loose from the concerns of character and becomes an aspect of narrative.

Thus, Steinberg and other critics interested in the early chapters of *Ulysses* seem to me to have erred in assuming that if the narrator is not an *unreliable character* in the story (like the lawyer in Melville's "Bartleby, the Scrivener," for example, or the narrator in Ford's *The Good Soldier*), then the narrative can be trusted. Frank Kermode writes in an essay entitled "Novels: Recognition and Deception" that "we have bothered too much about the authority of the narrator and too little about that of the narrative,"[14] and this distinction between the authority of the narrator and the narrative is an extremely important one for the reading of *Ulysses*.

The tone of the opening chapter of *Ulysses*, then, seems to oscillate: in certain parts of the narrative *Ulysses* announces itself as a comedy, but for the most part it is dominated by the rather bitter and serious Stephen Dedalus. The copresence of the naive aspect of the narrative and the well-written, precise narrative norm makes it difficult for the reader to form a clear perception of a unified narrator.

And yet, this one narrative strand found in the first chapter of the novel is quickly overshadowed by the narrative norm and the stream of consciousness technique in the rest of the "Telemachiad." The mimicry of a type of text rather than a character will resurface in later chapters—most obviously in "Cyclops" and "Oxen of the Sun." But after chapter 1, this naive parodic style vanishes. Despite Joyce's developing interest in representing the inadequacies of language, despite the warning about the enterprise of novel writing in the first chapter, it is character, not narration, that is the most important subject of the first six chapters of the novel. Simultaneous with Joyce's perceptions of the limitations of both the conventional novel and his own previous fiction was an interest in further developing a method with which to present the workings of consciousness. The "Proteus" chapter is, as critics have suggested, the culmination of the "Telemachiad," not only chronologically, but stylistically as well; here the stream of consciousness technique reaches its peak in transcribing an educated, artistic mind. The use of stream of consciousness was experimental for Joyce when he wrote the "Telemachiad"—it carried further the "direct" representation of the mind of the artist begun in *A Portrait*. It is the drama of the character's mind, rather than the drama of novel writing, that is still paramount. As S. L. Goldberg has pointed out, the paragraph is still a dramatic unit of consciousness, the "artistic medium of a particular *act* of understanding."[15]

In the next three chapters of *Ulysses*, devoted to Leopold Bloom, this interest in character is still paramount. In these chapters, the reader finds the same texture of narration as in the "Telemachiad": a combination of third-person narration, dialogue, free indirect discourse, and the stream of consciousness of the character. The denotative norm of the "Telemachiad" persists in these chapters: "By lorries along sir John Rogerson's quay Mr Bloom walked soberly, past Windmill lane, Leask's the linseed crusher, the postal telegraph office" (*U* 5.1–2); "The metal wheels ground the gravel with a sharp grating cry and the pack of blunt boots followed the trundled barrow along a lane of sepulchres" (*U* 6.637–39). The denotative norm continues to establish our sense of external reality and our sense of a narrative presence by assuring us that despite the introduction of a new character who sees the world differently from Stephen Dedalus, the world is the same. This second triad of chapters continues to build up our sense of what the world of Dublin and the world of the novel are like. The temporal symmetry of this second triad with the "Telemachiad" and the persistence of the same basic rules of narration encourage us to group the first six chapters together as providing the norm of the book.

As in the "Telemachiad," one finds in these chapters a sympathy between narrator and character that again involves the borrowing of linguistic habits. To turn the page from the heraldic image of Stephen Dedalus "rere regardant" and to encounter Leopold Bloom eating "with relish the inner organs of beasts and fowls" is to sense a difference in mood that depends in part on a change in style. The language associated with Bloom (both his stream of consciousness and some third-person narration) is more simple syntactically, more colloquial, and more redundant than Stephen's. (See, for example, the prose of the opening of the chapter.)

What is most interesting about the "sympathy" between narrator and character in Bloom's chapters, however, is its occasional comic manipulation. Although the exchange between character and narrator in these chapters follows rules set in the "Telemachiad," at times this exchange seems to pick up speed. In the following passage from "Hades," for example, Bloom and the narrator carry on a rapid and weird exchange of images:

> The whitesmocked priest came after him tidying his stole with one hand, balancing with the other a little book against his toad's belly. Who'll read the book? I, said the rook.
> They halted by the bier and the priest began to read out of his book with a fluent croak. (*U* 6.590–94)

The narrator describes the priest's belly as "his toad's belly"; then it is Bloom, presumably, who thinks, "Who'll read the book? I, said the rook." Again, the third-person narration resumes in what seems like the initial style, except for the presence of the word "croak." Soon after this passage, Bloom looks at the priest and thinks "Eyes of a toad too," and the word "too" must refer to the "toad's belly" mentioned in the narrator's statement. There is a strange kind of play between narrator and character, almost a parodic form of sympathy between the two. This is a kind of "sympathy" that reduces the distance between the telling of the story and the story itself, a distance that will be manipulated in increasingly bizarre ways as the book progresses. This passage in "Hades" looks forward to the exchanges between narrator and speaker in "Scylla and Charybdis":

> —Yes, Mr Best said youngly. I feel Hamlet quite young. (*U* 9.387)

—Bosh! Stephen said rudely. A man of genius makes no mistakes. His errors are volitional and are the portals of discovery.

Portals of discovery opened to let in the quaker librarian, softcreak-footed, bald, eared and assiduous. (*U* 9.28–31)

Hugh Kenner pointed out another anomaly of the second triad of chapters that emphasizes the artifice of the text. In his article, "The Rhetoric of Silence," Kenner cites several omissions in the text, some of which are highly significant to the plot. Chief among these gaps is a missing scene between Molly and Bloom, in which she tells him when Boylan is coming to Eccles Street ("At four"), and Bloom tells her he will attend the Gaiety Theatre (the cue she needs to assure her Bloom will not be home at four). Based upon Bloom's later recollection of Molly's words ("At four, she said" [*U* 11.189]) and Molly's recollection of Bloom's statement that he would be dining out ("he said Im dining out and going to the Gaiety" [*U* 18.81–82]), Kenner deduces that the painful scene between the two is omitted or repressed in the narrative. Since we cannot locate this conversation among the exchanges between Molly and Bloom that are recorded, Kenner concludes that they must have occurred offstage, like Molly's adultery or Bloom's visit to the insurance office on behalf of Paddy Dignam's widow.[16] Although this particular gap in the conversation can be recognized only retrospectively, when the missing lines are recollected, this playfulness in the selection of dramatized details puts into question our initial assumption that the narrative is recording all significant action. But, as Kenner says, we can reconstruct the scene in our minds, based on our knowledge of the characters and our sense of the empirical world that Joyce goes to such lengths to depict.[17] As Stephen discovers in "Proteus," the world is "there all the time without you ... world without end" (*U* 3.27–28). Narrative selection rather than empirical reality is questioned; the concept of omission presupposes that something in particular is being omitted.

In the second triad of chapters, we move closer to the comic play to come. In fact, I would argue that the mind of Leopold Bloom and the more comic and parodic tone of his chapters predict the direction of the rest of the narrative. It is Bloom's rather than Stephen's sensibility that dominates the *kind* of book *Ulysses* will become. The opening of the book to the subliterary as well as the literary and the movement from statement to cliché are predicted by the movement from Stephen Dedalus to Leopold Bloom. In some ways, the general tone and feeling of the book and some of the narrative strategies of the later chapters are also predicted in the book's first half

By the end of "Hades," we have been introduced to the two main characters in a thorough way. In the stream of consciousness of each character, in each private memory emerges a particular way of making sense of the world and the self. In "reading" the world, the characters rely on different tools of interpretation: Bloom on clichés and bits of popular information, Stephen on abstruse allusion and esoteric philosophy. Both characters, however, are concerned with making sense of their pasts, not by an act of retrospection, as can be found in the novels of James or Proust, but in random associations that surface while they live their lives. "It is the 'stream of consciousness' which serves to clarify or render intelligible both the element of duration in time and the aspect of an enduring self. The technique is designed to give some kind of visible, sensible impression of how it is meaningful and intelligible to think of the self as a continuing unit despite the most perplexing and chaotic manifold of immediate experience."[18] Amidst the sense of the "immediate experience" of life that we get in the first six chapters of *Ulysses* is the faith in character not as a "construct" seen from the outside but, nevertheless, as a "self" that is constant.

Thus in the early chapters of *Ulysses* the characters carry the main burden of interpreting the world. "Proteus" is the culmination of Stephen's attempt to interpret his surroundings. In fact, his portentous announcement, "Signatures of all things I am here to read," is one of the most explicit declarations of character as interpreter in literature. As Fredric Jameson has said of psychological novels in general (and this applies to the early chapters of *Ulysses*), the character "from within the book, reflecting on the meaning of his experiences, does the actual work of exegesis for us before our own eyes."[19] In subsequent chapters, the reader and the writer participate more strenuously in the hermeneutic process. But in the beginning of the book, the major "burden" of interpretation is placed on the characters.

By providing a norm in its first six chapters that later would be subverted, the novel encompasses its author's changing interests; it can thus be said that the book, as well as Joyce, the author, changes its mind. When he wrote the first six chapters, Joyce did not yet fully realize the direction the second half of the novel would take. But his decision to leave the first chapters substantially intact was made after writing the entire novel. The opening section of the book was left as a kind of testimony to an older order, a norm for the reader at the same time as it is an anachronism in terms of the book as a whole. Consequently, the opening of the novel does not prepare the reader for what follows. A novel usually offers its reader built-in strategies for interpreting the world it presents. The concept of development in most novels insures that the early parts of the work in some way prepare the reader for what is to come (Henry James's *Prefaces* devote considerable space to this idea of preparation). But the first six chapters of *Ulysses* lead the reader to have certain unfulfilled expectations, that is, they make a certain contract that is subverted (for instance, that the normative voice will be sustained throughout the novel, that character will be the major concern). Although Joyce, unlike Kierkegaard, never openly confessed to this kind of "deception,"[20] *Ulysses* begins by deliberately establishing narrative rules that are bent and finally broken later on.

In *Ulysses*, Joyce leaves the "tracks" of his artistic journey. Throughout his career Joyce transformed and developed his materials, but in the process he tended to outgrow a specific form and move on to another. Before writing *Ulysses* he had abandoned poetry for the short story and the short story for the extended narrative record of the growth of the artist's mind in *A Portrait*. Then, as S. L. Goldberg has observed, discovering that the record of the growth of the artist's mind was severely limited by the artist's awareness,[21] he began *Ulysses*. Realizing that Stephen had "a shape that [couldn't] be changed,"[22] he became more interested in Leopold Bloom. And, finally, finding obsolete the idea of a narrative norm that tells a story, with "Aeolus" as a clue and with "Wandering Rocks" and "Sirens" as the new formal beginning, he went beyond the novel to something else. In each case, the changes in form and style reflect the shedding of an artistic belief no longer sufficient to his vision.

2

"Wandering Rocks" and "Sirens"

The Breakdown of Narrative

In a letter to John Quinn, Joyce pointed out that "Scylla and Charybdis" was the ninth chapter of eighteen, the last chapter of the book's first half.[1] Indeed, this division has more than numerical significance, for both "Lestrygonians" and "Scylla and Charybdis" concern themselves primarily with developing our knowledge of the two main characters, the kind of novelistic enterprise paramount in the first six chapters. After the strange intrusive headings in "Aeolus," the return to the narrative mode in these chapters restores a comforting novelistic convention. Although rhetorical play continues in both chapters, and even some typographical play in "Scylla and Charybdis," it is not until "Wandering Rocks" and "Sirens" that we witness the breakdown of the initial style and a departure from the novelistic form of the book's first half. "Lestrygonians" and "Scylla and Charybdis," then, are less relevant to our discussion of style than the succeeding chapters.

However, before proceeding to "Wandering Rocks" and "Sirens," I would like to comment briefly on a specific aspect of the literary self-consciousness in "Scylla and Charybdis," namely, Stephen's public display of his theory on Shakespeare. In its own way, Stephen's verbal fancywork is as showy and attention-getting as the headings of "Aeolus," and, with his literary theory, as with the headings, the book can be said to turn back on itself to comment on its own creation. Like the headings, which call into question the idea of the origin of the writing, Stephen's theory deals with the relationship between creating consciousness and creation. The important distinction, however, is that the primary vehicle for the literary criticism in "Scylla and Charybdis" is character rather than narrative, and the comment on origins is given a naturalistic, dramatic context. The showmanship primarily attaches to Stephen: "Speech, speech. But act. Act speech. They mock to try you. Act. Be acted upon" (*U* 9.78–79), Stephen directs himself during his strategic, experimental performance. Even the greater rhetorical play in the third-person narration seems closely linked to Stephen's theatricality. As Robert Kellogg has noted, much of the verbal play in the narrative seems to be an extension of Stephen's "powerfully patterned imagination."[2] This relationship between the theatrics in the narrative and the theatrics of the character is more exaggerated than, but still in keeping with, the kind of "borrowing" between character and narrative seen in the earlier chapters.

Stephen's critical premise—that the writer reveals his psychological obsessions in disguised and multiple forms in his work—can be applied to Stephen's literary theory itself, for his elaborate reading of Shakespeare is, of course, an expression of his own feelings about paternity, betrayal, and the relationship between the artist and his work. The basic image of the artist fathering himself is a comfort to a young writer who scorns his natural parents and thinks of himself as "made not begotten" (*U* 3.45). Aside from the light it sheds on Stephen, however, the literary theory has important implications for *Ulysses* as a whole. One could relate Stephen's theory to the revelation of Joyce's own psychological obsessions in *Ulysses*, as Mark Schechner does in his book *Joyce in Nighttown: A Psychoanalytic Inquiry into "Ulysses."*[3] For our purposes, however, a more relevant application of the theory is to Joyce's deliberate use of rhetoric and style to reveal and disguise himself in his work. In its broadest implications, Stephen's theory represents more than a straight biographical approach to literature: it recognizes the subtle, intricate relationship between the artist's self-exposure and disguise in his work. One is reminded of Stanislaus's comment that Joyce's style is such that he seems to confess "in a foreign language."[4] As Stephen shows with Shakespeare, the consciousness of the artist is fractured in his work; it can be dispersed, however, not only among multiple characters but among multiple styles as well. In a sense, Joyce reveals himself in the rhetorical masks of the second half of *Ulysses* as well as in the "signature style" of the early chapters, and, paradoxically, it is in the gestures of imitation and disguise that we come to recognize him.

In later chapters of *Ulysses*, self-referential literary criticism is conveyed largely by rhetorical display in the narrative rather than by the verbal grandstanding of the characters. In fact, Stephen's literary pyrotechnics pale next to the book's showpiece of literary criticism, "Oxen of the Sun." Once again in *Ulysses*, we find that what begins on the level of character reemerges on the level of narration later on. It is in "Oxen" that Stephen's parable will give way to parody and his craftiness will be transferred to the craft of the writing.

"Wandering Rocks"

From the highly charged psychological dramas of Stephen Dedalus and William Shakespeare in "Scylla and Charybdis," we move to the dispassionate, almost deadpan narration in "Wandering Rocks." Jackson Cope has called the narration of this chapter "meticulous," and observes that the "drastic shift in stylistic technique" in "Sirens" is "all the more marked for coming upon the heels of the meticulous narration of 'Wandering Rocks.'"[5] But the simplicity of the narrative is deceptive and its "meticulousness" excessive. Although the familiar techniques of narration in the book's first half continue—interior monologue, free indirect discourse, dialogue, and the initial style of third-person narration—something strange happens nonetheless.

Like Gradgrind, the narrative spews forth a compendium of facts. Streets are named, the characters' courses are charted; the chapter ostentatiously creates that "complete picture" of Dublin from which the city itself could be reconstructed. But a seeming paradox arises from the way in which this is accomplished. While establishing the sense of fact in the text, the "meticulous" documentation suggests the strangeness of reality. Reality is "defamiliarized," to borrow a phrase from the Russian formalists, a process due to the type of narrative mind in the chapter. This narrative mind exhibits what I would call a "lateral" or paratactic imagination: it catalogues facts without synthesizing them. It documents the events that occur but fails to give the causal, logical, or even temporal connections between them. The discontinuity of the sections of "Wandering Rocks" is the most obvious example of this lack of synthesis. The temporal connections between the events presented in successive sections are deliberately obscured. For example, successive sections often refer to events occurring simultaneously, but there is no reference to this simultaneity in the text.[6] Indeed, within a single section, strange juxtapositions occur. For example, the narrator documents Father Conmee's movement along Mountjoy square east and then suddenly interpolates a description of the movements of Mr Denis J. Maginni, professor of dancing—movements that occur presumably at the same time but in a different place (U 10.40–41, 53–55). Even within a sentence, two actions are associated whose connection is arbitrary by the standards of novel writing, for they have no connection besides the mere coincidence in time (and a whimsical connection between the types of movements described): "Corny Kelleher sped a silent jet of hayjuice arching from his mouth while a generous white arm from a window in Eccles Street flung forth a coin" (*U* 10.221–23).

Time and space are the unifiers in the universe of the chapter: the characters moving through Dublin are related by *coincidence* in time and *proximity* in space. Instead of plot as conspiracy (as reflected in Stephen's theory on Shakespeare), or at least as motivated drama, we find the characters' actions plotted according to the coordinates of time and space. The apparently arbitrary and accidental connections between events and people in "Wandering Rocks" deepen the skepticism about any absolute idea of order introduced in "Aeolus."

But if the narrative confounds our expectations of plot by connecting two events arbitrarily, it also fails to acknowledge certain connections when they do occur. The narrator mentions a "onelegged sailor" in section one of the chapter ("A onelegged sailor, swinging himself onward by lazy jerks of his crutches, growled some notes" [*U* 10.7–8]) and again in section three ("A onelegged sailor crutched himself round MacConnell's corner, skirting Rabaiotti's icecream car, and jerked himself up Eccles Street" [*U* 10.228–29]). The repetition is strange because there is no acknowledgment in the narrative that the sailor is the *same* one in both descriptions. The narrative inability to progress from the indefinite to the definite article illustrates a strange failing in the "narrative memory." A crucial component of the development of narrative is precisely this ability to synthesize knowledge while accumulating it. In the previous example, the kind of conceptualization and logical subordination of events that one would expect in narrative discourse is again strangely absent.

This absence of connective fiber is reflected in other curious examples of verbal repetition. The following piece of dialogue appears at two different points in the narrative (with the only difference being the addition of a comma after the word "answered" in the second variation): "—Hello, Simon, Father Crowley said. How are things?"(*U* 10.740, 881) "—Hello Bob, old man, Mr Dedalus answered, stopping" (*U* 10.741, 882). Similarly, in a phrase in the initial style of third-person narration, we are told that "the young woman abruptly bent and with slow care detached from her light skirt a clinging twig" (*U* 10.201–2), and later in the same chapter this phrase is repeated with slight modification: "The young woman with slow care detached from her light skirt a clinging twig" (*U* 10.440–41). Although the two narrative descriptions document the same event, there is no awareness of this congruence in the narrative.

This verbatim repetition imparts a curiously mechanical quality to the narrative, as if a writing machine, rather than a human imagination, produced it. As in the previous description, the minor characters in the novel are tagged with characteristic descriptions or epithets. This mechanical system of classification has an important effect upon characterization in the novel. Whereas the repetition of phrases from a character's interior monologue helped establish the density of the character's inner life, the repetition of phrases in "Wandering Rocks" signals an odd reversal. The phrases are no longer subordinate to a sense of character; rather, the minor characters are reduced to the status of phrases. The existence of the "young woman" seems to be totally contingent upon the particular phrase that identifies her, as if she and her linguistic tag were identical. Similarly, "Marie Kendall, charming soubrette," and "Mr Denis Maginni, professor of dancing, &c." are comically inseparable from their advertisements. It is as if these linguistic labels exhausted the potential of the characters, as if Thom's Dublin Dictionary were equated with the real life of Dublin. Sentences that would normally refer us to the world of external reality begin to seem like cross-references in a textbook. As in "Aeolus," the process of inventory emphasizes the artifice of the writing.

Thus, masses of facts accumulate in the text with either arbitrary conceptual links or no links provided by the lateral imagination of the narrative. This strange cataloguing activity is reflected in the syntax of the prose itself. Sometimes the prose is paratactic and choppy ("Father Conmee perceived her perfume in the car. He perceived also that the awkward man at the other side of her was sitting on the edge of the seat" [*U* 10.128–30]). However, one of the most interesting stylistic phenomena in the chapter is the threading together of "facts" in long, winding sentences (either grammatically paratactic or hypotactic), such as the following:

> Lawyers of the past, haughty, pleading, beheld pass from the consolidated taxing office to Nisi Prius court Richie Goulding carrying the costbag of Goulding, Collis and Ward and heard rustling from the

> admiralty division of king's bench to the court of appeal an elderly female with false teeth smiling incredulously and a black silk skirt of great amplitude. (*U* 10.470–75)

and

> An elderly female, no more young, left the building of the courts of chancery, king's bench, exchequer and common pleas, having heard in the lord chancellor's court the case in lunacy of Potterton, in the admiralty division the summons, exparte motion, of the owners of the Lady Cairns versus the owners of the barque Mona, in the court of appeal reservation of judgment in the case of Harvey versus the Ocean Accident and Guarantee Corporation. (*U* 10.625–31)

Although formally connected, the clauses and phrases of the sentences often bear arbitrary and irrelevant conceptual connections to one another. Here are Jamesian sentences sorely lacking the interpretive intelligence to wrestle with subtle connections and relationships. In these particular examples, the lengthy clauses are initiated by the similar phrases "having heard" and "and heard." A Pandora's box opens up in the narration: not only are the activities and thoughts of the characters illustrious objects in the narrative catalogue but so too are the immediate past experiences of the characters, even if they have been documented previously in the narration. The narrative could then presumably continue to catalogue and recatalogue these experiences ad infinitum.

In fact, from that which was *actually heard* by the characters, the narrative passes to the *hearsay* meticulously documented in the last section of the chapter: "On Northumberland and Landsdowne roads His Excellency acknowledged punctually salutes from rare male walkers, the salute of two small schoolboys at the garden gate of the house *said to have been admired* by the late queen when visiting the Irish capital with her husband, the prince consort, in 1849" (*U* 10.1277–81; my italics). And the documentation of what might have happened is complemented in the last section by the documentation of what failed to happen: the viceregal carriages pass "unsaluted," John Henry Menton holds "a fat gold hunter watch not looked at in his fat left hand not feeling it," and Mr Denis J. Maginni walks "unobserved." The mushrooming sentences comically undermine any sense of telos in the writing. As in a comic cartoon, the plot of the novel seems to grow uncontrollably; everything seems potentially related to, indeed contaminated by, everything else (a kind of contamination that reaches epidemic proportions in "Ithaca"). Instead of Aristotle's definition of plot as an imitation of an action, this narrative gives us plot as infinite potentiality. For in documenting what doesn't happen in the chapter, Joyce plays with the categories of potentiality: the sentences of the chapter present a story in which boy doesn't meet girl nor fall in love nor get married ("Heard melodies are sweet, but those unheard/Are sweeter . . ."). The limitations imposed upon novel writing by the exigencies of plot making are ignored, and the reader's expectation of the functional relevance of narrative details is undermined. In "Wandering Rocks," the text includes the possibilities of writing usually "ousted" by any particular linear movement of plot. This is the aesthetic transvaluation of Stephen's interest in "Nestor" in the "ousted possibilities" of history.[7] Plot is the novelistic counterpart of history; especially in "Aeolus," "Wandering Rocks," and "Ithaca," Joyce investigates the possibilities that are ousted by conventional novelistic plot.

But the grammatical counterpart of plot is syntax, and in revealing the infinite potentiality of the plot, the narrative also reveals the infinite expansibility of the sentence. The sentences parody the arbitrary structure of prose writing. The narrative's attempt to catalogue all the action of the chapter is comically outpaced by the possibilities that present themselves as potential members in the catalogue. The sentences themselves huff and puff in a futile attempt to say all that can be said. The taciturnity of the initial style is replaced by the over-eager attempt to include everything. Roland Barthes' analysis of Flaubert's sentences is comically illustrated in "Wandering Rocks":

> La phrase est un objet, en elle une finitude fascine . . . mais en même temps par le mécanisme . . . de l'expansion, toute phrase est insaturable, on ne dispose d'aucune raison structurelle de l'arrêter ici plutôt que là. . . . Elle est comme l'arrêt gratuit d'une liberté infinie.
> [The sentence is an object in which finitude entrances . . . but at the same time by a mechanism . . . of expansion, every sentence is insaturable; there is no structural reason to stop here rather than there. . . . It is like the arbitrary limit to an infinite freedom.][8]

If the headlines of "Aeolus" revealed the potentially limitless number of sentences about Dublin, the sentences of "Wandering Rocks" reveal the potentially infinite expansibility of the sentence itself. Conversely, they reveal the gratuitousness of any chosen terminus for the sentence, a gratuitousness also found in the narrative of "Eumaeus." The syntax of a sentence progressively limits the potential choices of that sentence—its beginning limits the possibilities of its end. However, in the sentences of "Wandering Rocks," Joyce plays against this expectation of narrowing possibilities and ultimate closure, as successive clauses follow each other exhaustively in the prose.

In "Wandering Rocks," the book continues the exploration of its own choices begun in "Aeolus." It prepares for the investigation of potentiality in later chapters: "Circe" (the psychic potentiality of the characters); "Sirens," "Oxen of the Sun," and "Eumaeus" (stylistic and syntactic potentiality); and "Ithaca" (the potentiality of the plot). It is interesting that all of the examples I have cited from "Wandering Rocks" that illustrate an interest in the categories of potentiality were *added* to the chapter after its publication in *The Little Review*.[9] Joyce interpolated these passages into the text while he was working on the later chapters of the book. Despite the chapter's apparent simplicity, it thus anticipates the bizarre narrative activity of the chapters to come.

"Sirens"

In the "overture" of the "Sirens" chapter, *Ulysses* abandons even the pretense of being a traditional novel. Here conventional units of narration are fractured: short lines of non sequitur replace the paragraph, and splintered phrases replace the sentence. In turning the page from the lengthy paragraphs that conclude "Wandering Rocks," the reader comes upon a kind of shorthand or code in which Joyce seems to be playing linguistic games of notation. In the overture, the reader is offered an incomplete and abbreviated transcription of reality.

I have used the term "overture" as a convenient label for the opening section of the chapter because it does function as a musical overture, introducing the phrases and themes that are "orchestrated" in the narrative. However, the analogy between music and language does not, to my mind, supply the raison d'être of this strange section, as critics have suggested in discussing the "art" of the chapter. For example, Stanley Sultan contends that the "justification" for the section is that it "imitates an operatic overture."[10] But to see the chapter merely as an imitation of a musical form is to ignore how the stylistic antics in "Sirens" are anticipated in previous chapters and continued in subsequent chapters. The breakdown of the logic of narration and the willful arbitrariness of the writing in "Sirens" are first seen in "Aeolus" and extended in "Wandering Rocks." In addition, the linguistic games in the overture are anticipated in the games of notation found in "Calypso" ("Mkgnao . . . Mrkgnao! the cat cried") and in "Aeolus" ("The door of Ruttledge's office whispered: ee: cree"). And, finally, the variations played on the phrases of the overture in the narrative of "Sirens" illustrate a kind of rhetorical exercise which becomes increasingly obvious in later chapters that do not have music as their "art." The text as a *verbal composition* supersedes the text as an imitation of a musical composition.

The relationship of music and writing can be most fruitfully regarded not as an airtight analogy but as a kind of experimental premise in the chapter. The critical question then becomes, How does Joyce play on this relationship, that is, what happens to the text when this experiment is conducted? In a sense, the "Sirens" chapter is Joyce's experimental and, I think, parodic answer to Walter Pater, the tutelary genius of the chapter, who said that all art constantly aspires to the condition of music. The chapter shows us how language is and is not music—it plays a number of variations on this basic idea. In the process, the text displays its artifice, its status as a verbal composition. The experimental premise of the chapter thus liberates the stylistic behavior of the text. Joyce's experiments with the relationship between language and music issue in particular kinds of verbal antics that, in turn, have important implications for the reading of the text.

The overture attempts to reproduce literal music as well as formally to imitate its structure, for the overture is largely an encoded transcription of sound: it gives us the sounds of a voice, a piano, a garter snap, a laugh, applause. In "Sirens," Joyce turns the novel over to sound, that is, he writes a chapter that focuses on the "music" of Dublin—on its literal music (there is music played throughout the chapter), on its dialogue, and on its noises. In his games of notation in the overture, Joyce plays with the idea of reducing sound, verbal and nonverbal, to its written equivalent. For example, the phrase "Will lift your tschink with tschunk" reproduces a toast—both the words of the toast ("will lift your glass with us") and the sound of clinking glasses ("tschink with tschunk"). Perhaps the most famous example of sound reduced to its written equivalent is the representation of flatulence at the end of the chapter ("Pprrpffrrppffff").

In the overture, Joyce exploits the distance between the printed word and the sound it represents. In *The Stoic Comedians,* Hugh Kenner has observed of Joyce's games of notation in *Ulysses* that "there is something mechanical,

Joyce never lets us forget, about all reductions of speech to arrangements of twenty-six letters."[11] It seems to me that in "Sirens" there is a special poignancy to the gap between sound and written language: Joyce shows us in the chapter that no matter how hard the writing may try to capture the living music of Dublin, the text, like all texts, is silent. A crucial component of the chapter's irony is its revelation of the way in which writing is *not* music. One can say that the relationship between the transcriptions in the overture and real sound is like the relationship between a musical score and music. Like the musical symbols of a score, the signs of the overture remind us of what is lost in the transcription of sound.

As a kind of musical score, the chapter lays bare its inner workings. The overture in particular exposes the chapter's structure and composition by offering a "breakdown" of the narrative system into its constituent elements. Like a musical overture, the first section of "Sirens" offers an encapsulated version of the narrative. It provides a kind of table of contents, a chronological catalogue of what we can expect to find. The "contents" of the chapter are, as I have mentioned, the sounds of Dublin out of which the text will be constructed. In the overture, we are shown the elements before they are woven into a comprehensive semantic system. They are neither classified in narrative categories (like direct dialogue or third-person narration) nor developed into dramatic symbols (like "Jingle jingle jaunted jingling," which becomes a symbol for Boylan's car, and then for Boylan, and then for the cuckolding of Leopold Bloom). It is as if Ibsen reduced Nora's door slam to the status of mere noise.

Behind their meaning as acoustic transcriptions, however, the lines of the overture are themselves words on a page: the overture breaks down the contents of the chapter even further into the autonomous words and phrases that constitute the chapter. In confronting the almost meaningless overture, we are reminded that the literary text is comprised not of characters, nor plots, nor philosophies, but words.[12] In this way, the overture calls attention to the writer's tools: ultimately, we are meant to marvel at the creation of a story out of such basic ingredients. Again, there is a reminder of the text as a rhetorical exercise, a narrative fiat. "Sirens" provides a more self-conscious beginning to the narrative than any other chapter, for in the overture, the chapter ritualizes its intention to begin. Explicitly announcing its own end with the word "*Done*," the overture provides an introduction to the narrative proper with the word "Begin!" Because a novel tends to hide the laws of its composition so that we concentrate on what it is saying, this exposure of structure makes us aware of the text as a constructed system.[13]

Like "Aeolus," "Sirens" is a chapter that emphasizes the artifice of the text—the drama of the writing usurps the dramatic action. But the most interesting experiments in this chapter are the more local, verbal games played in the sentences of the narrative. A kind of breakdown of the style occurs that mirrors the anatomy of structure, for the narrative norm from the preceding chapters seems to be dissected and reassembled like a Tinker toy. Phrases are repeated, rearranged, slightly distorted. Statements in the serious, literate, precise prose of the narrative norm suffer the indignities of constant revision—they are pulled apart and examined, their literacy and assertiveness collapsing under the scrutiny. As in "Aeolus," we are drawn in "Sirens" to the surface of the language: in "Sirens," however, the play of the language almost seems to interrupt the telling of the story.

Recognizable examples of the narrative norm can be found in "Sirens," serving their characteristic function of documentation. For example, "Miss Douce's brave eyes, unregarded, turned from the crossblind, smitten by sunlight" (*U* 11.460–61) is identifiably in the initial style of the book. The precision and formality of its diction, its slight syntactic and semantic dislocations (that is, the awkward separation of the adjective "unregarded" and the figure "brave eyes"), and the obvious attention to sound are hallmarks of the initial style. However, rather surprisingly, an entire paragraph seems to "mushroom" out of this statement:

> Miss Douce's brave eyes, unregarded, turned from the crossblind, smitten by sunlight. Gone. Pensive (who knows?), smitten (the smiting light), she lowered the dropblind with a sliding cord. She drew down pensive (why did he go so quick when I?) about her bronze over the bar where bald stood by sister gold, inexquisite contrast, contrast inexquisite nonexquisite, slow cool dim seagreen sliding depth of shadow, *eau de Nil*. (*U* 11.460–65)

The succeeding sentences in the paragraph combine interior monologue with continued third-person narration, a juxtaposition that occurs in other chapters. But what is strange about the page is that the first narrative statement is immediately rewritten and explored: it gives birth to an exuberant narrative excursus. The initial sentence generates its own qualifications that are, in turn, repeated and qualified at an accelerating pace. The second sentence (omitting the word "Gone") explores the implicit pun in the first

(Miss Douce is both smitten with love for Boylan and struck by the harsh light of the sun). Similarly, the third sentence begins to repeat and expand on the second, when, quite inexplicably, it fixates on producing variations of itself and begins to rearrange the phrase "inexquisite contrast." This narrative exuberance is made more comic because it is itself based on a distorted echo of both a comment by Miss Kennedy ("Exquisite contrast," *U* 11.68) and a narrative comment about her and Miss Douce ("Ladylike in exquisite contrast," *U* 11.106). The phrase "in exquisite" becomes "inexquisite"; through some rather deaf-eared transcribing, the phrase becomes its opposite.

Thus, in the midst of the narrative, language circles back on itself, as if, by some strange compulsion, three steps backward must accompany any one step forward.[14] As in the preceding example, the narrative excursus sometimes involves an inaccurate repetition of a phrase already uttered. Simon Dedalus asks Miss Douce for some whiskey and she replies, "With the greatest alacrity." Suddenly, however, the phrase is repeated in the narrative in slightly altered form: "With the greatest alacrity" is transformed into "with grace of alacrity," and an entire passage is spawned from this distortion:

> With grace of alacrity towards the mirror gilt Cantrell and Cochrane's she turned herself. With grace she tapped a measure of gold whisky from her crystal keg. Forth from the skirt of his coat Mr Dedalus brought pouch and pipe. Alacrity she served. (*U* 11.214–17)

Here the sounds of phrases are repeated while their sense is ignored. As in the child's game of telephone, the original statement is lost in the translation, but the writing seems not to notice. (Instead of the absolute pitch we might expect to find in the chapter about music, we find much less than perfect hearing. At times we seem to be in the same unfortunate predicament as Bald deaf Pat who "seehears lipspeech" [*U* 11.10][15]

This deaf-eared transcribing places the emphasis on the phonetic rather than the semantic characteristics of words. An interest in the sounds of words begins to dominate the writing. Throughout the narrative, we find rhetorical figures of sound, such as rhyme, assonance, alliteration, elision—sentences like "lightward, gliding, mild, she smiled on Boylan." If we have seen the language of "Sirens" imitate literal sounds, we also see it here as itself a form of arranged sound. Aural associations guide the movement of the sentences: "Encore, enclap, said, cried, clapped all" (*U* 11.757–58). A personal pronoun metamorphoses into a laugh right before our eyes (or ears, as the case may be). "Pat is a waiter who waits while you wait. Hee hee hee hee" (*U* 11.916). In experimenting with language as patterned sound, Joyce liberates all kinds of aural associations and combinations. The rhetorical schemes and aural poetry of the initial style are now exaggerated into bizarre verbal behavior—sounds migrate within a sentence, as in the example "Mr Bloom reached Essex bridge. Yes, Mr Bloom crossed Bridge of Yessex" (*U* 11.228–29).[16]

As the chapter experiments with the sounds of words, the machinery or narration begins to creak and groan. Joyce deliberately sabotages the devices of narration used so effectively in the early chapters of the novel. The third-person narration becomes deliberately awkward: the writing has a comical, gestural component, as if a drunken clowning were enacted by the language itself. The moment the narration attempts to walk a straight line, it begins to wobble. A confident narrative statement such as "From the saloon a call came, long in dying" suddenly gives way to the awkward strains of "that was a tuningfork the tuner had that he forgot that he now struck. A call again. That he now poised that it now throbbed" (*U* 11.313–15). An excess of labor is needed for the simplest narrative functions (the reader is reminded of the comic style first glimpsed in "Telemachus"). With the punctiliousness and defensiveness of a drunk trying to prove he can still speak coherently, the narrative must labor to communicate even the simplest ideas: "He, Mr Bloom, listened while he, Richie Goulding, told him, Mr Bloom, of the night he, Richie, heard him, Si Dedalus, sing *'Twas rank and fame* in his, Ned Lambert's house" (*U* 11.816–17). Indirect discourse becomes increasingly indirect and awkward: "First gentleman told Mina that was so. She asked him was that so. And second tankard told her so. That that was so" (*U* 11.816–17). Narrative statements documenting external reality are misplaced, as if the narrative were a broken record telling us something we have already heard and no longer need to know: "Blazes Boylan's smart tan shoes creaked on the barfloor, said before" (*U* 11.761). (Boylan, we have been told already, has left the bar and is on his way to Molly's.)

In "Sirens," the book examines its own resources and plays with the kind of language it has once taken seriously. The third-person narration in the early chapters seems to have outlived its usefulness, and, indeed, it disappears after the "Sirens" chapter (as I said previously, I will discuss its brief reappearance in "Nausicaa"). The serious, literate documentation of reality becomes in "Sirens" almost an illiterate verbal gesture ("Bald deaf Pat brought quite flat pad ink" [*U* 11.847]). And the lyrical strand of the initial style associated with Stephen Dedalus turns into a verbal fiasco of excessive alliteration. In the following passage (a description of Simon Dedalus singing an aria), Joyce gives us his most parodic interpretation of Pater's observation that all art aspires to the condition of music:

> It soared, a bird, it held its flight, a swift pure cry, soar silver orb it leaped serene, speeding, sustained, to come, don't spin it out too long long breath he breath long life, soaring high, high resplendent, aflame, crowned, high in the effulgence symbolistic, high, of the ethereal bosom, high, of the high vast irradiation everywhere all soaring all around about the all, the endlessnessness. (*U* 11.745–50)

In this passage, Joyce invokes the spirit of Walter Pater, plagiarizes Dan Dawson in "Aeolus" (see Dawson's speech in *U* 7.327–28), and parodies the lyrical flights to which both he and Stephen Dedalus have sometimes been prone (see the epiphany on the beach in *A Portrait* and the lyrical descriptions in "Telemachus"—"Woodshadows floated silently by through the morning peace from the stairhead seaward where he gazed [. . .] White breast of the dim sea [. . .] Wavewhite wedded words shimmering on the dim tide" [*U* 1.242–47]). In *Ulysses on the Liffey*, Richard Ellmann suggests that this passage parodies the sentimentality of the characters listening to the music,[17] but it seems too tame to go beyond parody of character to a parody of lyricism and all pretensions to fine writing, even the book's own. The book borrows from the high-flown oratory of a character mocked in a previous chapter: excess infiltrates the writing.

In "Sirens," the play of rhetorical figures first seen in "Aeolus" leads to a more insistent verbal tinkering with the prose. If the verbal play and the headlines in "Aeolus" diverted us from the action in the micro-narrative, in "Sirens" the surface of the prose is even more absorbing, at times even obstructionist. In its self-delighted preening, the narration almost seems to ignore what is happening in the plot.[18] The play of the language is, in fact, a kind of linguistic diversion from the main event of the day, which occurs offstage: Molly's adultery with Boylan. For while the writing amuses itself with linguistic games, while the characters, including Bloom, amuse themselves with music, Boylan amuses himself with Molly. To put it another way, the reader is absorbed by the verbal surface of the prose just as Bloom momentarily escapes his loneliness, specifically his thoughts of his wife's adultery, by listening to music. The writing, like the music for the characters, is a form of play that substitutes pleasure for pain. The rhetorical play in part derives from the "gap" between reality and language: if language is basically defective as an instrument for transcribing the sounds and experiences of life, it still makes an exceptional Tinker toy. If it can never really aspire to the condition of music for fear of becoming ridiculous, its patterns of sound can generate interesting distortions of sense. The knowledge of the "gap" between reality and language leads, then, to a sense of liberation as well as loss.

And yet, paradoxically, the deliberately oblique treatment of the action functions as a strategy for capturing the pain being repressed. The avoidance makes us aware of the pain, just as Bloom's sudden reminder of Molly's meeting with Boylan (occasioned by the coincidence of his watch stopping at four-thirty) hits him with greater force because he has tried to forget it. An example of this oblique treatment is the sentence "Bloom looped, unlooped, noded, disnoded" (U 11.704). Twisting language in a verbal imitation of Bloom's game with an elastic band, the writing expresses Bloom's pain not by direct statement but in the rhythms of the prose. The prose bides its time, Bloom bides his time; both gestures make us aware of what is not confronted, either verbally in the narration or mentally by Bloom. Another example of this oblique treatment of emotion is the following: "Under the sandwichbell lay on a bier of bread one last, one lonely, last sardine of summer. Bloom alone" (U 11.1220–21). In this example, the avoidance comes in the form of metaphoric substitution. In "Sirens," our sense of the emotional as well as the empirical reality is stubbornly maintained throughout the verbal machinations of the prose.

3

"Eumaeus"

The Way of All Language

By the time he reaches "Eumaeus," the reader is prepared for outrageous experiments in *Ulysses*; after "Cyclops," "Oxen of the Sun," and "Circe," he no longer expects the relative tameness of the initial style. The first sentence of the chapter informs him of the book's return to narrative after the expressionistic drama of "Circe." In this first sentence, we recognize the sound of other chapter openings in *Ulysses*, such as "Stately, plump Buck Mulligan came from the stairhead" and "By lorries along sir John Rogerson's quay Mr Bloom walked soberly," where the physical action is described in faintly pompous, inaugural tones. But in "Eumaeus," precision is exaggerated into punctiliousness; the literate diction cedes to faded elegance and cliché.

> Preparatory to anything else Mr Bloom brushed off the greater bulk of the shavings and handed Stephen the hat and ashplant and bucked him up generally in orthodox Samaritan fashion which he very badly needed. (*U* 16.1–3)

Circumspect, in a succession of phrases, the sentence seeks to modify and amplify its subject. Beginning portentously with the phrase "preparatory to anything else," it betrays its pretensions with slang expressions ("buck him up"). Redundant, idiomatic, it finally collapses into anticlimax. Although the reader no longer expects to find the initial style, he might wonder why this sentence would be produced by a man who could write, "Two shafts of soft daylight fell across the flagged floor from the high barbicans: and at the meeting of their rays a cloud of coalsmoke and fumes of fried grease floated, turning" (*U* 1.315–17).

As the first sentence indicates, the language of "Eumaeus" is pretentious, verbose, and clichéd. It displays a love of elegant variation, convoluted phrases, and Latinate diction: "Possibly perceiving an expression of dubiosity on their faces, the globetrotter went on, adhering to his adventures" (*U* 16.574–75). Where one word will do, it insists on a phrase ("his expression of features"). But its most salient characteristic is its commonplaces, idioms, proverbs, and clichés:

> . . . on his expressed desire for some beverage to drink Mr Bloom in view of the hour it was and there being no pump of Vartry water available for their ablutions, let alone drinking purposes hit upon an expedient by suggesting, off the reel, the propriety of the cabman's shelter, as it was called, hardly a stonesthrow away near Butt bridge where they might hit upon some drinkables in the shape of a milk and soda or a mineral. (*U* 16.5–11)

As can be seen from the previous examples, the style has pretensions to elegance. Sometimes the writing tries to be coy and cute: "The keeper of the shelter in the middle of this *tête-à-tête* put a boiling swimming cup of a choice concoction labelled coffee on the table and a rather antediluvian specimen of a bun, or so it seemed" (*U* 16.354–56). It specializes, however, in little verbal twists on clichés ("gone the way of all buttons," "on the tapis," "ventilated the matter thoroughly"), or in coinages ("Sherlockholmsing it") and forced puns ("Telegraphic, Tell a graphic lie") of a type Lenehan would offer in "Aeolus." The style, in fact, is not the "namby-pamby" style of a Gerty MacDowell but a style that exaggerates the qualities of the more educated, garrulous talk of the storytellers, would-be rhetoricians, and resident Dublin wits at their worst moments: "So as neither of them were particularly pressed for time, as it happened, and the temperature refreshing since it cleared up after the recent visitation of Jupiter Pluvius, they dandered along past by where the empty vehicle was waiting without a fare or a jarvey" (*U* 16.39–42). The elaborate use of classical allusion to describe rain ("the visit of Jupiter Pluvius"), and then the slight twist on the accepted phrase ("visitation"), plus the word "dandered," could originate with a Lenehan but not with a Gerty MacDowell. "Looking back now in a retrospective kind of arrangement" (*U* 16.1400–1401), the narrator says, and this recalls the pretentious critical vocabulary of Tom Kernan, as mocked by Mr Power: "—Trenchant, Mr Power said laughing. He's [Tom Kernan's] dead nuts on that. And the *retrospective arrangement*" (*U* 6.149–50). Stanislaus once described the language of "Eumaeus" as "flabby Dublin journalese, with its weak effort to be witty,"[1] and there is something in "Eumaeus" of the headings (both the pomposity of the late Victorian headings and the smart slang of the "modern" headings) and of the conversation in "Aeolus." The common denominator of all these styles, including Gerty MacDowell's, is their pretense to some kind of fine writing.

The elegance is faded and the language misfires—all deliberately, of course, on Joyce's part. For in "Eumaeus," Joyce chooses the "wrong" word as scrupulously as he chooses the right one in the early chapters. Comedy arises from the narrator's misuse of language—"originality" enters through the back door of error. In phrases like "nipped in the bud of premature decay" and "redolent with rotten corn," we see the narrator's reach exceed his grasp. Language in the chapter glances off its object. A succession of phrases is offered, none of which captures meaning fully. In the following example, we see the narrator trying and failing to duplicate subtle novelistic description: "He displayed half solicitude, half curiosity, augmented by friendliness"—the mathematics of the situation (half and half, plus some more) tells us that too many phrases are needed. As in the language of "Cyclops" and "Nausicaa," sentences that begin with fanfare cannot maintain their high tone. In "Eumaeus," however, it is as if the sentences forget where they begin. (See the sentence beginning with the word "Accordingly" and ending with the words "Dan Bergin's" on pages U 16.18–24).) There is something vaguely senescent about this writing, from the wandering sentences to the half-remembered idioms. It is as if all the allusions, clichés, and idioms of a lifetime floated somewhere in the memory and were summoned forth for the sake of the story. The movement of the narrative mind is like the stream of consciousness of the early chapters slowed down, its associations grown fuzzy. It is as if the silent monologue of the early chapters had become a rambling and tedious after-dinner speech. The narrative is indeed the "narrative old" that Joyce described to Gilbert.[2]

But the "memory" invoked in the chapter is best regarded not as a personal but a collective one, specifically, a linguistic memory. The cumulative effect of all these clichés is to make "Eumaeus" into a kind of encyclopedia of received phrases. If the language of "Eumaeus" is enervated, it is not merely to reflect the fatigue of the characters or a narrator but to reveal that language is tired and "old," used and reused so many times that it runs in grooves. The language of "Eumaeus" is the public, anonymous "voice of culture" first heard in the headings of "Aeolus," a transpersonal repository of received ideas. Just as the narrative of "Aeolus" offers a compendium of rhetorical figures, the narrative of "Eumaeus" offers a compendium of clichés, from a catchword of popular melodrama ("balderdash"), to bureaucratic jargon ("embark on a policy," "Accordingly, after a few such preliminaries"), to proverbs ("as things always moved with the time"), to the low Dublin idiom of the dun in "Cyclops" ("hang it, the first go-off"). Although one can describe the habit of mind or the tone in the chapter, one's final impression of "Eumaeus" is of a body of language—as Gerald Bruns says, "a world of banal locutions within which both narrator and story struggle into being."[3] Clichés in "Eumaeus" are not relegated through indirect discourse to the mind of a character, as in "Nausicaa," or separated typographically from other writing, like the headings of "Aeolus." In "Eumaeus," all writing has become cliché. Joyce gives us, then, a picture of all language in the debased state of the word "love" in the parody of "Cyclops." More than Flaubert in *Bouvard et Pécuchet* or the *Dictionary of Accepted Ideas*, Joyce focuses on received *locutions*, the ready-made phrases that express the received ideas of society.

Both description and discourse pass through the crucible of cliché. Instead of the narrator's borrowing the language of the characters, as he does in free indirect discourse, in "Eumaeus" the discourse of the characters is assimilated to the language of narration (as it is also in "Oxen of the Sun"). "Mr Bloom, likely to poohpooh the situation as egregious balderdash" is a translation of Bloom's reactions into a language he would never use. Neither the prissy "poohpooh the situation" nor the blustery "egregious balderdash" could possibly originate with Leopold Bloom. Similarly, the following passage of Bloom's thoughts is paraphrased:

> It was a subject of regret and absurd as well on the face of it and no small blame to our vaunted society that the man in the street, when the system really needed toning up, for a matter of a couple of paltry pounds was debarred from seeing more of the world they lived in instead of being always cooped up since my old stick-in-the-mud took me for a wife. After all, hang it, they had their eleven and more humdrum months of it and merited a radical change of *venue* after the grind of city life in the summertime for choice when dame Nature is at her spectacular best constituting nothing short of a new lease of life. (*U* 16.539–47)

We recognize this as having elements of Bloom's thought, in its plans for the welfare of society, in its use of the formulae of public wisdom, even in its getting its clichés confused (compare "lease of life" with Bloom's "out of the land of Egypt and into the house of bondage" [*U* 7.208–9]). But this is not the sound of Bloom's mind—from its beginning in the tones of the newspaper editorial, to its shift to the low Dublin idiom, to its conclusions in the tones of a pretentious advertisement in a travel magazine. (Its anger is also alien to Bloom.) This is a picture of Bloom's mind cheated of all its vitality and curiosity. One has only to compare this passage with a passage of stream of consciousness in an earlier chapter to see the distortion:

> The chemist turned back page after page. Sandy shrivelled smell he seems to have. Shrunken skull. And old. Quest for the philosopher's stone. The alchemists. Drugs age you after mental excitement. Lethargy then. Why? Reaction. A lifetime in a night. Gradually changes your character. Living all the day among herbs, ointments, disinfectants. All his alabaster lilypots [. . .] Enough stuff here to chloroform you. Test: turns blue litmus paper red. Chloroform. Overdose of laudanum [. . .] Paragoric poppysyrup bad for cough. Clogs your pores or the phlegm. Poisons the only cures. Remedy where you least expect it. Clever of nature. (*U* 5.472–84)

The depiction of the act of imagination here is different from the one in "Eumaeus," even though in both passages Bloom relies on the formulae in his memory. In "Lotus-Eaters," his manipulation of these formulae is creative, intelligent, funny. "Eumaeus" gives us a travestied form of Bloom's stream of consciousness, a reduction of it to its least common denominator.

What the stream of consciousness technique and the third-person narrative norm in the early chapters had in common was that they purported to present "reality" directly, either psychological or material "reality." In "Eumaeus," this pretense of unmediated vision is exposed once more. The chapter marks the climax of the increasing indirection of the narration seen in "Cyclops" and "Oxen of the Sun." The indirection is flagrantly advertised in various aspects of style: rhetorically in the technique of indirect discourse; semantically in the use of elegant variation, euphemism, and cliché; and syntactically in the circumlocutions of the sentence. In "Eumaeus," Joyce shows us language that is patently inadequate to the task of capturing the subtle nuances of behavior or even the quality of a physical action—a travesty, that is, of the initial style. Instead of language that is able to fix essences in confident phrases, this is language that casts a net of words in the forlorn hope of capturing meaning. It names rather than presents emotional and psychological behavior: "Mr Bloom actuated by motives of inherent delicacy, inasmuch as he always believed in minding his own business moved off but nevertheless remained on the *qui vive* with just a shade of anxiety though not funkyish in the least (*U* 16.116–19). The linguistic tools available are impediments to the capturing of the complexity and subtlety of reality: trying to capture nuance with phrases like "inherent delicacy" and "*qui vive*" is like trying to whittle with a sledgehammer. Wolfgang Iser's description of one of the styles in the "Oxen of the Sun" chapter is equally appropriate to "Eumaeus": "As language approached, reality seemed rather to withdraw than to come closer."[4] The twists and turns of the phrases, the elegant variation, the attempt of the writing to wrap itself around its object in "Eumaeus" reveal the essential discrepancy between language and the reality it seeks to describe. If the circumlocution and the modifying phrases of Henry James's style convince us that language is a subtle and pliable enough instrument for capturing the nuances of life, the travestied style of "Eumaeus" reveals Joyce's essential skepticism about language. In "Eumaeus," he demonstrates once again that life is mediated through the abuses of language.

One can say that "Eumaeus" is a version of the writer's struggle to write with a language that is contaminated, a language that is no longer a transparent medium. In the preface to his *Essais critiques*, Roland Barthes discusses the writer's struggle with language, and I quote him at length because I think he describes the view of language Joyce expresses in "Eumaeus." According to Barthes:

> *La matière première de la littérature n'est pas l'innommable, mais bien au contraire le nommé; celui qui veut écrire doit savoir qu'il commence un long concubinage avec un langage qui est toujours antérieur. L'écrivain n'a donc nullement à <<arracher>> un verbe au silence . . . mais à l'inverse, et combien plus difficilement, plus cruellement et moins glorieusement, à détacher une parole seconde de l'euglument des paroles premieres que lui fournissent le monde, l'histoire, son existence, bref un intelligible qui préexiste, car il vient dans un monde plein de langage. . . . [N]aître n'est rien d'autre que trouver ce code tout fait et devoir s'en accommoder. On entend souvent dire que l'art a pour charge d'exprimer l'inexprimable: c'est le contraire qu'il faut dire (sans nulle intention de paradoxe): toute la tâche de l'art est d'inexprimer l'exprimable, d'enlever à la langue du monde, qui est la pauvre et puissante langue des passions, une parole autre, une parole exacte.*

[The primary substance of literature is not the unnamable, but on the contrary the named; the man who wants to write must know that he is beginning a long concubinage with a language which is always *previous*. The writer does not "wrest" speech from silence . . . but inversely, and how much more arduously, more cruelly and less gloriously, detaches a secondary language from the slime of primary languages afforded him by the world, history, his existence, in short by an intelligibility which preexists him, for he comes into a world full of language. . . . [T]o be born is nothing but to find this code ready-made and to be obliged to accommodate oneself to it. We often hear it said that it is the task of art to *express the inexpressible*; it is the contrary which must be said (with no intention to paradox): the whole task of art is to unexpress the expressible, to kidnap from the world's language, which is the poor and powerful language of the passions, another speech, an exact speech.][5]

"Eumaeus" represents "the world full of language," something that only Flaubert before Joyce had treated so fully in fiction. Through interruption and displacement in the early chapters of *Ulysses*, Joyce dramatized the struggle between writing and rewriting, personal signature and the world's language, in "Eumaeus," he deliberately stages an "accommodation" to writing that is "previous."

There is no particular exponent of language who encroaches on the writer's ego: the "fear" of other writing in "Eumaeus" is generalized beyond individual predecessors (as in "Oxen of the Sun") or even generic models (as in "Cyclops"). Joyce does not display the "anxiety of influence" which Harold Bloom describes, that Freudian battle of Titanic egos;[6] instead, he reveals a more general anxiety about writing as an echo of other writing and language that has been tainted by its prior use. Joyce is quoted as having remarked to a friend: "I'd like a language which is above all languages, a language to which all will do service. I cannot express myself in English without enclosing myself in a tradition."[7] Again, one can see Joyce's desire to transcend the limitations of language and the classifications of reality offered by his predecessors.

The problem posed by this linguistic inheritance, however, is not only that it is a threat to the writer's ego but also that it assaults intelligence and meaning. It is the Flaubertian language of stupidity. The clichés and proverbs, the public wisdom of "Eumaeus," exemplify the premature "conclusions" leading to stupidity. The clichés are a system of classification through which life in all its complexity is forced. This anonymous voice of culture expounds a rigid system of meaning, whether in its old wives' tales or its scientific formulae. It is not that these "conclusions" are always untrue, but that they pretend they are the only possible truth. They organize the world in terms of type and generalization that belie the contingency of individual fact.

If in the style of scrupulous meanness Joyce tried to pare away the numerous associations of words, in "Eumaeus" he deliberately decided to let the linguistic memory loose on the page to devour the individual style. If the style of scrupulous meanness was in part a defense against a lapse into the stupidity of language, the style of "Eumaeus" suggests that no one is exempt from this stupidity. For by the time we reach "Eumaeus," we realize that everyone is implicated in it. Wayne Booth's "stable irony" is no longer possible, for no one, no writer or reader, can remain outside the ring of stupidity that Joyce draws. The condescending irony of Flaubert to his characters in *Madame Bovary* and of Joyce to the "submerged population" in *Dubliners* and in "Nausicaa" is obsolete. The narrative of "Eumaeus" embodies, with gross exaggeration, our inescapable stupidities; no one, Joyce seems to be saying, even the most "scrupulous" writer, can prevent the presence of at least some cliché in his writing.

But if he abandoned the defense against stupidity available in the style of scrupulous meanness, Joyce substituted another defense. On one level, the writing of "Eumaeus" functions like the parodies of "Cyclops": it attempts to disarm criticism through self-mockery. There is something redemptive about conceding one's stupidity. Both the writer's and the reader's implicit defense against stupidity is to recognize it. We recognize a cliché as a cliché—a reader who does not would not be the one for whom the book was created (and only someone like Gerty MacDowell or a cliché expert like Joyce could produce such a thorough list of received locutions). The attempt to outdo a Gerty MacDowell in producing clichés is a strategy that can he used after stable irony is obsolete. But there is a greater sense of defensiveness about the writing in "Eumaeus," for in turning his writing over to cliché, Joyce asserts his own consciousness over the kind of inadvertent slips into cliché displayed by even the best writers. The compulsiveness and comprehensiveness of the catalogue of clichés in "Eumaeus" makes one sense that Joyce felt the worst thing that he could do was to accidentally include a cliché without recognizing it as such. There is a driven quality to the writing, as if by including all possible clichés, Joyce could prove himself their master. Instead of mocking eloquence and emotion by rewriting it in parodic form (as in "Cyclops"), Joyce subjects all writing to "stupidity" right away. In this sense, the writing takes no risks. It is like lying down to prevent a fall.

But on the other hand, the writing of "Eumaeus" is a virtuoso display of what a writer can do once he accepts the inadequacy of language: it is both a demonstration of the problems of language and a linguistic performance. If everybody succumbs to cliché some of the time, no one but Joyce would think of writing in cliché for a whole chapter. By intensifying the use of clichés, by making them come at the reader so thick and so fast at every comma, Joyce exposes their absurdity. He destroys the context in which clichés might appear natural (as in a nineteenth-century sentimental novel, for example, in which some cliché is permissible and, indeed, expected). But Joyce also asserts his own ability to tell a story using only this execrable language, to put more of an obstacle in his way than any other writer, and then to proceed to keep our attention by showing us just how wonderfully bad the style is. In fact, what is startling about the clichés in "Eumaeus" is that Joyce deliberately does nothing to revitalize them in the way he does in "Cyclops," for example, or in *Finnegans Wake*. In "Language of/as Gesture in Joyce," David Hayman shows effectively how Joyce often cleverly returns the language of cliché to gesture (for example, by turning the expression "I could eat you up" into "We could ate you, par Buccas, and imbabe through you, reassuranced in the wild lac of gotliness" in *Finnegans Wake* [FW 378. 2–4]).[8] Conversely, in "Eumaeus," he gives us the narrator's deliberately feeble attempts to revive cliché in expressions like "the horse at the end of his tether," which applies to a literal horse. A phrase like "gone the way of all buttons" is the kind of phrase that would become a pun in *Finnegans Wake* (one can imagine that the substitution of "buttons" for "flesh" in the phrase "gone the way of all flesh" would at least produce "gone the way of all buttoms"). The performance in "Eumaeus" consists of Joyce's *refusal* to revitalize cliché, his insistence on using the worn-out style to tell the story.

The enormous confidence behind the writing and the "risk" that Joyce really does take in "Eumaeus" is most apparent when we realize the chapter's place in the book. In "Eumaeus," what could have been the dramatic and allegorical climax of the plot coincides with the nadir of the writing. "Eumaeus" represents the recognition scene between Stephen (Telemachus) and Bloom (Odysseus), and this has a special place in the plot of the story.

The "Eumaeus" chapter is Joyce's deliberate "sabotage" of both style and the dramatic climax. The coming together of Stephen and Bloom is rendered entirely in vacuous clichés and vague phrases: "Side by side," "tête-à-tête," "with a certain analogy," Joyce's Odysseus and Telemachus are united. What other writer would render this climax in the following way?

> The queer suddenly things he popped out with attracted the elder man who was several years the other's senior or like his father [. . .] Though they didn't see eye to eye in everything a certain analogy there somehow was as if both their minds were travelling, so to speak, in the one train of thought. (U 16.1723–24)

and

> —Yes, Stephen said uncertainly because he thought he felt a strange kind of flesh of a different man approach him, sinewless and wobbly and all that. (U 16.1723–24)

Almost everything possible is done to the language here to destroy the emotion and eloquence of the dramatic climax. In the first quotation, for example, the succession of clichés, the vagueness, and the comic literalization of the metaphor "train of thought" all serve to deflate the language and the event. It is possible to imagine certain parts of the second quotation written "straight" in another novel: "He felt a strange kind of flesh . . . sinewless." But characteristically in the chapter, Joyce deliberately overwrites the phrase, making it redundant ("a strange kind of flesh of a different man") and mocking Stephen's important perception and the temporary eloquence of the writing with the sloppy "and all that." Similarly, the phrase "the elder man who was like his father" is conceivable in another novel, but the insertion of the phrase "several years the other's senior" deliberately sabotages the simile (and thus the allegorical unity of Odysseus and Telemachus). The eloquence of the writing and the significance of the drama are deflated: both style and climax are revealed to be clichés—one linguistic, the other dramatic.

And yet, somehow, by "sacrificing" the moment of climax, Joyce gets something back. The clichéd writing is an artistic strategy to allow emotion and inarticulate eloquence to enter the narrative obliquely. In language that deliberately claims very little, he finds a way to suggest emotion while avoiding sentimentality, and significance while avoiding dramatic climax. Somehow the very lameness and incompetence of writing creates the proper significance of the moment of meeting: displaying neither the solemnity of myth nor the neat doubleness of the "mock-heroic," the moment possesses, to use Joyce's idiom, "a certain sort of significance." By destroying eloquence, he allows emotion to be felt. The climax of the story is transcribed in the language of cliché because there is no other narrative means available that has not been "scorched." The clichés are, in effect, both the sabotage of style and a means of allowing the narrative to continue.

In "Cyclops," the exposure of the book's limitations allows the book to continue and expand. One can view the destruction of "literature" in "Eumaeus" in the same paradoxical way: literature is destroyed as the book expands. I have charted a movement away from "literature" in *Ulysses*, in the introduction of the subliterary text of the newspaper in "Aeolus" and the subliterary clichés of "Cyclops." The inclusion of the subliterary is, however, a part of the larger enterprise of the book, which is to expand its borders to include what is outside of it. The intrusion of the headings in "Aeolus" signifies not only the usurpation of narrative authority and the appearance of the public language of journalism but also the book's incorporation of something it had excluded. If the headings displace the narrative, it is because the narrative, in a sense, displaced journalism in its original narrative contract. It implicitly agreed to exclude it. In *Ulysses*, Joyce progressively incorporates in the novel what has been banished from it previously: other forms (for example, drama, catechism, newspaper) and other styles.

The text, like the self, is a circle that excludes everything outside itself. Through the devices of interruption and displacement, Joyce has dramatized what Stephen learned in "Proteus," that what is outside is "there all the time without you."[9] Now in "Eumaeus," the total displacement of the literate narrative by cliché expands the limits of the book as literature *and* the limits of the "self" (both the narrative "self" and the "self" of the characters), for the language is both subliterary and transpersonal (in contrast, allegory, for example, is transpersonal but not subliterary).

"He is a purely literary writer," T. S. Eliot observed of Joyce to Virginia Woolf. "He is founded upon Walter Pater with a dash of Newman."[10] The clichéd style of "Eumaeus" (unlike the pastiche in "Oxen of the Sun") can be regarded as Joyce's deliberate refusal of this kind of mantle. In "Ithaca," he rejected "literature" in a different way: by pretending to use the "neutral" language of the sciences. By the close of "Eumaeus," he had taken both his indictment of the "anonymous voice of culture" and his use of it as far as it could go in *Ulysses*.

4

"Ithaca"

The Order of Things

"Ithaca" represents the climax of the book's movement away from "literature," a movement initiated in the subliterary headings of "Aeolus." The narrative of the chapter dons the antiliterary mask of science. Its technical, denotative language, like the prose advocated by Thomas Sprat's Royal Society, represents science's "answer" to metaphor and fine writing. But Joyce's use of this kind of language in a book that began as a novel is subversive to literature in a more profound way: no other modern novel works quite as hard to dispense with most of the beauties of style. Joyce called "Ithaca" the "ugly duckling" of *Ulysses*,[1] but in a book that he called his "damned monster-novel,"[2] the ugly duckling is likely to be the favorite child. In reading "Ithaca," one senses that a page has been turned in literary history. From now on, it would seem, the most interesting creative project for the modern writer is to create ugly ducklings rather than swans. If the style of scrupulous meanness was Joyce's early answer to the fine writing and purple prose of his contemporaries, the language of "Ithaca" mounts a far more radical attack on the idea of literary style.

The chapter that deliberately dispenses with the beauties of style dispenses with other niceties of novel writing as well. In it, Joyce plays with our conceptions of narrative as well as style. "Ithaca" is an anatomy of a chapter: it offers us an outline of events. Instead of the suspense of a linear plot, it advances direct questions and answers; instead of the human voice of a narrative persona, it offers a catalogue of cold, hard facts. The book seems to interrogate itself in the catechism, implicitly promising to fill in the blanks by telling us the present and past perceptions, actions, and feelings of the characters. Joyce wrote to Budgen that in the "mathematical catechism" of "Ithaca," all events would be "resolved into their cosmic, physical, psychical etc. equivalents," so that the reader would "know everything and know it in the baldest and coldest way."[3]

Both the coldness and the mechanical cataloguing in "Ithaca" are anticipated in "Wandering Rocks." The mind represented in the narrative of "Ithaca" resembles the alienated, "lateral" imagination found in the earlier chapter: it meticulously strings together facts without establishing any sense of priority among them. This narrative mind amasses facts with no regard for normal conventions of significance and relevance. In an exaggerated form of inductive observation, the lateral imagination of "Ithaca" peruses the world, exhaustively cataloguing its contents, whether they are objects in a drawer, books on a bookshelf, or thoughts in someone's mind. In "Wandering Rocks," characters are treated as physical objects moving in space; in "Ithaca," the equation of people and objects is evidence of a general tonal and emotional leveling that surpasses anything in the early chapters. The real strangeness of the writing is described beautifully by Frank Budgen: "It is the coldest episode in an unemotional book. . . . The skeleton of each fact is stripped of its emotional covering. One fact stands by the other like the skeletons of man and woman, ape and tiger in an anatomical museum at twilight, all their differences of contour made secondary by their sameness of material, function and mechanism."[4]

There is a curious sense of displacement about the writing, as if one story were being written, while another, more important story were taking place. Instead of human feelings, we are given a scientific record of phenomena. For example, Bloom's awareness of Stephen's potential significance as an adopted son and Stephen's awareness of Bloom's potential meaning as an adopted father are recorded in terms of auditory and visual sensations: "He heard in a profound ancient male unfamiliar melody the accumulation of the past" (*U* 17.777–78) and "He saw in a quick young male familiar form the predestination of a future" (*U* 17.780). One has only to compare some of these passages with earlier passages in the book to see how the emotions and situations of the characters are now transcribed in a language of mathematics and statistics: "Reduce Bloom by cross manipulation of reverses of fortune, from which these supports protected him, and by elimination of all positive values to a negligible negative irrational unreal quantity" (*U* 17.1933–35). We strain for signs of human characters and are told of physical objects; we try to understand the relationship among characters and encounter mathematical tangents and algebraic equations.

There seems to be a mechanism of avoidance in the narrative that resembles Bloom's sudden scrutiny of his fingernails at the mention of Blazes Boylan in "Hades." In that chapter, Bloom psychologically displaces his anxieties onto a physical object; in "Ithaca," it is as if the story were displaced onto objects, as if the mechanisms of avoidance characterized the behavior of the text. This narrative displacement, in fact, sometimes dovetails with Bloom's own mechanism of avoidance, as in the answer to the question "By what reflections did he, a conscious reactor against the void of incertitude, justify to himself his sentiments?" (U 17.2210–11). The answer includes a disquisition on everything from the "frangibility of the hymen" to the "apathy of the stars" (U 17.2212–26). A. Walton Litz has observed, rightly I believe, that this answer "is a reflection of Bloom's thoughts as he strives for equanimity by sinking his own anxieties in the processes of nature."[5] Bloom's strategy for dealing with his domestic situation merges with the narrative strategy. The rational organization of the catechetical form seems to shade into Bloom's habit of rationalizing. The contiguous relationships catalogued throughout the narrative seem like psychological sidling, a way of not reaching a destination or climax, a means of avoiding a final realization.

I would like to be as clear as possible about the "minds" represented by the writing in "Ithaca." On one level, it is Joyce, of course, who deliberately "resolves" the events into their physical equivalents. One can imagine Joyce delighting in the creation of this obstacle to his writing—to fashion the end of the plot in this language and form is itself a tour de force. Joyce thus sets the task for himself of sabotaging the climax (as he did in "Eumaeus"), and yet, in his way, of creating the "right" ending for the book. To abandon the arsenal of literature's weapons, like dramatic climax, tone, style, and linear narration, and still to tell the story is the kind of challenge Joyce enjoyed. The "lateral imagination" is the psyche represented in the text. Although I occasionally use the term "narrator" for ease of reference, I prefer the concept of the consciousness or mind of the text, since Joyce does everything possible in "Ithaca" to destroy our sense of a narrating, human voice. To say that the text avoids or displaces is not to psychoanalyze Joyce but to describe the behavior of the text. One of the conventions of this particular stylistic mask in "Ithaca" is that we are told too much and not enough; the book performs a gesture of disclosure and withholding. Lastly, the habit of mind represented in "Ithaca" resembles the mind of Leopold Bloom in its displacement: at certain specific points in the text when the narrative catalogues objects or focuses on nature, it is paraphrasing the thoughts of Leopold Bloom.

Empirical reality is not totally obscured in this process—what actually happens in the chapter can be determined. As Budgen maintains, it is the emotional drama of the characters that is obscured by the writing. Yet, paradoxically, one of the effects of the disparity between the emotion we expect and the intellectualization that we find is that the chapter *is* touching in its own way.[6] It is through the intellectualizing and the coldness in "Ithaca" that Joyce is able to communicate the loneliness of Leopold Bloom, just as it is through cliché in "Eumaeus" that he is able to convey the sense of Bloom and Stephen's relationship. Somehow its coldness and its ostensible lack of interest in the emotional drama of the characters allow the narrative to be moving in certain places without immediately turning parodic, as it does in the "Cyclops" chapter, for example.

So, in the midst of the fussy, almost scholastic description of "What rendered problematic for Bloom the realisation of these mutually selfexcluding propositions," two short pairs of questions and answers appear. The preceding lengthy passage has described Bloom's experience with the "clown in quest of paternity" and his gesture of marking a florin to see if it would be returned. Now we come upon the following: "Was the clown Bloom's son? No. Had Bloom's coin returned? Never" (U 17.973–88). The simplicity of these questions and answers is striking—the contrast in the writing brings the reader up short. He feels that he is confronting an important passage in the text. The starkness of the statement, telling us of the frustration of Bloom's desire, elicits our understanding of the depths of Bloom's loneliness. The complete avoidance of sentimentality here allows for the entrance of the reader's sympathy.

Even within one sentence, the punctilious, denotative style will suddenly give way to a short, fragile phrase of beauty. The question is asked, "Alone, what did Bloom feel?" The answer is: "The cold of interstellar space, thousands of degrees below freezing point or the absolute zero of Fahrenheit, Centigrade or Réaumur: the incipient intimations of proximate dawn" (*U* 17.1245–48). The soft, Latinate sounds of the final phrase surprise us after the preceding barrage of facts. In "Ithaca," lyrical passages of the type parodied in other chapters of *Ulysses* are left to stand without becoming parodic. In the midst of the scientific jargon, we come upon the following line in one of the answers: "The heaventree of stars hung with humid nightblue fruit" (*U* 17.1039). The one statement we can make about this line is that no matter what it is supposed to mean, we know from the sounds, the verbal compression, the images, and the allusion to *The Divine Comedy* that this is poetry. The line is not, however, a parody of lyricism, although one can imagine something like it on the lips of one of the "eloquent" speakers parodied during the course of *Ulysses*.[7] Somehow, it is as if the coldness and ugliness of the rest of the narration have earned the narrative the right to this lyricism without parody, as, in a different way, the scrupulous meanness of the early Joyce allowed the lyricism at the end of "The Dead" to exist. No prior context of stylistic hyperbole undermines the significance of these isolated lines as it does in "Cyclops" and "Nausicaa," no surrounding sentimentality turns this line "namby-pamby." The coldness of the narration in "Ithaca" functions to clear the air of phrases like "Love loves to love love." The writing represents a way to tell the story using the English language without parody.

But the disparity between the human story and the writing in the narrative leads to comedy as well as pathos and has important philosophical implications for the reading of the text as well. The reader finds himself bombarded with a wealth of data. If, as Joyce said in his letter, the reader is told everything, it seems as if he is told everything that he does not really need to know. The text's implicit promise to supply all the details of the plot is overzealously fulfilled. The most exhaustive answers respond to the simplest of questions.[8] What constitutes an answer becomes problematical, even in the case of the simplest questions of plot. For example, the question "What did Bloom do at the range?" receives the following response: "He removed the saucepan to the left hob, rose and carried the iron kettle to the sink in order to tap the current by turning the faucet to let it flow" (*U* 17.160–62). The process of making tea is anatomized into a series of smaller actions, as details of information are given in the text that one would normally assume rather than state. The carrying of the kettle to the sink and the motive for the action ("in order to tap the current . . . to let it flow") are details that are usually taken for granted. It is not only the wealth of detail that makes this answer so strange and unexpected but also the type of information included. A similar description of Bloom's domestic ritual in "Calypso," for example, is almost as detailed: "He scalded and rinsed out the teapot and put in four full spoons of tea, tilting the kettle then to let the water flow in" (*U* 4.271–73). But this description is unified by the aura of domesticity that surrounds Bloom; the details of the description mirror

Bloom's delight in the trappings of his domestic activity. The later description suggests instead that the narrator and the reader are unfamiliar with the act of making tea.

Similarly, the description of certain common events like a handshake, a sunrise, and a bump on the head are documented with such precision that they are almost unrecognizable. The action of Bloom and Stephen shaking hands is not named as such; rather, their geometric relationship is described. They are described as "standing perpendicular at the same door and on different sides of its base, the lines of their valedictory arms, meeting at any point and forming any angle less than the sum of two right angles" (*U* 17.1221–23). This is, of course, another example of the resolution of the characters into their mathematical equivalents, but to analyze a common action so scrupulously is to make the narrative very strange. Like Zeno Cosini in Italo Svevo's *Confessions of Zeno*, who thinks of the twenty-six movements necessary to the action of walking, the narrator does not take anything for granted, even the relative position of two people shaking hands. Like the narrator in "Wandering Rocks," he amasses an abundance of facts without classifying them in the conceptual categories on which both literary and nonliterary discourse generally rely. He plows through a mass of facts laboriously, as if a name were a labor-saving device of which he had never heard.

The laboriousness of this kind of description is comic; as in "Cyclops" and in the final paragraphs of "Wandering Rocks," the writing becomes an obvious performance, an exhibition of excess. The particular comic quality of much of the narration in "Ithaca" derives from a sense of the extravagance of the writing (this is different, of course, from actual *stylistic* hyperbole). Here Freud's analysis of the comedy of the clown is applicable, for he says that we laugh at a clown because his actions "seem to us extravagant and inexpedient. We are laughing at an expenditure that is too large."[9] The term "burlesque" applies to the excessive expenditure of energy in the writing, not only in its meaning as a literary technique that employs a grand style to describe a trivial matter, but also in its associations with physical comedy.[10] For if one reads the description of the handshake between Stephen and Bloom, the description itself begins to seem like a Rube Goldberg invention—a ludicrously elaborate mechanism with pretensions to efficiency and accuracy, a dogged, meticulous effort with small results. The description comically perverts the fundamental law of science, which is economy, and offers a comic translation of the epic impulse to go the long way around.

In its overprecision, the narration engages in what Stephen Heath has called a transgression of "the threshold of functional relevance below which things are taken for granted," a threshold that "divides the narratable from the non-narratable."[11] This transgression is a form of what the Russian formalists have called the "defamiliarization" or making strange of the text (the type of thing we saw in "Wandering Rocks"). This kind of overprecision can serve varied functions in a literary text. For instance, in *Gulliver's Travels*, the purpose of the microscopic perspective is primarily satiric; it throws into relief the absurdity of human society. But this is not the purpose of the defamiliarization in "Ithaca." Rather, the overprecision shows what the stream of consciousness suggested in the early chapters: that reality is infinitely expansible by being infinitely divisible. A clue to this view of reality is found in one of the answers of the catechism. The response to the question "Were there obverse meditations of involution increasingly less vast?" ends with a tongue-twisting disquisition on the infinite number of microscopic organisms

> of the universe of human serum constellated with red and white bodies, themselves universes of void space constellated with other bodies, each, in continuity, its universe of divisible component bodies of which each was again divisible in divisions of redivisible component bodies, dividends and divisors ever diminishing without actual division till, if the progress were carried far enough, nought nowhere was never reached. (*U* 17.1057–69)

This examination of the Chinese box of the world represents another point in the chapter where Bloom's obsessive calculations merge with the overprecision of the narrative. But it describes also the divisibility of reality that is implied in the narrative. The narrative promise to fill in the gaps of the plot is fulfilled surprisingly in a microscopic notation of reality that threatens to continue forever.

This demonstration of the infinite divisibility of reality tells us something about the relationship between writing and the reality it represents. The "threshold of functional relevance," transgressed in the answers of "Ithaca," pertains to the conventions of discourse. As Heath says, it refers to the narrative choices made in the text. The microscopic notation in "Ithaca" transforms even the smallest detail of reality into a "narratable" fact. But it is the breakdown of the plot into discrete questions and answers that is the primary model of the infinite divisibility of experience and the expansibility of writing. Ironically, no answer is definitive because it has the potential to generate another, more specific question, which leads to another answer, and so on.

The narrative of "Ithaca" also demonstrates that events are infinitely expansible into larger sequences of which they are a part. Again, the precision of the writing leads to an expanding answer. (And again, a specific answer in the catechism represents this expansibility. See Bloom's "[m]editations of evolution increasingly vaster" [*U* 17.1042].) For example, the running of tap water is "explained" by tracing the water back to its source; the action of turning on the water is seen as a stage in a physical process that begins with the reservoir. Similarly, in a parody of the scientific investigation of causes and effects, the boiling of water is traced back to the coal that heats it, to the "decidua" of the forest that became the coal, to the energy of the sun that formed the coal (*U* 17.257–71). The details of the plot move outward from the actions of the characters, as the narrative spins a web of actions and reactions, antecedents and causes.

The narrative traces the antecedents of cognitive as well as physical events. Perceptions have a "history" that can be traced in the text. Bloom's perception of the gaslight spawns a description of a prior identical perception. Similarly, the sight of Bloom lighting the fire leads to a list of the previous actions of this sort that Stephen remembers. It is as if the stream of consciousness of the early chapters were turned inside out, as "remembrances of things past," both the characters' and the book's, are inventoried. Each event narrated can be seen as a point in a chain of events; each event has a potential relationship with another. "Really, universally, relations stop nowhere," says Henry James in his Preface to *Roderick Hudson*, "and the exquisite problem of the artist is eternally but to draw, by a geometry of his own, the circle within which they shall happily *appear* to do so."[12] "Ithaca" is a demonstration that "relations stop nowhere" and a refusal to limit the representation of experience in a personal "geometry." The lateral imagination sweeps backwards and forwards both in time and in space.

In "Ithaca," as in the last passages of "Wandering Rocks," plot and digression are almost synonymous, as the conventions of relevance are undermined. The "facts" included in the answers seem increasingly arbitrary: the answer to the question "Did it [the water] flow?" (*U* 17.163) includes the record of steps taken by one Mr Spencer Harty to prevent a worsening drought as well as Mr Harty's hypothetical solution, recorded parenthetically, to the contingent possibility of the drought's becoming severe.[13] Logically, of course, the details of Mr Harty's plans are less relevant to the plot than the actions of Stephen and Bloom. But the idea of plot, based on the concepts of relevance and closure, are parodied, as the surplus of data makes the separation of the relevant from the irrelevant more problematical. Our progress towards the book's end is impeded as the narrative goes off in all directions; we are overwhelmed by the excess of information and are unable to organize the data into patterns of significance. Joyce plays with our desire to organize the material of the book—the parentheses in the above answer seem to be a wink from the author: What can a parenthetical thought be in a sentence so full of random associations?[14]

Just as we are hoping for the resolution of the plot, then, the narrative opens up to include almost everything imaginable. In addition to the exhaustive tracing of the causes and effects of events in the plot, the narrative increasingly speculates on potential causes and effects of hypothetical events. Joyce expands the realm of relevant "fact" by including the conditional tense as well as the past and present; conjecture and hypothesis enter the narration. Early in the chapter the narrator asks, "For what personal purpose could Bloom have applied the water so boiled?" and the answer "To shave himself" generates other questions related to the desirability of shaving at night.[15] In the midst of its "progress" to limit indeterminacy, the narrative begins to entertain (and I stress this word) various kinds of possibilities and potentialities: "If he had smiled why would he have smiled?" "What various advantages would or might have resulted from a prolongation of such extemporisation?" "Why might these several provisional contingencies between a guest and a hostess not necessarily preclude or be precluded by a permanent eventuality of reconciliatory union between a schoolfellow and a jew's daughter?" (*U* 17.940–42).

In certain passages, Bloom's daydreams occasion the narrative journey into the hypothetical. The prime example of this convergence is the three-page description of Bloom's suburban dream house.[16] Bloom's obsessiveness and the obsessiveness of the narrative come together to produce the most detailed of descriptions of a nonexistent place. Bloom's psychic energy and the narrator's descriptive energy are lavished on this dream house—again, one has the sense of an extravagant expenditure of energy. The specificity of the description is funny: "What additional attractions might the grounds contain?" "What improvements might be subsequently introduced?" "What facilities of transit were desirable?" (*U* 17.1551, 1567, 1573), asks the narrator, offering us one of the most exhaustive anatomies of desire in literature.[17]

Not only do the questions investigate the real and hypothetical details of plot, but they also conduct a search for the *relationship* between events or objects. Especially in the first half of the chapter, many of the questions seek to organize the world of facts into a series of relationships. This demand for comparison in the catechism is the second major means by which Joyce shows us that "relations stop nowhere." Throughout the catechism, the questions of the inquirer induce the respondent to make comparisons (this is not to suggest that they are two different personae, but to differentiate between functions). Almost every question includes words of comparison. In some, these comparative words are applied in heaping portions. The comparative question that begins the chapter, "What parallel course . . . ?" is followed by many others, which inquire about "common facts of similarity between reactions," "common study," "points of contact," "previous intimations," and "glyphic comparisons," to name a few. The major comparisons requested in the questions pertain to the relationship of Stephen and Bloom. The leading questions of the catechism promise to structure a final sorting out of their relationship.

And so, the various points of contact are outlined according to the principle of identity and difference. The ways in which Stephen and Bloom are similar and dissimilar are catalogued: their opinions, their ages, their temperaments, their ancestors' languages, their drinking speed, the trajectory of their urination. They are substituted linguistically for one another ("Substituting Stephen for Bloom, Stoom . . ."), charted geometrically ("Standing perpendicular . . ."), their thoughts are "reduced to their simplest reciprocal form." The inquirer conducts a search for their common denominator.[18]

Again, the "lateral imagination" of the narrator is apparent, as he ranges over a set of facts, drawing connections. The most unlikely analogies are made: it seems that everything can potentially be compared to everything else (for example, Milly Bloom and the cat). Conversely, two entities (like Stephen and Bloom) can he compared and contrasted in a number of ways: every detail of the characters' biography and behavior can be potentially assimilated to the comparison. The questions encourage an analytical exercise in constructing binary oppositions. They seem more like theoretical constructs imposed than natural congruencies discovered. The binarism of the narrator allows anything to be classified, and the comedy of the comparisons, in many cases, derives from their sheer irrelevance. As Hugh Kenner observes of the mind of the narrator, it "loses nothing, penetrates nothing, and has a category for everything."[19]

Kenner discusses the analytic enterprise of the chapter as a kind of parody of "metaphysical intuition, or of allied aesthetic modes of knowledge." "Ithaca" does indeed parody the attempt to find an intelligible pattern, religious or secular. In *The Order of Things*, Michel Foucault has written brilliantly of Don Quixote's attempt to transform his own world into the Renaissance world of resemblance and similitude—it seems to me that the same kind of semiotic hope is parodied in "Ithaca." In attempting to connect the dots, the narrator becomes a kind of comic Thomas Browne, searching high and low for quincunxes. The desire for an intelligible pattern overwhelms the search.

What the catechism of "Ithaca" parodies is not the idea of relationship but the idea of a system that purports to halt the play of potential relationships. All sorts of relationships *do* exist in unexpected places—coincidences, repetitions, puns—but these "facts" cannot he reduced to a schema. Critics have had difficulty in agreeing on the particular system parodied in "Ithaca" (for example, the Christian catechism, nineteenth-century books of knowledge, or nineteenth-century science) because it is the *idea* of a taxonomic system itself, not any particular system, that is parodied. Science, logic, mathematics, theology, and literary criticism are all implicated in the parody, for they are all systems of ordering and containing knowledge. In fact, almost any kid of criticism that has been revered at one time or another ("new," old, structural, exegetical) is in some way represented or anticipated in the parody in "Ithaca." For example, the binary divisions classifying Milly Bloom and the cat (*U* 17.886–908) can be thought of as a perfect parody of structuralist criticism. It is, perhaps, particularly ironic to think of the Christian catechism behind the form of the chapter: the book adopts the mask of dogma and belief in order to reveal a radical skepticism of order and authority.[20]

The questions and answers of the catechism offer various suggestions for ordering the world of facts—by similitude, by hypothesis, by causality, and so on. Facts are classified into categories, categories dispersed, new categories formed. Despite the prominence of the catechetical form, the underlying impulse for the movement of the chapter is rhetorical. In "Ithaca," Joyce employs the rhetorical topoi of "inventio," the first part of classical rhetoric.

The narrative proceeds by ingenious "arguments" from analogy, difference, contraries, cause and effect, example.[21] Some examples of topoi used in "Ithaca" are: "If he had smiled why would he have smiled?" (hypothesis, *U* 17.2126); "What past consecutive causes [. . .] did Bloom [. . .] recapitulate?" (causes and effects, *U* 17.2042–43); "Prove that he loved rectitude . . ." (proof by example, *U* 17.1634). Analogy and difference are found, of course, throughout.[22] The performance of the catechism is really a school performance in the rhetorical classification of facts. For the Ciceronian orator, these rhetorical topoi represented the machinery for an investigation of a subject—they were the means of generating true statements about something. Using these topoi for comic purposes, Joyce plays with the idea of the human wish to arrive at truth. Like the system of nineteenth-century positivism, the system of rhetoric was originally a testimony to man's belief in his capacity for wisdom. However, in "Ithaca," the topoi ordinarily used in the service of investigation do not include or prove anything. If each of the book's last chapters is an experiment in ordering experience, "Ithaca" is the climax and the microcosm of this enterprise. It shows the arbitrariness of any system of classification, either of the book or, by implication, of the world. Instead of "truth" about his subject, Joyce offers us an exercise in the many ways in which the subject can be discussed.

The real subversion of the comprehensive classification of knowledge is implied, then, in the questions themselves. The series of comparative questions reveals that a line can be drawn between any two points, but it is impossible to connect all the dots. Each pair of questions and answers carves up a segment of reality but tells us nothing about the whole of the universe of the book. If "reality" and the meaning of it are investigated in each pair of questions and answers, there is always another question to he asked, another comparison to be explored. One can imagine an infinite series of questions and answers. René Girard, in discussing the "conversion" at the end of certain novels, says that "the conclusion must be considered as a successful effort to overcome the inability to conclude."[23] "Ithaca" is a parody of such closure; the book's "inability to conclude" is emphasized rather than overcome. If, as Hugh Kenner suggests, the catechism is like a huge filing system,[24] it is a system that has no necessary final entry.

In fact, by the end of the chapter, the connections made by the narrative mind become looser and looser. Instead of forging connections between characters, the respondent sinks into a spasm of verbal association, in a realm of imagination that fuses the child's world with the mythic. The answer to the question of the identity of Bloom's companions is "Sinbad the Sailor." The answer generates, however, a series of alliterative names that rhyme with Sinbad (Tinbad the Tailor and Jinbad the Jailor), and finally, the principle of alliteration itself gives way to the final reply "Xinbad the Phthailer," as the association becomes freer (*U* 17.2322–26). This kind of language looks back to the "moo-cow" story that begins *A Portrait* and forward to the language of *Finnegans Wake*. Although the final answer is a paraphrase of Bloom's response to Molly, its implication is that the book has now embarked on a course of generating all sorts of linguistic connections from this fertile medium of dream language. The mind that peruses the world, cataloguing and making connections, could conceivably continue in its effort forever, in a language even more unlikely to encourage a halt in the play of connections than that of the rest of the chapter. The chapter stops, as if the mind went to sleep or the power of the machine were cut off, but it doesn't really end.

In "Ithaca," we see that the wealth of possible connections can never be catalogued completely. There is no system that can include or account for them all. Among other things, "Ithaca" is about ordering: the way characters order their world, the way authors order their texts, the way readers order their interpretations, and the way people order the world they live in. The chapter incorporates Joyce's ideas about making sense of the world and about making sense of a literary text. Just as the wealth of life exceeds the book's representation of it, so the surplus of meanings in the book exceeds the reader's interpretation of it.

The "roles" of interrogator and respondent in the catechism represent both the characters trying to make their way through the world and the reader trying to make his way through the book. In playing "twenty questions" with itself, the chapter makes explicit the questions and answers usually embedded in the linear narrative. During the course of the chapter, these narrative questions and answers have converged at certain points with Leopold Bloom's attempt to solve his personal problems. The questions that they ask and answer are questions that Bloom asks himself (indeed, the language of logic is used to underline this problem-solving activity). At the end of the chapter, it is Bloom's dialogue with Molly that now converges with the narrative, and the narrator's role as a kind of substitute or surrogate for the characters is explicitly noted. Molly's questions to Bloom are actually referred to by the narrator as "the catechetical interrogation," Bloom is called the "narrator" and Molly the "listener," who sometimes interrupts to ask questions. The slackening pace of the narration is observed in the narration itself, as the interrogator asks "What limitations of activity and inhibitions of conjugal rights were perceived by listener and narrator concerning themselves during the course of this intermittent and increasingly more laconic narration?" (*U* 17.2271–73). The dialogue of the characters and the dialogue of the chapter become one.

But the reader, too, is represented in the catechism, for the interrogation in the text parodies the kind of activity we ourselves usually perform. Both the characters and the reader go through the book trying to solve enigmas. It is the central irony of the chapter that despite the exhaustiveness of the interrogation process, fundamental questions remain unanswered, both for the characters and for the readers. Just as Bloom reminds himself of all his unfinished business and some unsolved enigmas, we too recognize that everything has not been resolved in the chapter. The pedagogical "mask" of the chapter, in fact, has interesting implications for the notion of the "ideal reader," who, like the ideal student, tries to arrive at a vision of truth. What we understand from this final simulated educational exercise in "Ithaca" is that there are no ideal readers for the text, no perfect students who can arrive at a definitive reading of the book. It is not surprising that the conception of the ideal reader has a religious source: it originated in St. Augustine's "On Christian Doctrine" and applied to the Christian who had the "preunderstanding" necessary to read and interpret scriptures. The notion of this "ideal reader" and the student of the Christian catechism dovetail in "Ithaca": the "mysteries" of the text cannot be taught or learned in any absolute way; there is no privileged position from which to arrive at "truth" or knowledge.[25] That the book is about writing and reading fiction as well as the characters in Dublin is something I have tried to demonstrate throughout—but "Ithaca" shows us that the play of the text will always exceed the reader's attempt to grasp it.

The multiple possibilities of meaning in *Ulysses* and a parody of the attempt to arrive at a conclusive reading are comically presented in an hermeneutic metaphor within the chapter. The narrator's question "What in water did Bloom, waterlover, drawer of water, watercarrier, returning to the range, admire?" (*U* 17.183–84) is answered in a Rabelaisian catalogue of Bloom's thoughts on the meaning of water: "Its universality: its democratic equality and constancy to its nature in seeking its own level [. . .] its infallibility as paradigm and paragon." (*U* 17.185–216). In one sense, the catalogue of Bloom's thoughts on the "potency of water as a symbol" can be seen as a projection of his desire to mean something to somebody. But the catalogue also represents a "reading" of water—the book, in this instance, like Stephen in "Proteus," attempts to read a "signature" in the material world. We recognize in this kind of reading a parody of the basic activity of symbol making and deciphering, the kind of activities engaged in by everyone, but by writers and readers especially. Indeed, one has only to think of Joyce's statement to Budgen that Odysseus is "the complete man" (representing son, father, husband, and warrior)[26] to realize how writers, as well as characters and readers, are represented in this disquisition. On the one hand, the passage is a parody of the writer's attempt to create symbolism and the reader's attempt to exhaust the significance of what he reads. The passage parodies the desire for epiphany, as it catalogues the "whatness" of the object. Any one of these interpretations of water, serving as the basis of a metaphor in a poem, for example, would not be comic; it is the completeness and ingenuity of these multiple readings that parody the search for significance and the creation of symbolism.

On the other hand, the passage offers a range of potential meaning, that is, a surplus of meanings, and this is, in fact, what *Ulysses* itself offers to the reader. The meditation on water, to quote William Gass, an expert meditator, shows how things "become concepts": somewhere between the perceiver and the object, significance resides.[27] For after all, water, like Homer's Odysseus, *is* a perfect paradigm. If the passage parodies the desire for the exhaustion of meaning, for a final, conclusive interpretation, it reveals a surplus rather than a dearth of meanings.

Despite the representation of events in what Joyce called "the coldest, baldest way," a sense of possibility mitigates the alienation of the cosmic perspective. The abstract record of events somehow confirms the richness of the story. The leveling of experience that derives from the form and style of "Ithaca" ultimately does not feel like an aggressive cancellation of possibilities or a ruthless satire of belief but imparts instead a sense of the various possibilities that exist in life. *Ulysses* is full of meaning, but this is not to say that its final meaning is the affirmation of life. It is a book that is beyond what we generally mean by affirmation or negation; it shows us all kinds of truths about life but doesn't sum it up in any one statement of meaning. The overabundance of details and styles invites the reader to pare away the excess until he arrives at some kind of interpretation. The history of Joyce criticism reveals how personal this winnowing process is. As Arnold Goldman pointed out in *The Joyce Paradox*, *Ulysses* allows us to see the progression of the style toward the computerlike abstractions of "Ithaca" as life denying, the triumph of mechanism (as Kenner does in *Dublin's Joyce*), or we can see the characters' survival, in spite of the stylistic progression, as ultimately life affirming (as does S. L. Goldberg, for example[28]).

My own feeling is that while *Ulysses* is skeptical about meaning and belief, it is not "pyrrhonic" (to use Hugh Kenner's term for it[29]): anyone as concerned with life as Joyce is in *Ulysses* cannot be as much of an eternal pessimist as Kenner makes him sound in his brilliant but ultimately too dark readings of the book. Neither, however, is *Ulysses* a "self-consuming artifact" by which the reader is led to a vision of truth.

II

Compromising Letters

Joyce, Women, and Feminism

5

Joyce and Feminism

I

Joyce and feminism—a difficult conjunction, a seemingly forced connection between a man who is quoted as saying, "I hate women who know anything" and a movement that applauds women's intellects and rights. Perhaps the "and" conjoins opposites, such as black and white? This would be the view of some feminists who see misogyny expressed in Joyce's representation of female characters, particularly Molly Bloom in *Ulysses*. Sandra Gilbert and Susan Gubar, for example, view Molly as "a choice of matter over mind."[1] They regard Woman in Joyce as confined to her body, excluded from the production of culture. Particularly in *Ulysses*, they see Joyce's language as the triumph of a patriarchal literary heritage. In short, and in pun, they "refuse to be Mollified" (519) by "feminologist re-Joyceings"; they castigate those women critics who see in Joyce's subversion of social and literary conventions a natural alliance with feminism.

These harsh judgments are anticipated in Joyce's work itself, particularly *Ulysses* and *Finnegans Wake*, and even in his recorded dreams, all of which contain numerous examples of women accusing men of misleading and misrepresenting them. One of the best texts in which to examine these images of accusation is the "Circe" or Nighttown episode of *Ulysses*, in which the characters act out many of their deepest desires and fears suppressed during the day. Women from Leopold Bloom's past and present accuse him of sexual innuendo, voyeurism, and defamation of character. For example, here is Martha Clifford, a typist with whom Bloom has conducted a titillating and secret correspondence after her response to an advertisement placed by him in the *Irish Times*:

MARTHA
(*thickveiled, a crimson halter round her neck, a copy of the* Irish Times *in her hand, in tone of reproach, pointing*) Henry! Leopold! Lionel, thou lost one! Clear my name. (*U* 15.752–54)

"Clear my name," Martha cries reproachfully to her male betrayer/s, perhaps speaking for other female characters and readers who accuse the male writer of misunderstanding and misrepresenting women. In a chapter where transformations abound and identities slip and slide, Martha accuses a multiple male betrayer: Henry, the penname with which Bloom signs his secret letters to her ("Henry Flower" is the full signature); Leopold, Bloom's real first name which Martha never learns; Lionel, the male lead in Flotow's opera *Martha*. This composite list of male betrayers enjoined to "clear" Martha's name suggests that perhaps "James" (as in "James Joyce") could be added to the list of men whose words to and about women endanger their reputations, and who might be challenged to redeem them.

Indeed, Joyce dreamt of Molly Bloom herself reproaching him for his prurient interest in women's "business" and for his presumptuous attempts to lend voice to female desire. In a dream important enough for Joyce to relate in two different versions to two different friends (Herbert Gorman and John Sullivan), Molly Bloom herself rejects his attempts to represent her. In one version, Joyce said, "Molly came calling on me and said, 'What are you meddling with my old business for?' She had a coffin in her hand and said, 'If you don't change this is for you.'"[2] Here, Molly expresses her murderous anger toward her creator for his interest in woman's private, that is, sexual "old" (smelly?) business. In another version of the dream, Molly flings a child's black coffin at Bloom (presumably Rudy's) and says, "I've done with you." Joyce, indignant, tries to intercede by delivering a "very long, eloquent" and passionate speech "explaining all the last episode of *Ulysses* to her." Molly smiles at the end of Joyce's "astronomical climax," then flings at him "a tiny snuffbox, in the form of a little black coffin" and says, "And I have done with you, too." In recording this dream, Joyce explained that his godfather had given him a similar snuffbox when he attended Clongowes Wood College (*JJ* 549). Here Molly flings at him the symbol of intercourse, the coffin-shaped snuffbox that may remind us of the symbol of "Plumtree's Potted Meat" in *Ulysses*. The snuffbox thrown in Joyce's face is also, as Joyce tells us, a patriarchal legacy. Molly cuts off her male critic as well as male creator, the one who tries to pen woman's desire and then has the audacity to explain it. It is as if the "real" Molly accuses Joyce of offering a constructed woman as a naturalistic Everywoman.

Finally, as Bonnie Scott points out in *James Joyce,* Anna Livia Plurabelle (ALP), the multi-formed female presence in *Finnegans Wake,* comments on Molly Bloom's ill treatment at the pen of their joint creator.[3] ALP describes the "Penelope" chapter of *Ulysses* as "a colophon [last word] of no fewer than seven hundred and thirtytwo strokes tailed by a leaping lasso," in which "the vaulting feminine libido" is "sternly controlled and easily repersuaded by the uniform matteroffactness of a meandering male fist" (*FW* 123.05–10). Anna Livia ridicules the male writing which tries to "lasso" the feminine libido (the "lasso" is also the male pen) and the stern male fist that tries to grasp it (sexually and intellectually). This is the fist that makes Molly wait (like Penelope) the whole of *Ulysses* to be given "the last word."

II

How do these examples of female accusation, staged in Joyce's fiction and infiltrating his dreams, address the charges of feminist readers like Gilbert and Gubar, for example, who claim that women in Joyce are "sentenced" to a purely material existence? These charges are compelling. For one thing, the history of male critical response to the women in Joyce, and to Molly in particular, seems to lend support to a charge of Joyce's confining women to their bodies: Molly has been read by influential critics as the womb (Tindall, *James Joyce*), Nature (Ellmann, *Ulysses on the Liffey*), and the goddess of the "animal kingdom of the dead" (Kenner, *Dublin's Joyce*). And yet, this particular feminist reading ignores the way in which Joyce's texts partly deconstruct the symbolic, encoded forms of their own representations and expose the workings of male desire. Joyce's dream accounts and fictional passages implicitly acknowledge that the male writer's representation of woman is never "objective," but rather involves a combination of *hubris,* assault, fascination, even envy. When men write to and about the Other, emotions are never expressed simply or directly. Feelings about the Other are highly ambivalent, changeable, and disguised even from oneself. Desire circulates consciously and unconsciously through the writer's representation of the Other; art embeds this desire in the text.

In the "Scylla and Charybdis" chapter of *Ulysses,* Stephen Dedalus describes his theory of artistic creation in a long disquisition on Shakespeare. According to Stephen, Shakespeare's plays are full of the torments in his life, especially sexual ones; he speaks of Shakespeare's plays as "the creation he has piled up to hide him from himself" (*U* 9.475). Although Stephen's theory is grandiose and sometimes muddled, Joyce, too, believed that art is not simple self-expression or autobiography, but a complicated embedding, disguising, dispersing of the author and his desire in the text. Joyce's later work in particular reveals the ambivalent nature of writing, in relation to desire. In *Finnegans Wake*, Shem the Penman figures this dual nature of writing in the word "squirtscreen[ed]" (*FW* 186.07), which captures the sense of writing as expression of the self (Shem's "ink" is his own excrement) and self-defense (a squid squirts ink in self-defense); writing is a burst of expression ("squirt") but also a "screen." Perhaps writing is even a "skirtscreen," by which the penman hides behind his mother's skirts or hides the female body, her body functioning as a defense against the anxiety of writing, or writing functioning as a defense against the power of her body. In 1904, Stanislaus Joyce wrote that it might be contended of James's style that he "confesses in a foreign language."[4] James came to realize that disclosure and disguise were inextricably linked, particularly in the arena of sexuality.

Thus a catalogue of misogynistic images or female stereotypes in Joyce's work fails to account for his undermining of the grounds of representation. And Gilbert and Gubar's emphasis on Joyce's linguistic "puissance" and patriarchal mastery ignores his radical skepticism of the possibility of "lassoing" essences, including that of the "vaulting feminine libido." Indeed, the deconstruction of presences poses a relationship between the metaphor of woman and a writing practice that disrupts patriarchal signature and conventions. Again, one can think of Joyce's dream of Molly, which seems to acknowledge that woman in writing is beyond his control and might stand for a play of language that always exceeds the writer's intention. Julia Kristeva links the disruption of patriarchal discourse in Joyce and some other avant-garde male writers with the feminine or maternal repressed by Western culture: as Kristeva calls it, "the inseparable obverse of [the writer's] very being, the other [sex] that torments and possesses him."[5] This idea is anticipated in the description of *Finnegans Wake* as a "letter self-penned to one's other" (*FW* 489.33–34). If paternity is the "legal fiction," as Stephen Dedalus says in "Scylla and Charybdis," woman becomes the figure for illegitimacy, errancy, and forgery rather than patriarchal signature, a significance to which I will return.

III

Increasingly, Joyce's texts unmask male anxieties of women's power. In the earlier texts, these anxieties are represented as largely character based, the personal fears and desires of male characters like Stephen Dedalus or Gabriel Conroy; increasingly, however, the later texts reveal these fears to be inscriptions of cultural anxieties. Joyce shows that desire, like language, cannot be a purely personal phenomenon. At the beginning of *Ulysses*, Stephen says that history is a "nightmare from which [he is] trying to awake," referring to his own past and Irish history. His latent reference to the profoundly troubling dream of Woman (the "night-mare") is made more explicit when he jokes that the nightmare might give him a "back kick" (*U* 2.377–79). *Finnegans Wake* reworks the image so as to expose the way in which culture validates male fear and subordination of the female. The nightmare reappears, this time explicitly as Woman being "ridden" by male desire in the form of "The galleonman jovial on his bucky brown nightmare" (*FW* 583.08–09). The galleonman's joviality and casual assumption of the superior position do not mask the potential of the bucky "night-mare" to bring unquiet dreams to her male rider. And, as Bernard Benstock has pointed out in regard to the struggle between the narrative voice and Margareen in book 1, chapter 6 of the *Wake*, the "functioning narrator" undertakes "ploys" in order to "'objectify'—and therefore dispel—the strong feminine influence. By posing behind numerous journalistic styles and guises he seeks to prevent her female voice from usurping the directional tone."[6]

In exploring the institutionalization of cultural myths, Joyce exposed the power relationship suppressed within the binary oppositions that underwrite culture, i.e., the pairs of words like male/female and presence/absence in which one of the terms of the pair is privileged over the other. In unmasking the binary oppositions, Joyce is a precursor of deconstruction. Indeed, Jacques Derrida himself announces his debt to Joyce, especially *Finnegans Wake*, in "Plato's Pharmacy" and in "Two Words for Joyce."[7]

But in unmasking the power relations inscribed in culture and the workings of male fear and desire of the Other, Joyce implies that no one can stand outside this process. As Cheryl Herr puts it from a Marxist perspective in *Joyce's Anatomy of Culture*, "Joyce's fictions both operate within the philosophical structures that marked his early rearing and critique their ideological surface."⁸ Herr is speaking here of bourgeois ideology in particular, but her statement applies to patriarchal ideology in general. As Joyce's own dreams and letters attest, to expose the workings of male paranoia, desire, guilt, and ambivalence in one's fiction is not necessarily to free one from the same feelings. Contending that Joyce exposes the workings of ideology and desire and subverts conventions is not the same as claiming that he completely transcends his own time. On the other hand, his skepticism of order, system, and style led to a radical critique of phallogocentrism, in which the disruptive metaphor of woman played an important part.

What I am describing is never an unambivalent progress toward a uniform idea or embodiment of woman. ALP's comment notwithstanding, Joyce's "male fist" is neither "matteroffact" nor "uniform" when it comes to the feminine. Indeed, Joyce's representation of the feminine is often double-minded, containing the traces of past desires and fears. His "critique" of the ideological surface of patriarchal culture in general, and his greater self-consciousness about the mechanisms of the cultural construction of the female, seem often to coexist with the longing for a natural "home" in the maternal body. To be more specific, although Joyce's work from *Dubliners* to *Finnegans Wake* moves toward a radical questioning of the notion of origin, it retains the signs of longing for just such an origin or home, a longing Stephen expresses when he calls mother love "The only true thing in life," or when he imagines the "strandentwining cable of all flesh" leading back to Edenville (*U* 3.37). Joyce, everywhere more self-conscious than his fledgling artist, still encodes in even the most postmodern of his works, *Finnegans Wake* and the latter parts of *Ulysses*, the desire for that place of birth, of origin, while simultaneously showing the impossibility of ever getting beyond culture, beyond language, to a natural, single "home."⁹

At times, this longing for an origin takes the form of a search for a "natural" language. For example, according to Richard Ellmann, Joyce chose as analogue to the concept of perfect pitch in "Sirens" "Molly's natural comprehension of the hurdy-gurdy boy without understanding a word of his language" (*JJ* 439). Bloom sentimentally calls Molly's ability a "Gift of Nature." Joyce himself was fascinated by the idea of the "secret" language of women. He kept a dream book in which he recorded some of Nora's dreams with his interpretations. In one such dream, Nora is lying on a hill amidst a herd of *silver* cows and is made love to by one cow. Joyce's sister Eileen appears. Joyce's interpretation of the dream is revealing:

> That silver seems to her [Nora] a fine metal (and not a cheaper form of gold) shows a freedom from conventional ideas, a freedom more strongly shown by the fact that she feels no repulsion at being made love to by a female beast. Here there is no fear either of goring or of pregnancy. An experience more in life and therefore not to be avoided. Eileen appears as a messenger of *those secret tidings* which only women bear to women and the silver mountain torrent [an element in the dream], a precious and wild element, accompanies the secrecy of her messages with the music of romance. (*JJ* 437; my italics)

Here Joyce fantasizes about a secret female language, an elsewhere outside patriarchal mastery, a kind of female annunciation ("no goring, no pregnancy"). Of necessity, it is an elsewhere whose very condition depends upon the exclusion of men. Paradoxically, woman represents an "experience more in life" and therefore "not to be avoided," yet an experience which the fallen Adam cannot have.

But the image of woman as the Truth of Nature is itself shown to be a fiction. As Stephen Heath reminds us in "Ambiviolences," Anna Livia is the "Bringer of Plurabilities" (*FW* 104.02).[10] Both Woman as Nature and Woman as Fiction are conveyed in the name ALP—the source of every river *and* German for "nightmare" (*alptraum*), the dream and the nightmare from which the male writer cannot awake. Another phrase from *Finnegans Wake* condenses this longing for a source before language and the impossibility of arriving at that source. In his excellent work *Joyce's Book of the Dark*, John Bishop cites the following line from *Finnegans Wake*, applying it to the work as a whole: it "make[s] you to see figuratleavely the whome of your eternal geomater" (*FW* 296.30–297.01). He says "the passage moves us behind the occulting and shame-invested 'fig leave' (hence 'figuratleavely') into a 'momerry' of first 'whome' ('womb,' 'home')."[11] But it seems to me the "figuratleavely" suggests not only the desire to remove the fig leaf to view the source, but also the inescapable *figuration* involved in the representation of Woman. If the desire to lift the veil of Woman is everywhere portrayed in the text, its impossibility is insistent. The "misses in prints" (*FW* 20.11) are never stripped of their "feminine clothiering" (*FW* 109.31)—one figuration leads to another, never passing beyond to a realm where the Truth of Woman is found.

In Joyce's works, then, woman is not revealed but constantly revised. Even epiphanies ("sudden spiritual manifestations") of women are rethought and rewritten. For example, the powerful image of the bird girl which sears Stephen's imagination in *A Portrait* is progressively deromanticized. That beautiful Irish muse with "long slender bare legs" metamorphoses into the limping Gerty MacDowell, finally to become Biddy Doran the hen foraging in the midden heap in *Finnegans Wake*. The female is seen variously: she is ALP as the River Liffey, libidinously circulating through *Finnegans Wake*, ALP the letter writer, attempting to save her husband's reputation, and Issy, the daughter, whose letter threatens to expose her father's incestuous desires. She is both Nature and Culture, her body identified with both Mother Earth and the materiality of writing.

It is finally not as "flesh-without-word" that Woman functions for Joyce most powerfully, but as an "allaphbed" figuring the erotic and material potential of language. The phrase "misses in prints" suggests the errancy and waywardness of language which for Joyce, particularly in his later works, is figured by women. Biddy Doran's midden heap in *Finnegans Wake* is an image of the contaminated, uncontrollable material of language, and the slipperiness of its sounds and associations. The female figures the comic, almost slapstick potential in language that eludes patriarchal control. Penelope as weaver, the hen as gatherer and scavenger, remind us of the texture of writing, its material body, its bricolage. Anna Livia is a thief, a retriever and interpreter of other people's language ("where in thunder did she plunder" [*FW* 209.12]). Her theft of language serves as a model of its citationality. She provides a figure for an illegality, something outside of the patriarchal rebellion that is a killing of the literary forefather by the male heir apparent. She offers, metaphorically, a way out of the discourse of Freudian rebellion, offers instead a term for the Derridean "drift" in language.

Thus, although male rivalry and relationship dominate much of Joyce's texts and filial rebellion is an enormously important figure as well as theme, the "feminine" figured and as figure becomes increasingly important. One must recognize the danger of the "genderization" of writing as feminine and of viewing the male avant-garde as writing the "feminine," for the undecidability that characterizes "feminine" writing might appear to reinscribe Woman in her old stereotypes. This seems to me always a danger in Joyce's work. But ultimately I believe that Joyce relied on stereotypical binary oppositions, as Stephen Heath says in "Joyce and Language,"[12] to "deride and overturn them" by unmasking them and, further, by blurring the oppositions in the play of his language.

IV

In Joyce's early fiction, the staging of rebellion against the patriarchy exists still within some of its more dominant myths. For, although the early works explore cultural inscriptions of power, they seem less concerned with the role of the female in relation to patriarchal law. In *Dubliners* Joyce depicts the general entrapment of the "submerged population" of Dublin, as Frank O'Connor once called it, the underclass victimized by its own pathetically limited expectations and by the masters—the British and the Church of Rome—that rule the country. Women do not figure prominently in the majority of these stories. When they do, as in "Eveline" and "Clay," they display the general Dublin "paralysis" of their male counterparts, but, like the child in "Counterparts," these women suffer by being the oppressed of the oppressed. Like the "slavey" in "Two Gallants," women in Dublin, "good girls" included, wait for the favors of men. Even Gretta Conroy, whose vivid moment of romance is central to the story "The Dead," is locked in her husband's story as well as his fantasy, and can reveal only glimpses of her own desire. The register of female roles is more limited than that of the males— overbearing mothers (Mrs. Mooney, Mrs. Kearney), repressed spinsters (the eponymous "Sisters," Maria in "Clay," Julia and Kate Morkan in "The Dead"), frustrated wives (Gretta, Mrs. Chandler), objects of fantasy (the girl in "Araby"), the new political woman (Molly Ivors). The frustration of the female characters is signaled by this limited repertory of roles, but their marginality also arises from Joyce's basic scheme for the stories, to depict the stages of development from youth to maturity of a male protagonist.

The story of female development must be largely inferred: a character like Maria might be seen as the human consequence of Eveline's decision not to go with her sailor Frank; Mrs. Kearney, the frustrated and manipulative mother in "A Mother," might be what the pregnant and unwed Polly Mooney will become. Mrs Sinico in "A Painful Case" is the fleeting image of what a woman could have meant in a man's life, a kind of Jamesian promise of the lived life. (Interestingly, it is the woman who dies as a result of the man missing his opportunity.) The significance of the female, however, is suggested in strange ways in *Dubliners*—in the seemingly misplaced title of the first story, "The Sisters," which focuses on a young boy's fascination with a dead priest, or in "The Dead," which itself might be called "The Sisters," because the Morkan sisters, who play an auxiliary role in the plot, haunt the story almost like shades, with the thought of their impending deaths muted and displaced.[13]

In the early portraits of the artist, *Stephen Hero* and *A Portrait*, women seem to be once again cast in roles auxiliary to male development—as sexual tutors (the prostitute), muses (E. C., the bird girl), and symbols of the entangling snares the developing male must avoid (temptress of the villanelle, E. C., Dante with her hysterical Catholicism). The development of the Daedalean artist seems to entail a flight from women, particularly the mother, as a condition of growth. She is one of the "nets" he must fly by. In order to enter the symbolic world of language and the Father, the boy must remove himself from "the sufferings of women, the weakness of their bodies and souls" (*P* 245).

Joyce himself curtails the role of the female between *Stephen Hero*, the long unpublished novel in which both his mother and Emma Clery have explicit and extended roles, and the much shorter *Portrait*. May Dedalus, whose conversations are recorded in the earlier version of Stephen's story, is deprived of most of her lines and much of her role in *A Portrait*. And, as numerous critics have observed, Emma Clery is transformed from a character with a body and a name, to an object of mystery and intrigue—an ambivalent focus of desire, fear, and friendship whose presence—like the "characters" of *Finnegans Wake*—is signified by her initials (E. C.).

It is as if the image of the female were abstracted by Joyce so that Stephen must incarnate it himself, for ultimately Stephen seeks to convert abstract beauty and desire into poetry. As he has his "epiphany" of the bird girl at the end of part IV, Stephen feels "her image pass into his soul for ever" (*P* 172). But he begins to realize that the image must pass out as well, if he is to be a "priest of the eternal imagination" and transmute the spirit into a material image. The muse is crucial to this incarnation; somehow it is her spirit that must be embodied. One might say with Molly that all poets merely "want to write about some woman," but the female is more than a topic here; she is projected as the muse of representation, of embodiment. Her image haunts his days and his nights, as he struggles to refine it into poetry.

In part V Stephen seeks to find an image for E. C., between temptress and muse, inspiration for a wet dream and for poetry. In the process of figuring her, the young artist hopes to capture her elusive power, yet, he questions his own images, disturbed that he cannot fully represent her. He tries first one, then another image, crossing out as he goes along, debating how to figure her in language. In the following passage, for example, he first clothes her in Elizabethan garb, then rejects the sluttish image he has summoned:

> Eyes, opening from the darkness of desire, eyes that dimmed the breaking east . . . And what was their shimmer but the shimmer of the scum that mantled the cesspool of the court of a slobbering Stuart. And he tasted in the language of memory . . . dying fallings of sweet airs . . . and saw with the eyes of memory kind gentlewomen in Covent Garden wooing from their balconies with sucking mouths . . .
> The images he had summoned gave him no pleasure. They were secret and enflaming but her image was not entangled by them. That was not the way to think of her. It was not even the way in which he thought of her. Could his mind then not trust itself? Old phrases, sweet only with a disinterred sweetness like the figseeds Cranly rooted out of his gleaming teeth. (P 233)

In the first passage Stephen searches for the "right" image for Emma; in the second, he cancels out the image he has summoned from the literary stockpile. Like the "figseeds" plucked from Cranly's teeth, these phrases are leftover erotic (forbidden) fruit, conducive to erotic fantasy but not to poetry. Just like Molly Bloom in Joyce's dream, E. C. eludes Stephen's representation of her. "Her image was not entangled" by his words, a strange phrase that suggests it is she now who flies by the nets.[14]

The maternal image, too, seems beyond Stephen's control, surfacing at a crucial moment like the return of the repressed. The moment occurs in *A Portrait* during Stephen's trip to Cork, his father's hometown, when he searches for his father's initials in a school desk. Instead, in the midst of his search for his paternal origins, he is startled to find the word "foetus" carved in the desk like a scar. As Maud Ellmann says in a brilliant discussion of this episode, Stephen, searching for his father's (and thus his own) initials, discovers instead an image that draws him back to the body of the mother. In the midst of the scripting of the artist in the patriarchal tradition, the word leads back to "a prior nameless unbegotten world." The mother's anonymity flouts the name of the father. Her "namelessness," Ellmann says, "engraves itself upon the flesh [i.e. the navel] before the father ever carved his signature."[15] "The name of the father . . . necessarily entails a fresh unstained creation. The patronyms of all link back to that 'creation from nothing' . . . which Stephen mocks and then repudiates . . . The scarletter on the belly tells another story that has neither a beginning nor an end: that neither flesh nor words can ever say where they come from or claim a unitary origin" (101). Ellmann rightly sees anonymity, rather than the authority of the proper name, in the maternal image. Maternity, then, is a different kind of "fiction" than paternity, a fiction of a source before law and identity, the "allaphbed" of Anna Livia. Stephen's discovery seems to have a significance in the narrative and his consciousness that is never fully explained or rationalized in the text. It is as if it were itself a kind of scar. Unlike the epiphany at the end of part II in which the prostitute initiates Stephen into sexual experience, the word "foetus" cannot be assimilated to the pattern of the artist's quest. Indeed, the image of the artist as "foetus" reverses the direction of development in an alarming way.

In *Ulysses*, too, Stephen is suddenly and gratuitously reminded of the maternal image in another scene which juxtaposes maternal mark with the name and seal of the father. In "Nestor," scrawny Cyril Sargent, one of Stephen's students, copies out his sums; reminded of his own youth, Stephen gazes at an inkstain on the boy's face:

> On his cheek, dull and bloodless, a soft stain of ink lay, dateshaped, recent and damp as a snail's bed.
> He held out his copybook... [A]t the foot a crooked signature with blind loops and a blot. Cyril Sargent: his name and seal.
> . . .
> Ugly and futile: lean neck and thick hair and a stain of ink, a snail's bed. Yet someone had loved him, borne him in her arms and in her heart. But for her the race of the world would have trampled him underfoot, a squashed boneless snail . . . Was that then real? The only true thing in life?
> . . .
> *Amor matris*: subjective and objective genitive. With her weak blood and wheysour milk she had fed him and hid from sight of others his swaddlingbands. (*U* 2.126–67)

The inkstain, the blemish on the face, is the mark of the mother's anonymity in the text. It reminds Stephen of maternal stain rather than the "fresh unstained creation" of the father. Between birthmark and ink, the stain blurs the boundary between nature and culture. This scarletter reminds us that Moses, the child in swaddling bands, was shielded by a woman, his patriarchy dependent upon her protection. The wasted body of Stephen's mother appears throughout *Ulysses* to remind Stephen that one ignores the sign of the mother at one's peril. *Amor matris* is subjective and objective genitive—it works two ways.[16]

Throughout *Ulysses*, Stephen wrestles with the nightmare of his own history, especially its origin in the maternal body, his conception, the result of what he calls "an instant of blind rut." Indeed, Stephen's theory of literary creation in "Scylla and Charybdis" and patriarchal literary culture itself in "Oxen of the Sun" neutralize the power of the mother by effacing her role in culture.

In "Scylla and Charybdis," Stephen speaks of the "mystical estate" of fatherhood. Paternity, he says, may be a "legal fiction," that is, only a fiction of origin, and yet it is the *founding* fiction of the Church of Rome and of Western civilization itself, including literary creation, In contrast, here, as in the "Nestor" chapter, Stephen speculates that *amor matris* may be "the only true thing in life," a product of nature instead of culture. The statement hides the complexity of the maternal image for Stephen. Moreover, although he acknowledges the mother's power, he renders it impotent; essentialized as Womb, she is excluded from participating in culture by means of her function as its unproblematic "true" body. Stephen's theory of creation, then, pre-empts the role of the mother and leaves the male artist self-sufficient, free to create a world. If Joyce was intrigued with Nora's dream of a female language outside of patriarchal mastery, a kind of female annunciation without male interference, Stephen's myth of creation seeks to efface the role of the mother in the production of language.

As Dorothy Dinnerstein suggests in *The Mermaid and the Minotaur*, the invisibility of fatherhood paradoxically contributes to its power, as if man conceded to woman the visible and claimed for himself, compensatorily, the much greater world of the spiritual and invisible.[17] She further suggests that patrilineage arises out of envy of woman's procreative power. In "Oxen of the Sun" Stephen says (quoting the Gospel of John), "In woman's womb the word is made flesh but in the spirit of the maker all flesh that passes becomes the word that shall not pass away. This is the postcreation" (*U* 14.292–94). He acknowledges the body of the mother only to appropriate its womb for paternal postcreation. Stephen acknowledges the reproductive power of the mother, but it is the paternal "postcreation" of the word that produces true immortality.

In the "Oxen of the Sun" chapter of *Ulysses* it is as if Stephen's defensiveness were played out across the span of literary history. The chapter represents the suppressed relationship between reproduction and textual production. The symbol of the chapter is the "womb," and it applies to the chapter in two ways. In a sense, woman's womb *funds* the male discussion: it is the object of male debate and is praised, jeered at, legislated. In the changing styles of literary history, woman's economy changes as she is alternately valued and devalued, her body rhetorically flowered and deflowered. But the symbol of the chapter is also the womb in the sense that the womb is borrowed by male writers who are pregnant with the word. "Oxen of the Sun" is the chapter most conducive to source-hunting for fathers whose signatures are hidden in the chapter's styles; it seems to suggest that Literature is the domain of the proper name, of paternity. Just like Mrs. Purefoy, relegated to a place offstage during the male discussion, women seem to be excluded from cultural production.

But we sense as well that writing functions in part as "skirtscreen," that is, as defense against the power of woman's body. Male anxiety surfaces despite the rhetorical styles that attempt to elide it, like the periodic sentences of Gibbon which almost obscure the birth of the Purefoy child. It surfaces in the explicit examples of male ambivalence toward the maternal image ("But thou hast sucked me with a bitter milk: my moon and my sun thou hast quenched for ever. And thou hast left me alone for ever in the dark ways of my bitterness: and with a kiss of ashes hast thou kissed my mouth" [*U* 14.377–80]). It surfaces in the mention of Lilith, "patron of abortion," a female fiction older than Eve, and one which was never tamed.

We are reminded of woman's body when Bloom stares at the red-rubied triangle, the delta, on the bottle of Bass Ale trademark or "mademark" that figures so prominently in *Finnegans Wake*. The anonymous power of woman's body is felt within the chapter as a power to undo the male patronym. The power functions as a kind of illegitimacy that runs counter to the "legal" fictions of patriarchal succession. And it is expressed in the spirit of errancy within the succession of styles that compromises that authority of the literary forefathers, in, for example, anachronism and multiple allusion that deliberately subvert the integrity of the *pater* texts expropriated. (For specific examples, see Lawrence, "Paternity, the legal fiction" 47.) The pregnant word gives birth to too many meanings. It is this undermining of patriarchal authority and its connection with the mother that Gilbert and Gubar overlook in calling the chapter the triumph of patrolingualism (534). If Joyce had wanted to write the epitome of the Egotistical Sublime, he could have done better.[18]

This spirit of the errancy and texture of language, the sense of language's body, bursts on stage in "Circe" in no other than the body of Mrs. Mina Purefoy upon which Father Malachi O'Flynn celebrates a Black Mass. "*On the altarstone Mrs Mina Purefoy, goddess of unreason, lies, naked, fettered, a chalice resting on her swollen belly. Father Malachi O'Flynn in a lace petticoat and reversed chasuble, his two left feet back to the front, celebrates camp mass*" (*U* 15.4691–95). Here we find a parody of the body of woman as unproblematic ground of culture, as pregnant Mrs Purefoy becomes the symbol of disruption (rather than "pure faith," as her name suggests?). (And the injunction "Be fruitful and multiply" is treated ironically, as unthinking obedience to the law is portrayed as irrational.) Stable forms merge into their opposites. With chalice on her body, a position recalling that of the dead priest, Father Flynn in "The Sisters," Mrs Purefoy provides her body to Father O'Flynn for the Black Mass. Here is the "abject" body of woman (to use Julia Kristeva's term), come back to haunt the priest of the eternal imagination who would expel it from the myth of postcreation and thus from language.

Ulysses, however, does contain two chapters in which woman's subjectivity is staged, chapters more in the spirit of Bloom's prurience and empathy than Stephen's fear. In "Nausicaa" Joyce rewrote Stephen's epiphany on the beach, using, as Fritz Senn has shown in his essay "Nausicaa," many details from the earlier episode.[19] In fact, one can say that in "Nausicaa," Joyce opened up the possibility of female desire only glimpsed in *A Portrait* in the young girl's frank gaze: "She was alone and still, gazing out to sea; and when she felt his presence and the worship of his eyes her eyes turned to him in quiet sufferance of his gaze, without shame or wantonness" (*P* 171). From the perspective of *Ulysses*, this section from *A Portrait* now sounds like something Gerty could think as she watches Bloom. Only this time the dynamics are self-conscious, the topoi of desire scripted by the characters themselves. One effect of the transposition is deflationary, deromanticizing. If the eyes of Stephen's young girl had called him and "his soul had leaped at the call" (*P* 172), Bloom responds to Gerty's gaze with a different kind of rise. The players have changed to Odysseus and Nausicaa, and the chapter carries an air reminiscent of Odysseus' embarrassment upon his naked intrusion on the young girls' play. It is an air that brings us close to the dynamics of desire in *Finnegans Wake*, a banality and hopelessness that will return with Issy and Earwicker.

If in the "Oxen" chapter we see the changing economy of woman's body encoded by the male pen in different ages, "Nausicaa" presents that body clothed in the rhetoric of nineteenth-century popular romance. We are given the world in what Joyce described as a "namby-pamby jammy marmalady drawersy" style of Victorian ladies' magazines (*Letters I* 135). The art of the chapter is painting, and indeed the scene on the beach is like a Victorian reproduction of woman's desire (a writing of "what woman wants"). In the light of Derrida's work on postcards it is tempting to envision this scene as not even a painting but a postcard—a romantic, anonymous, mass-reproduced fantasy, the caption, perhaps, reading "love loves to love love" (a line from "Cyclops" perfect for "Nausicaa"). Although it is Gerty's fantasy to the extent that she accepts the encoding of her desires in such language, even courts the titillation of euphemism and longs to have the "suppressed meanings" in her look discovered, the fantasy is rooted in the patriarchal view. Gerty is "troped" according to the dual roles of angel in the house and femme fatale. The free indirect discourse, blending the resources of first- and third-person narration, suggests that the troping of her mind comes from outside as well as inside, providing the space of a separate view. Indeed, it is voyeurism that fuels Gerty's part of the chapter as well as Bloom's; Bloom watches Gerty watching him watch her. He projects his desires onto her, including his desire to be seen as exotic stranger rather than lonely Jew. Joyce once told Arthur Power, "Nothing happened between [Gerty and Bloom] . . . It all took place in Bloom's imagination."[20]

I have previously written of this chapter as a puzzling instance of Joyce's condescending to a particular style, suggesting, as the preceding chapters have not, "that there is some Olympian ground upon which the writer and reader can stand to be exempt from the charges of stupidity" (*The Odyssey of Style* 122–23). I now believe that the male gaze *is* contaminated by the "namby-pamby . . . marmalady" style of romance, *is* implicated in just such a troping. Indeed, Joyce himself was "implicated" in the encoded, banal desire circulating in this chapter, by a typically complicated set of revisions and mirrorings of life and art. Gerty MacDowell is based on Marthe Fleischmann, a young woman Joyce met in Zurich. In 1918 Joyce sent Marthe Fleischmann some love letters and a postcard addressed to "Nausikaa," signed "Odysseus" (see *Letters II* 426–36). As Heinrich Straumann records on the basis of an interview with Fleischmann, Joyce stared at her in wonder when he first saw her entering her apartment because she reminded him of the girl he had seen wading on the beach in his home country (*Letters II* 428). Thus, Gerty's desire is filtered through Joyce's desire for young "Nausicaa," who in turn reminded him of his prior representation of the girl on the beach in Ireland and the bird girl in *A Portrait*.

It is in "Penelope," however, that Joyce attempts to lend presence to woman's subjectivity in the flowing, unpunctuated sentences of Molly Bloom. As we have seen, Joyce's dream seems to acknowledge that woman and woman in writing are beyond his control, as the character he creates exceeds the boundaries he created. (One thinks of Issy in *Finnegans Wake* described as an "uncontrollable nighttalker" [*FW* 32.07–08].) Therefore, Molly's chapter presents a dilemma: how can she represent what is beyond Joyce's control, language emanating from somewhere else, and still somehow provide an ending of the book and a release from the stark, patriarchal abstractions preceding it? How can she seem like a new beginning without seeming to offer a "truth," the possibility of which the styles of the rest of the book have subverted?

Perhaps one can say that Molly represents the *problem of woman represented by the male pen*, a staging of alterity that reveals itself as masquerade. Patrick McGee says in *Paperspace*: "Molly's word represents less what Joyce thought a woman was than what he could not think, possess, or come to be."[21] The masquerade cannot represent something wholly outside the writer's knowledge, not wholly outside the dominant discourse. Somewhere, between subject and object, Molly is figured as that which exists elsewhere, beyond the mastery of the male pen.[22]

This elsewhere, however, will be refigured, rewritten, repositioned, displaced in *Finnegans Wake*. For it was not until *Finnegans Wake* that Joyce wrote a whole book in which he tried to represent what could not be thought or possessed, a book, in other words, that does not limit the sign of the unthinkable or the other to the interstices and final chapters. For one thing, the concept of the interstitial loses its meaning in a book that so radically blurs the boundaries between inside and outside as well as the binary oppositions of male and female. The alphabet itself is gendered, its letters combining in transgressive ways. As Shari Benstock puts it in an article entitled "Nightletters," woman's desire runs through the letters of the book signifying not a voice or presence, as has previously been suggested, but a writing always elusive, a desire that can never be possessed.[23] And although Anna Livia, like Molly, has "the last word," it returns us to the book's beginning. Indeed, the circulation of her "untitled mamafesta" might be a figure for the wayward path of the writing of desire, a reminder that desire is always encoded and disguised, in letters "selfpenned to the other."

V

Joyce once wrote to Nora, "I *know* and *feel* that if I am to write anything fine or noble in the future I shall do so only by listening at the doors of your heart" (*Letters II* 254). The combination of adoration and titillation in this image of Joyce as "evesdropper" and "earwitness" captures the complexity of his attitude toward women and suggests the kind of images with which he represented them. In a sense, Joyce's works are letters of desire to the female that circulate through the texts of culture, letters published for all the world to see. They are "compromising letters" where women are concerned, just such a letter as Joyce referred to in a dream he recorded after the publication of *Ulysses*:

> A young woman tells me with less and less indignation that I have written a compromising letter to her. The contents do not shock her much, but she asks me why I signed it "Ulysses." I affirm that I have done nothing of the kind; before I can swear to it she disappears. She was dressed in black. (*JJ* 548)

The dream suggests that *Ulysses* is the "compromising letter." The young girl denies that the contents of the book shock her, a denial that is suspect, given the shocked reaction of most early readers of the novel. Her shock is displaced onto the book's signature, "Ulysses." However, by a process of symbolic substitution, we can try to discover what the condensed symbol "Ulysses" stands for. The title "Ulysses" refers, of course, to the name of Ulysses, Latinized version of Odysseus, Greek counterpart to Leopold Bloom. Bloom's "other" name, in his clandestine and "compromising letters" to Martha Clifford, is Henry Flower. At the end of chapter 5 of *Ulysses*, Bloom imagines himself reclining in the tub, gazing at his penis, "the limp father of thousands, a languid floating *flower*" (my italics). By a "commodius vicus of recirculation" we can trace the disguised signature back to the phallus of its author. Despite displacement and other defenses, the dream conveys Joyce's sense that he has exposed himself. Although he says that the girl becomes "less and less" indignant, by a process of inversion typical of dreams, this probably suggests her increasing indignation and his increasing humiliation. "I affirm that I have done nothing of the kind," Joyce defends himself in the dream. But strangely, he "affirms" his denial, thus suggesting it is his guilt that he affirms. We might remember that in *Finnegans Wake* one of the names for James Joyce is "Shame's Voice."

Finally, in the dream the girl seems to question the substitution of the book's title for the author's signature, perhaps objecting that the private "letter" of desire has itself been "exposed" in the letters of the published book.

The dream draws on Joyce's correspondence with Marthe Fleischmann. In the love letters he sent her, he "disguised" his signature by signing his name with Greek "e's" (just as Bloom signs the name Henry Flower in his clandestine letters to Martha Clifford). As noted, he also sent her a postcard (which was subsequently lost), written to "Nausikaa" and signed "Odysseus." The "compromising letter" in this case is in the form of a postcard, its message, as Derrida says in *The Postcard*, both exposed to the world and yet curiously encoded for deciphering by its recipient.[24] The fact that it is now lost adds an ironic confirmation of the wayward path of desire. Heinrich Straumann, who first learned of the postcard by interviewing Marthe Fleischmann, bemoaned its loss, which he found "particularly unfortunate in view of what the experience evidently meant to Joyce" (*Letters II* 429).

What it and similar experiences of the female "meant" to Joyce is played out in Joyce's dreams, letters, unpublished drafts, and published works, and there is no simple way to decipher it. The desire is in no simple sense Joyce's; indeed, the substitution of the signature "Ulysses" for that of "James Joyce" in Joyce's dream functions to acknowledge that the desire encoded is neither singular nor merely personal. It is a desire variously woven through all the compromising, sent, suppressed, published, borrowed, and lost letters that he wrote to and about women.[25]

6

Women Building the Foundation

Gertrude Stein begins her book *Wars I Have Seen* by saying, "I do not know whether to put in the things I do not remember as well as the things I do remember. To begin with I was born, that I do not remember but I was told about it quite often. . . ."[1] I have heard about the early days of the Joyce world only through stories, mostly from friends who were there at the time when the International James Joyce Foundation was formed. I had not yet read Joyce in 1967 when Tom Staley, Fritz Senn, Murray Beja, and Berni Benstock, along with others, were inspired to create a foundation that sponsored an international symposium in European cities in which Joyce lived at some point in his life.

A small number of women attended the first International James Joyce Symposium in Dublin in 1967. Margaret Solomon was one of the few women listed in the program of both the first and second symposia, in 1967 and '69. The introduction to Solomon's book *Eternal Geomater: The Sexual Universe of "Finnegans Wake"* (1969) provides a telling entry to the topic of early women Joyceans. What struck me about Solomon's introduction was the following: the only critic whom Solomon mentions is Adaline Glasheen, the woman who helped launch *Finnegans Wake* criticism in the early issues of *A Wake Newsletter*. In her introduction, Solomon does not make typical obeisance to her predecessors and excuses its absence by saying: "I hope Joycean critics will not be offended by my failure to mention, in many instances, the work others have done on particular passages. Scholarship on *Finnegans Wake* must progress through community labor, and I have been helped considerably by an exhaustive reading of all available critical material."[2] I mention this not to suggest that Solomon failed to pay her "dues" to her colleagues (indeed, Berni Benstock's work is prominently mentioned in a later chapter), but to suggest that the few early women Joyceans played a significant role for each other, particularly in what Solomon called the "sexplication" (viii) of *Finnegans Wake*. Glasheen was clearly an important colleague for Solomon in the endeavor she refers to as the "community labor" of exploring *Finnegans Wake*, a kind of labor that the *Wake* invited and in which women often excel. (It is interesting that much of the early work by women focused on the *Wake* or *Dubliners* rather than *Ulysses* and *A Portrait*.) The ratio of male to female critics of Joyce was overwhelming. In a 1969 *Modern Fiction Studies* special issue on Joyce, all the contributors were men, and the Selected Checklist of Joyce criticism published that year included few women commentators among the hundreds listed: Elizabeth Bowen, Rebecca West, Margaret Church, Maria Jolas, and Hélène Cixous among the most notable; two Catholic "sisters" who wrote essays on ritual in Joyce and Joyce and Hopkins; and a few who discovered his work via other writers and discussed it in essays on "Joyce and . . ."—Proust, Ibsen, Beckett, and the French symbolists.[3]

The collection *Women in Joyce*, edited by Suzette Henke and Elaine Unkeless in 1982, reflected some of the tensions in the first wave of feminist attention to Joyce, which tended to focus on Joyce's fictional representations of and personal relationships with women.[4] Many women Joyceans, like some Marxist Joyceans, felt a need to justify the critical attention and sympathy they lavished on him. *Women in Joyce* is symptomatic of a certain critical moment in which feminist criticism's treatment of Joyce divided into those critics who viewed him as an ally in the critique of gender stereotypes and the oppression of women and those who, like Carolyn Heilbrun in her two-page "Afterword" to the volume, accuse him of misogyny despite acknowledging his literary achievement. The fact that Heilbrun, a pioneering feminist but not herself a "Joycean," was strategically relegated to the outside of the collection proper, suggests that the editors and other contributors subscribed to a view of Joyce more congenial to feminist aspiration. On a personal note, I might add that this antipathy to Joyce on Carolyn Heilbrun's part led us to decide, mutually, that she would not direct my dissertation on Joyce at Columbia, despite my admiration for her.

In 1979, fresh from graduate school and in the first year of my first faculty appointment, I attended my first International James Joyce Symposium, held in Zurich, where Joyce lived at the end of his life and where he is buried. That year, with much fanfare, the James Joyce Pub opened in Zurich, having traveled piece by piece from Jury's Hotel in Dublin. The Zurich James Joyce Foundation was only a gleam in Fritz Senn's eye; David

Lodge came to the symposium to gather material for his parody of academic conferences, *Small World*, and found plenty to write about.[5] Hans Gabler presented an experimental prototype for his critical edition.

By 1979, two Margarets, Solomon and Church, served on the Board of Trustees. Margot Norris had published her important book *The Decentered Universe of "Finnegans Wake": A Structuralist Analysis*. Marilyn French (author of the enormously popular *The Woman's Room*) had also published *The Book as World: James Joyce's "Ulysses"*; Julia Kristeva had written of Joycean jouissance in her essays in French (later published in English in *Desire in Language: A Semiotic Approach to Literature and Art*); and Hélène Cixous' *The Exile of James Joyce* had appeared in both English and French.[6] But, again, the predominant gender at that incredible event in Zurich was decidedly male. For a neophyte, the roster was a daunting and inspiring list of Who's Who in Joyce studies. Fritz Senn, who had organized the program, had set up a narrative panel on *Ulysses*, with different presenters every day for five days. I was thrilled to be on the panel, a participant by virtue of Fritz's characteristic openness to graduate students just emerging within the Joycean ranks. On one of the sessions I presented a paper on narrative voice in "Ithaca." At the end of the week, Fritz selected four panelists for a narrative wrap-up session on the sixth day. He himself participated, and invited Hugh Kenner, Arnold Goldman (who had written an excellent book on Joyce), and me. I felt like an understudy suddenly called to perform. Out of fear, I considered declining. A sense of opportunity led me to accept. I offered one small and basically inarticulate comment on the panel; to my surprise, I heard Hugh Kenner endorse my observation (thankfully, I was on the side of his good ear). I will never forget the way he tossed off the words, "as Karen said. . . ." Like Stephen Dedalus, I felt that the ciborium had come to me!

In 1982 at the Centennial Symposium in Dublin, Marilyn French, a plenary speaker, generously hosted a number of Joyceans for drinks and discussion in her room in a posh hotel that no one else could have afforded. A number of women present bemoaned the fact that here were so few women plenary speakers and few panels with feminist content. The next year, at the Joyce conference in Provincetown, Massachusetts, the Women's Caucus was born, largely through the dedicated efforts of Bonnie Scott and Suzette Henke. On Friday, June 13, 1983, the *Boston Globe*'s Arts and Films section carried an article entitled "Feminist Joyceans Demand More Say." The story read, "Few had expected feminism to become a major issue. . . . At a luncheon Tuesday, however, the long-simmering issues of the role of women in Joyce studies reached the boiling point." Although its metaphor placed women at the stove, the article went on to give credence to our political action. According to the article, "23 of the country's best-known female Joyceans led by Bonnie Scott, of the University of Delaware . . . yesterday demanded a greater voice in the decisions of the Joyce 'industry'" in a letter to Murray Beja, then President of the International James Joyce Foundation. My own participation at that conference was enabled by my mother-in-law, who agreed to accompany me to Provincetown to babysit for my one-year-old son. For many of us, feminist issues were bound up with our careers in multiple and pragmatic ways.

The Caucus helped considerably to increase the influence of women Joyceans within the Foundation's agenda. It ensured that more women would be on the board of the Foundation, consulted in the planning of the symposia, and invited as plenary speakers. But it also confirmed powerful intellectual currents that were propelling theory and criticism within the academy and beyond. If the act of solidarity that spawned the Caucus signified inroads of feminism into the American academy (despite the international emphasis of the foundation, the Caucus was largely a product of a group of American academics), the next year's symposium in Frankfurt revealed how much the American academy had been influenced by contemporary French thought. At the 1984 International James Joyce Symposium in Frankfurt, the symposium that could best be regarded as a major intellectual "event," post-structuralist and feminist approaches, sometimes in uneasy mix, were the news. Kristeva's "Joyce 'The Gracehoper' or the Return of Orpheus" and Derrida's "*Ulysses* Gramophone: Hear say yes in Joyce" originated as twin plenary talks, both enormously inspiring, both in difficult French.[7]

The plenaries marked an important turn in the conception of Joyce criticism with a feminist bent, just as it marked the influence of theory on the activities of literary criticism. Studies of women characters and thematic approaches to female oppression and subversion either condoned or critiqued in Joyce were overtaken by more fluid notions of sexual identity and identification. Kristeva admonished critics that "it has been a mistake to search in this ending of *Ulysses* [Molly's monologue] for a recognition of, or alternately a censuring of, feminine sexuality. More correctly, it [the process of identification in *Ulysses*] concerns the male-artist who, sated with a final appropriation-identification, restores to us a menad swallowed by Orpheus" (171). The "ubiquitous identificatory process" Kristeva described shifted the ground of critique from women to the psychic adventures of subjectivity (and with it, more complex processes of identification with the Other) and the reabsorption of sexuality into a body of language. In addition, it complicated her own earlier view of *écriture féminine* and Joyce's role as its avatar. Derrida, whose extraordinary talk demonstrated how modernist fiction anticipated post-structuralist theory, discoursed on Elijah/Molly and the "unforeseeable Other for whom a place must he kept" (59). Although Lacan had addressed the Joyceans at the 1975 Paris symposium, the Frankfurt symposium clearly emphasized that Joycean transatlantic travel worked both ways, not only in the exporting of Americans to European conferences.

By the late eighties, six women served as Trustees of the Foundation—Bonnie Scott, Christine Van Boheemen-Saaf, Rosa Maria Bosinelli, Shari Benstock, Carla Marengo, and I. I was fortunate to be elected Foundation President in 1990. In 1992, Foundation members approved a major change to the bylaws of the organization: election of trustees and foundation officers by the membership of the Foundation, and a rotating, rather than infinitely expanding, membership on the board. Until that point, trustees were elected by the existing board for permanent appointment, a procedure that created two problems: the difficulty of adding new blood to the organization and the lack of space on foundation stationery. (In time the change would lessen the dominance of those who had been active in the organization for decades.)

The second highlight of my Joycean career occurred in Ireland in 1992 at the 13th International James Joyce Symposium, when the Trustees were privileged to meet the first woman President of Ireland, the extraordinary Mary Robinson. Robinson was proud to claim Joyce as a quintessentially Irish writer, yet, for a president, unusually reluctant to subscribe to the customary chauvinism expected of heads of state. Joyce's Ireland, she said, "is not a place of regional interest, it's that fierce territory where nothing is taken for granted." His legacy, she told the enthralled audience, was one of "rebellion and uncompromising self-inquiry, which prevents us from ever feeling complacent about being Irish."[8] Eavan Boland, the Irish poet, spoke at the Women's Caucus luncheon that year and drew an equally adulatory crowd. The "women only" invitation policy for this event led to some protest on the part of a few male scholars, who complained at being excluded from a speech by such an important poet. (Subsequently, notice of the Women's Caucus was included in the program brochure.) In her plenary talk at a later International Symposium in Seville, Boland spoke of Joyce's complicated legacy to contemporary women poets: "The fact is," she said, "that I began my writing life learning the categories of Irishness and identity which he had spent all his resisting."[9] As Boland's comment makes clear, issues of gender were increasingly yoked to other cultural matrices, particularly to those of nationalism and language. Work on Joyce has continually mined his texts for their treatments of postcoloniality and race. If this procedure in some sense acknowledges that the Joyce industry replenishes itself by recourse to new theories, it also recognizes how fiction, particularly modern fiction, theorizes, with pride of place accorded to Joyce in psychoanalytic, deconstructive, postcolonial, and some feminist critique.

I believe that my own career as an academic woman has been indelibly affected by my continuing fascination with Joyce and involvement with the scholars and readers who share my preoccupation. I know of no other scholarly group that is as international, as welcoming of new generations of critics, and as conducive to forming lasting friendships as this one. Personally, my six-year tenure as the first woman President of the Joyce Foundation also helped prepare me for other administrative responsibilities. It taught me something about the assumption of certain public roles traditionally inhabited by men. Like the epic, the after-dinner speech is one not often practiced by women. As President of the Foundation, I followed Murray Beja, an inveterate emcee totally comfortable in his role. I tried to learn from Murray, who, like Berni Benstock before him, was born to his official role as charmer of new and old members alike. In one of my first after-dinner speeches as the new President at the Miami Joyce conference in 1993, I tried to emulate Murray's after-dinner style by telling a joke. Regina Barreca's book on women and humor aside, I have never found it very natural to stand up and tell jokes.[10] Like Freddy Malins in "The Dead," I tend to succumb to the suspense of joke telling even when I am the one telling the joke, and my anxiety about blowing the punch line is apparent. For whatever reason, at the Miami event, I had put myself in the unenviable position of telling a joke I didn't like and was not convinced was actually funny. Halfway through I knew it was a big mistake; the glass of wine I had gulped during dinner only made it worse. Here I was, as "off" as Freddy Malins (though certainly not as inebriated). The joke bombed. In the years that followed that first experience, I became accustomed to my public responsibilities, even relishing the welcoming and valedictory functions of the office performed, often in awe-inspiring European places of assembly. Even Stephen Joyce in the audience did not occasion undue alarm.

In 2008, Anne Fogarty is President of the International James Joyce Foundation, following Margot Norris, and many women have been and are members of the Foundation Board of Trustees. The changes in the Joyce organization reflect larger welcomed changes in the academy. And, as in the academy, still more needs to be done.

III

Bloom in Circulation

Navigating Identifications

7

"Eumaeus" Redux

The "Eumaeus" chapter of *Ulysses* inaugurates the *nostos* or final section of Joyce's novel. It represents the 1 A.M. wanderings of Stephen Dedalus and Leopold Bloom after they escape from "nighttown" and seek refuge in the cabman's shelter. In the logic of the plot, there is a kind of recuperation here, represented in the first sentence by Bloom's "preparatory" action of brushing off the shavings from Stephen's shoulder and "buck[ing] him up generally in orthodox Samaritan fashion" (*U* 16.2–3). It is as if the intense psycho-sexual drama of "Circe" were traded, with relief, for a more comfortable outing in the male world of cabman's shelters and almost deserted Dublin streets, the psychic depths charted earlier replaced by strictly surface transportation. (The art of the chapter, according to Joyce's schema, is navigation.) The "Bloom" of "Circe," in all his pantomimic glory and shame, is now dignified with his original title in the narrative, "Mr Bloom." One could say that the narrative is engaged in regaining a sense of bourgeois respectability.

The narrative, then, offers linguistic respite as well as geographic refuge. For the place of refuge is also a *commonplace*; the narrative contains a host of well-worn clichés. *Nostos* means home-coming; hence, the word "nostalgia." I have written previously that the language of the chapter represents the "public, anonymous 'voice of culture' . . . a transpersonal repository of received ideas."[1] But this Flaubertian notion of received ideas bears further scrutiny. What is the socio-economic terrain of the commonplace? To whom is it common? What are the investments of canvasser and poet in speaking or trying to evade this discourse? In "Eumaeus" Joyce shows us how language interpellates (to use Althusser's word) political subjects. The dominant cultural "voice" of "Eumaeus" mimes the hegemony of middle-class ideology and bourgeois common sense. The discourse of bourgeois productivity underwrites much of the narrative, an extension of, but not limited to, Bloom's own preoccupation with utility and profit. This ethic of productivity, summed up in Bloom's vision of Ireland as a country "[w]here you can live well, the sense is, if you work" (*U* 16.1139–40), is woven into the narrative in a tissue of economic idioms of accounting and investment. But the discourse of "Eumaeus" demonstrates the way ideology conceals contradictions in colonial Ireland; the commonplaces mask economic and political divisions beneath their universalizing rhetoric. "Calypso"'s art is economy, referring to the domestic economy of the Blooms; "Eumaeus" represents complexities of the Irish political economy. Jew and poet are seen as part of the weave of this socio-economic fabric, even in their alienation. In the play (and work) of the narrative of "Eumaeus," Joyce constructs an anatomy of socio-economic identifications and divisions at the turn of the century in Ireland.

By focusing on the socio-economic terrain of the language, we can recast questions of identity in the chapter, which have received much deserved critical attention, into the terms of social identifications. Emphasis then falls on a kind of social mapping in "Eumaeus," by which characters are placed in relation to an economy of production. In a largely sympathetic review of *Ulysses* in 1937, the British Marxist Alick West complained that the book shows no sign of productive activity, no work or workers: "Joyce shows ... little of the relations of production. There are no disputes between employers and labor, no struggle for wages, no strikes."[2] But, paradoxically, in this desultory chapter, work is a central concern. From Stephen's question to Bloom about the reason that chairs are put on tables (to sweep under the table) to Gumley's sleeping on the job ("evidently a glutton for work," Bloom surmises), labor leaves its traces. And twice we are reminded that Thursday "16 June, 1904" is payday.[3] The "disputes" West calls for are implied in the chapter—there are signs of overwork and underemployment. The ethic of productivity is belied in the plot and language. We might do well to remember that the Odyssean parallel to Joyce's "Eumaeus" is the episode in which Odysseus returns to Ithaca disguised as a beggar. *Ulysses* at this point shifts to a lower key on the socio-economic scale, which is imaginatively, if not geographically, outside the limits of the city "proper." (Although this can be said as well of "nighttown," I will return to the differences between the kind of hallucinatory psychic space of "Circe" and the feel of the quotidian in "Eumaeus.") The "vicinity" of the cabman's shelter is a social space through which poet and canvasser navigate their way carefully, past warehouse, police station, and unsavory loiterers. If one of the main projects of *Ulysses* is to put the "everyday" under a microscope, in this chapter what we see is a "miscellaneous collection of waifs and strays and other nondescript specimens of the genus *homo*" (*U* 16.327–28).[4] The beggar represents a kind of limit case on the social map—an insistent part of urban geography, yet outside the economy of production, a living sign of society's failures. Like John Corley, who asks Stephen for money, some of the characters in the chapter are reduced to the status of beggars (the prostitute, technically selling rather than begging, is said to have "begged the chance of [Bloom's] washing" [*U* 16.714–15]). If "Wandering Rocks" represents the Dubliners' encounters as they busily traverse the city, "Eumaeus," so much more lethargic in its comings and goings, reveals the déclassé nature of itinerancy. It plots the downward direction of social mobility that was an important fact of existence in Dublin, as well as a counter-desire to maintain a shabby and threatened gentility. These socio-economic tensions are plotted as well in the language, in the texture of its idioms and its odd mixture of verbal play and labor. The narrative itself enacts processes of labor and lassitude, productivity and wastefulness, thematized in the plot.

This kind of reading involves more than a reappraisal of an under-analyzed chapter of *Ulysses*. "Eumaeus" provides a challenge to two opposing critical views of the political implications of modernist and postmodernist style, for which Joyce's work has provided a central example. The first is that of early Marxists, like Lukács, who equated modernist formalism and technical experiment with retrogressive politics. This view inspired readings of *Ulysses* as a quintessential modern novel, in which stylistic experimentalism reflects a retreat from politics and the representation of social forces.[5] (It persists in the pejorative view of what has been called "ludic" postmodernism as opposed to a more radical or "resistance" postmodernism.) The second is the view purveyed by the Adorno/Brecht side of the German Marxist debate, and updated in Terry Eagleton's *Ideology of the Aesthetic*, which equates Joyce's "revolution" in language with radical politics. In speaking of Joyce's "Bakhtinian radicalism" and the *Wake*'s "profoundly political undermining of fixed signification [that] comes about through the movements of a promiscuous signifier," Eagleton is typical of the many recent critics who *assume* a link between radical style and progressive politics and read Joyce as exemplar of the postmodern play of language. "It is as though *Ulysses* and *Finnegans Wake* lift a protean dissolution of all stable identity from base to superstructure."[6]

The complex verbal play in "Eumaeus" frustrates both these assessments of the political valence of Joyce's stylistic play. First, far from retreating from social forces, the narrative dissects them. Rather than being merely a symptom of the isolated bourgeois consciousness, the writing in "Eumaeus" is a kind of diagnosis of the tension of this consciousness in its particular Irish colonial formation. Secondly, the obvious labor and banality of the prose makes it an unlikely candidate for Eagleton's allegory of the signifier. The language is not sexy enough to qualify as "promiscuous signifier." In other words, it is difficult to see this particular language as of the liberating, postmodern kind. Nevertheless, I shall argue that the *labor* of language in this soporific chapter has political and socio-economic purport, which is indissolubly linked to the representation of material conditions in the chapter. Eagleton's move from "base" to "superstructure" short-circuits Joyce's concern in "Eumaeus" to anatomize "real" economic conditions as well as economies of language.

In "Eumaeus," unlike "Cyclops," another public chapter in which politics plays an important role, exploitation subsumes the category of oppression. I mean by this that whereas Stephen elsewhere focuses on the psychological effects on the Irish artist of the domination of Ireland by the British government and the Roman Catholic Church, in "Eumaeus" the material effects of economic exploitation are felt as facts of everyday life in Dublin ("But in the economic, not touching religion, domain the priest spells poverty," says Bloom to Stephen [*U* 16.1127]). The economic here is featured as a bottom line. A "Marxist" Bloom analyzes those "wretched quarrels . . . erroneously supposed to be about a punctilio of honour and a flag," as "very largely a question of the money question which was at the back of everything greed and jealousy, people never knowing when to stop (*U* 16.1111–15). The "guardians of the law," he tells Stephen, are "never on the spot when wanted but in quiet parts of the city, Pembroke road for example . . . the obvious reason being they were paid to protect the upper classes" (*U* 16.79–82).

But the economic in Ireland is inextricably bound to Ireland's colonial status.[7] Dublin is kept in its place as a kind of urban village because of it. The keeper of the shelter is quick to comment that the resources of Ireland are diverted to the imperial power. Even the startling extent of prostitution in Dublin, as Richard Brown has remarked, depended upon the continuing presence of English soldiers far from home.[8] The economic fate of Ireland as metropolitan colony is figured in Lord John Corley's supposed genealogy. Corley, with "not as much as a farthing to purchase a night's lodgings" (*U* 16.145), is said to be the descendant of Lord Talbot and a woman "in service in the washkitchen" (*U* 16.140)—his mixed-class origins link issues of imperialism and exploitation, sexual and economic.[9]

Class discourse, then, is greatly complicated by the colonial situation, in which sailor, advertising man and poet alike see themselves in the "cracked lookingglass of a servant" (*U* 1.146). Some curious alliances emerge among classes through a collective sense of exploitation. But in this chapter, as opposed to "Cyclops," for example, both the sympathy that binds Bloom to the less fortunate, and the Irish nationalism that might be the political result of such inter-class identifications, are cast in the wider terms of European political and economic discourses. These include the socialist, syndicalist, and anarchist discourses that fascinated Joyce in Rome in 1906, when he first conceived of *Ulysses*, and in Trieste when he was writing it. In this quotidian chapter, traces of these discourses document the important revolutionary moment that included the 1904 setting of *Ulysses*.

As "a friendless expatriate small bank clerk," as Giorgio Melchiori describes Joyce in Rome,[10] he steeped himself in Italian socialism, reading avidly the socialist daily *Avanti!*, *L'Asino*, a satirical weekly paper, as well as books by the sociologist and historian Guglielmo Ferrero. At that time, Joyce identified himself as a socialist, writing to Stanislaus often about his "socialist tendencies" (*Letters* II 148). Joyce's reading of Italian socialism coincided with his thinking and writing about Irish politics, but Melchiori contends that what Joyce learned from witnessing the Italian Socialist Congress in October 1906 and from reading the Italian socialist press was "a totally different approach to politics: politics as ideology. It was a way of recovering his own original attitude, beyond the narrow limits of nationalism whether in its militant or in its vaguely nostalgic form" (Melchiori 47). As a writer from a metropolitan colony of the United Kingdom, Joyce could not have avoided knowing something about politics as ideology. But the point is that for Joyce, whose reservations about nationalism included the potentially bourgeois character of an Irish republic, socialism and syndicalism provided a more radical and economic understanding of the politics of the everyday. In *The Consciousness of James Joyce* and *Joyce's Politics*, Richard Ellmann and Dominic Manganiello demonstrate respectively the extent of Joyce's interest in revolutionary and socialist writings during the first decade of the twentieth century.[11] Joyce's library in Trieste included the first 173 Fabian tracts, Wilde's *The Soul of Man under Socialism*, and the writings of Tucker, Kropotkin, Proudhon, and Bakunin.[12]

An economic and class-bound understanding permeates the "Eumaeus" chapter, as it resurrects the earlier, more socialist concerns of *Stephen Hero*. Writing of the "socialist eclipse in twentieth-century Ireland," Terence Brown remarks:

> The socialist ideas and preoccupations of much of modern Europe have had curiously little currency in a country where ideology has meant protracted, repetitive debates on the national question with, up to very recently, little attention directed to class issues and social conditions. . . . There has been no Irish disciple of Brecht, have been no efforts apart from O'Casey's later plays written in exile, to produce a literature *engagé* on behalf of socialism. (105)

Joyce here does not produce a literature "on behalf of socialism"; skeptical of political programs, he neither wholly endorses nor wholly mocks socialist and syndicalist politics in the chapter. But he does present a view that reveals the pressing relevance of socialist economic and class analysis, particularly to the Irish situation.[13] He documents a particular historical moment in European history at the turn of the century, when the problems of the "real" produced revolutionary discourses that could neither be ignored nor wholly co-opted by bourgeois discourse. Certainly, part of the comedy of Bloom's politics is his bourgeoisification of socialist concepts, his argument, for example, for revolution "on the due installments plan" (*U* 16.1101). But, although he misquotes Marx in the chapter (transforming Marx's "From each according to his ability, to each according to his needs" into a jumbled mix of socialism and capitalism—"Everyone according to his needs or everyone according to his deeds" [*U* 16.247]), the effect of the radical political discourse remains. Although Bloom's dream of being savior to the masses may seem like a reformist fantasy of the bourgeois imaginary, still the basic idea of needs stubbornly clings to the discourse of desire. The semantic unit "need" surfaces in various forms sixteen times in the chapter. Four of these references appear in the stock expression "needless to say," a phrase that characterizes much of the circumlocution in the narrative, but the mass of "needless" phrases might serve as a kind of compensation for (and symptom of) the deficiency of material satisfactions.

The radical politics in the chapter, like much else, is handled by suggestion and indirection, not polemic. Disguised identity shades into political alias, most notably in the case of the shelter's proprietor, the purported anarchist, Skin-the-Goat. The link between Skin-the-Goat's anarchy and European, particularly Italian, anarchist and syndicalist discourses is smuggled into the chapter through a number of references: the rumor that the Invincibles were foreigners, probably Italian, because they used a knife; the sailor's story of a man killed in Trieste by an Italian chap; the argument about money that is conducted in Italian; even the potential puns on labor strikes and political murders in the references to a "dangerouslooking claspknife" held "in the *striking* [my italics] position" (*U* 16.579), and to "striking views" (*U* 16.1592) and "striking coincidence" (*U* 16.1775–76). Corrosive, potentially violent ressentiment pervades the atmosphere. Skin-the-Goat's rancorous political comments betray his "axe to grind" (*U* 16.985). In its engagement with a European political discourse, "Eumaeus" is Joyce's version of *The Secret Agent*, Conrad's novel of anarchism and political intrigue written in 1907, and part of Joyce's library in Trieste.[14] Bloom and Stephen in the streets of Dublin ironically repeat that other rather odd couple, Mr. Verloc and Stevie, although, in some ways, Bloom plays both Verloc and Stevie in Joyce's revision. In Bloom's encounter with the "good poor brute" of a horse, in his interest in the plight of the cabbies, Joyce rewrote Conrad's own parodic, pathetic scene of Stevie's sympathy toward cabby and horse, summed up in Stevie's inarticulate yet intensely felt declaration, "Bad world for poor people!" (Conrad 168). Joyce's reference to those at "the end of [their] tether" (*U* 16.952, 1874) is both a cliché and a literary allusion to Conrad's story, "The End of the Tether." Carla Bigazzi tells us that in Rome Joyce avidly read the satiric weekly *L'Asino*, which means "The Ass"; the motto of the paper was "The donkey is the people: useful, patient, and flogged."[15] Although Joyce and Conrad are skeptical of the grand notions of politics and represent scenes of injustice through Flaubertian comedy, exploitation is still a serious theme in their work.

Indeed, the kind of wordplay evident in the repeated expression "the end of [their] tether" is crucial to Joyce's treatment of exploitation in "Eumaeus," in which abstractions are comically literalized to return us to material conditions. Aaron Fogel points out that the scene with cabby and horse in Conrad is part of what he calls a "beast of burden" motif that presents a "primal scene of nineteenth-century inter-class social pathos."[16] Joyce picks up on this beast of burden motif in "Eumaeus," making the ubiquitous horse emblematic of the drudgery of alienated labor. I would suggest that what he constructs in the chapter is a kind of "puncept" involving overwork, "puncept" being a term coined by Gregory Ulmer to designate a metaphoric node created by verbal repetition and suggestion.[17] This "puncept" centers on the idea of the hackney and hackneyed. The word "hackney" appears only once, yet it is as if this concept ran like an invisible thread through the narrative, linking workers, horses, and even the laboring language. The dictionary definitions of "hackney" and "hackneyed" include: "a horse for ordinary driving," "a carriage for hire," "a prostitute, a person hired for dull, monotonous work," and, of course, "trite, overworked language," all prominent aspects of "Eumaeus." At the end of the chapter, Bloom thinks of Stephen's music as "a decided novelty for Dublin's musical world after the usual hackneyed run of catchy tenor solos" (*U* 16.1849–51). The phrase "hackneyed run" might remind us of the vehicles for hire mentioned in the chapter. In Bloom's thoughts, the "hackneyed run" applies to "tenor solos"; thus, we have not only vehicles, but "tenors" that are hired for dull, everyday work—Irish tenors, vehicles drawn by horses, perhaps the tenors and vehicles of metaphoric *conveyance*. (Bloom realizes elsewhere that it is "highly advisable to get a conveyance of some description" [*U* 16.15–16], an expression that links the movement of people and the movement of meaning.) Workers and language are impoverished by the system, an effect suggested in the phrase "beggaring description" (*U* 16.591) (which refers directly to the "inscrutable" face of the keeper of the shelter). Cabbies, horses, musical solos and language are all at someone's service for dull, monotonous work and have lost their freshness because of it. As Fogel points out about the beast of burden motif in Conrad, it includes not only the idea of the *beast of burden*, but of *la bêtise*—an almost overwhelming stupidity in the quotidian. In "Eumaeus," too, the poor beast of burden is also a poor *dumb* beast, a "big nervous foolish noodly kind of horse" (*U* 16.1789), as Bloom thinks of him in a moment of sympathy.

The habit of verbal suggestion, the linking of seemingly unrelated meanings through playful puns, establishes a kind of political unconscious. Contradictory inter-class identifications are suggested through this language play, most evident in the figural consciousness of "Mr Bloom." Tactfully charting his way between poet and cabby, Mr Bloom takes a middle course that displays a sometime solidarity with the working class, which would argue for the urgency of social change, and a counter-desire to maintain the status quo. Although Bloom solidly, sometimes even eloquently opposes violence in the service of change, still the language of "Eumaeus" betrays contradictory impulses within the petit-bourgeois breast towards social change through violence. In the following example, the language of the narrative oddly undermines Bloom's ostensible political opinions:

[H]e disliked those careers of wrongdoing and crime on principle. Yet, though such criminal propensities had never been an inmate of his bosom in any shape or form, he certainly did feel and no denying (while inwardly remaining what he was) a certain kind of admiration for a man who had actually brandished a knife, cold steel, with the courage of his political convictions (though, personally, he would never be a party to any such thing). (*U* 16.1054–60)

Manganiello cites this passage to show that "Joyce indicates that however just a political cause might be, violence can never provide a solution" (*Joyce's Politics* 5), but it seems to me both the syntax and imagery entail more contradiction than this summary suggests. Not only in the accumulation of qualifications and reversals in the numerous clauses, but also in the contamination of classes suggested in the imagery, the boundaries between Bloom and the perpetrators are blurred and social incrimination occurs. The parenthetical phrase ("while inwardly remaining what he was") seeks to reassure us of the integrity of Bloom's identity, made more emphatic by the presence of the parentheses graphically separating Bloom's "inward" being from the rest of the "subjects" in the sentence. But the boundaries seem to dissolve in the language—crime is made more bourgeois (in the "career" of wrong-doing) and the middle class is invaded by the "criminal" element (propensities become "inmates" of the bourgeois bosom). Despite Bloom's too-emphatic denial (an example of denegation), it is as if the language were refusing to maintain the boundaries to which Bloom's conscious mind clings.[18] At another point, Bloom thinks nostalgically about his more radical youth, when he took a position on "the evicted tenants question" more radical than Michael Davitt's: "he at the outset in principle at all events was in thorough sympathy with peasant possession as voicing the trend of modern opinion (a partiality, however, which, realising his mistake, he was subsequently partially cured of)" (*U* 16.1588–91). Which party does he subscribe to? Which part does Bloom play, since his "partiality" was only "partially" cured?

Thus, in this chapter of navigation, the issue of political movements and parties is present, an issue that involves the question of communal interests and identifications that might lead to change. Throughout *Ulysses*, we see a process of imaginative identifications with different others. Bloom, particularly, figures prominently in this context, for empathy is one of his most salient qualities. The chapter shows us Bloom's identification with the downtrodden, even with the "good poor brute" of a horse in whom he senses "a different grouping of bones and even flesh" (*U* 16.1783). As he passes the cabman's shelter earlier in the novel, Bloom remarks, "Curious the life of drifting cabbies. All weathers, all places, time or setdown, no will of their own. *Voglio e non.* Like to give them an odd cigarette. Sociable. Shout a few flying syllables as they pass" (*U* 5.223–26). Bloom wants to hail them, that is, to salute them in a gesture of solidarity. At the beginning of "Eumaeus," there are no "flying syllables," as Bloom tries, unsuccessfully, to hail a cab:

> But as he [Mr Bloom] confidently anticipated there was not a sign of a Jehu plying for hire anywhere to be seen except a fourwheeler, probably engaged by some fellows inside on the spree . . . and there was no symptom of its budging a quarter of an inch when Mr Bloom, who was anything but a professional whistler, endeavoured to hail it by emitting a kind of a whistle, holding his arms arched over his head, twice. (*U* 16.24–30)

Originally a nautical term, as the *OED* tells us, "hailing" means to salute from a great distance, as on a ship. Neither a "professional whistler" nor a navigator, Bloom will find himself both drawn to, and yet different from, the itinerant cabbies and sailors who frequent the cabman's shelter.

In *Ulysses* Joyce comically dramatizes what Althusser later described as the relation between such mundane gestures of "hailing" and the "hailing" or interpellating of subjects in society.[19] Althusser is concerned with the way individuals are "called" into a position in society, as if society addressed them personally to be productive contributors to its enterprise. Indeed, the idea of a "calling" is exploited by Joyce throughout his works, literally, in the "voices from beyond the world" that Dedalus thinks he hears invoking him as an artist. But throughout *Ulysses*, more comic and physical gestures of hailing and calling not only play with the idea of vocation but also demonstrate how these gestures of recognition (and, in some cases misrecognition) *construct* one's place in society, interpellating one into the existing power structure and dominant discourses. This process is most apparent in "Wandering Rocks," where the viceroy is "most cordially greeted on his way through the metropolis"(*U* 10.1182–83) and is "saluted" by "obsequious policemen" and others. In "Wandering Rocks," even Almidano Artifoni's "sturdy trousers" salute the viceroy (*U* 10.1282).

In "Eumaeus," where the issue of male identification and kinship is central, and the denizens of the cabman's shelter crowd around W. B. Murphy for some fellowship, this concept is recapitulated—in the salute Stephen gets from Corley, who needs money, and in Bloom's hailing the cab. The chapter offers a complex example for Althusser's notion of interpellation, because it reveals the contradictory identifications that coexist; here we see both what binds Bloom and the "drifting" cabbies, and what divides them. What Althusser's theory omits—the way gender can cut across class divisions—is also relevant to the chapter, coming as it does on the heels of the very threatening psychosexual material of the "nighttown" episode. Both "Circe" and "Eumaeus" are concerned with the *cultural* imagination and the bourgeois imaginary, but in the latter there is a sense of refuge in the banality of an "everyday" that is gendered male.

The sense of comfort and consolidation after the threats to identity in "Circe" seems to depend upon the absence of women. One lone prostitute circulates in the chapter, a reminder of nighttown, perhaps, as well as of the "Sirens" chapter, where Bloom first sees this particular streetwalker (*U* 11.1252). In "Eumaeus" the security of the petit-bourgeois adman, as well as the alienated artist, depends upon the regulation of the female, whose "siren song" represents potential snares for male subjects. Control of women's sexuality becomes a topic of discussion; when the prostitute appears to an "outwardly calm" but "flusterfied" Bloom, he spouts his ideas on the medical inspection and licensing of prostitutes (*U* 16.741–47). The "black straw hat" of the prostitute (*U* 11.1252), as Fritz Senn has pointed out, is the "black straw sailor hat" that was noticed during the afternoon, linking the streetwalker with the traveling sailor.[20] There is, thus, a suggestion of possible contagion, of this circulating sexuality threatening to spread; the threat is met with a kind of bourgeois regulation represented in the received wisdom of middle-class culture. Further, the control of female sexuality unites the men in the cabman's shelter, who circulate pictures and stories of women as part of kinship rituals. Women are "pictured" as commodities in a system of exchanges between men. The prostitute is only the crassest figure for women on the market, but others function similarly, like the savage women on the postcard that the sailor shows around to his rapt male audience, and, of course, even Molly, whose photograph, we are told twice, is "prudently pocket[ed]" by Bloom (*U* 16.1644, 1648) (and it is likely that the "prude" in "prudently" is meant to be heard, distinguishing "prudent" member from female "whore"). The chapter ends with a song of the sirens, extending the reference to Kitty O'Shea's "siren charms" (*U* 13.1382–83). Even the disaffected Stephen, who empathizes with the prostitute as victim, can be said to capitalize on her pain, using her as an emblem for the prostituted artist.[21] Concerned here, as elsewhere, with the symbolic aspects of "selling out," Stephen says, "In this country people sell much more than she ever had and do a roaring trade. Fear not them that sell the body but have not power to buy the soul. She is a bad merchant. She buys dear and sells cheap" (*U* 16.736–39).

The solidarity of the men, facilitated by the exchange of women and the swapping of stories, is, however, somewhat fragile, and divisions, as well as affiliations, between classes surface. The language of the chapter abounds in gestures of prudence, punctiliousness, and regulation, as if to maintain a boundary between vulgarity and bourgeois gentility. Despite his position as a Jewish outsider through much of *Ulysses*, here Bloom participates in, and draws comfort from, a bourgeois ideology that operates to consolidate his own position. The discourses of bourgeois rationality and regulation are woven throughout the chapter, comically and insistently constructed in the clichés and metaphors of the narrative. "Eumaeus" begins with Bloom's disappointed search for transportation: "bringing common sense to bear" on his dilemma, he realizes that he and Stephen must walk to the cabman's shelter (*U* 16.31). That the simple decision to walk is belabored reflects Bloom's self-congratulatory sense of his own prudent rationality. It also implicitly inaugurates the idea of the "pedestrian." Bloom likes to see himself as someone with feet firmly planted on terra firma, the force of his common sense "bearing" him down. (I will refer later to various puns in the chapter that play with the idea of the pedestrian.) Like "hackney," "pedestrian" suggests both language and physical movement, but if the meanings of "hackney" remind us of labor and drudgery, and thus of a solidarity in oppression, the meanings of "pedestrian" are more suggestive of class divisions. Bloom desires to separate clearly the "pedestrian" from the drifter, or as he thinks of it, the "peaceable pedestrians" from the "famished loiterers" (*U* 16.121–23) and "desperadoes" (*U* 16.120). The pedestrian who circulates through Dublin has direction and purpose, even social mobility, as opposed to the itinerants who wander aimlessly or loiter. It is as if bourgeois rationality were plotted geographically—Bloom never goes beyond "a certain point where he invariably drew the line" (*U* 16.92–93). Fritz Senn has observed that the word "point" is found twenty-three times in the chapter, with puns on both its abstract and material properties (Senn 5). (Bloom is described as a "levelheaded individual who could give points to not a few in point of shrewd observation" [*U* 16.219–20].) The prevalence of "points" is linked to the prudent graphing of the social map of Dublin—"points" become lines that fix boundaries, geographic, social, moral; "points" are pieces of common sense; "points" are punctuation marks in pedestrian prose; the sum total of all the "points" in the chapter is some notion of bourgeois rational economy.[22]

This "economy" is capitalistic—the ideology of bourgeois productivity, as well as rationality, underwrites the chapter. The language of "Eumaeus" is saturated with expressions of economic value, revealing how capitalist economies permeate the social relations of individuals. This ideology of productivity finds expression in double entendres: Bloom's "interest" (*U* 16.1216) in what individuals amount to, his concern with the "net result" (*U* 16.506) of social planning, his hope to "profit by the unlooked for occasion" (*U* 16.1217). We see him as a kind of broker in the market, someone who "credit[s]" assertions in conversation and "guarantee[s] them as well" (*U* 16.246). The notion of consciousness itself is constructed in relation to this ideology of productivity; metaphors of private property and productive labor structure the very concepts of consciousness and individuality; Bloom is described as luckily in "complete *possession* of his faculties" (*U* 16.62) and as "*minding* his own *business*" (*U* 16.117, my italics). The language reveals the "value" of rationality: as Bloom is constantly "putting two and two together" (*U* 16.1196). And when Bloom is "at a *loss* to fathom" Mulligan's cruelty to Stephen (*U* 16.295–96), we see the debit column in the economy of rationality. Even the turds of the horse are inscribed in this language of productivity—"the horse . . . added his *quota* by letting fall on the floor which the brush would soon brush up and polish, three smoking globes of turds" (*U* 16.1874–77, my italics). Quotas, rations and portions are found throughout the chapter, revealing the subtext of private property in the received ideas of the culture

Bloom's relation to Stephen is placed under the sign of this productive economy. Bloom sees Stephen as an investment in the future.[23] Scheming how Stephen can "utilise" his brains for "pecuniary emolument" (*U* 16.1840), Bloom calculates the benefits of nurturing Stephen's "voice production" (*U* 16.1822). The narrative comically transforms Stephen's agony over his artistic "voice" and vocation into Bloom's marketing scheme, his "gift" commodified so as to be exchanged on the market. Bloom suspects Stephen has "his father's voice to bank his hopes on" (*U* 16.1659). As he physically maneuvers Stephen around the city streets, Bloom, with all the tact of which he is capable, attempts to steer Stephen into productive work and productive conversation. He tries to prevent Stephen from a further slide into genteel poverty and to channel him into a solid middle-class existence.

Thus, class consciousness riddles the narrative and complicates the impression of it as the locus of the "common." Stephen and Bloom amidst "*hoi polloi*" of "jarvies or stevedores or whatever they were" (*U* 16.335–36) are represented in the narrative like Stanley and Livingston among the natives: "A few moments later saw our two noctambules safely seated in a discreet corner only to be greeted by stares from the decidedly miscellaneous collection of waifs and strays and other nondescript specimens of the genus *homo* already there engaged in eating and drinking . . ." (*U* 16.325–29). It is as if this human collection were indescribable because it is so foreign and so low. Even the naming of common objects in the narrative partakes of this kind of class consciousness—the biscuit is substandard and, hence, only a "socalled roll"; the coffee, not a respectable cup, is a "boiling, swimming cup of a choice concoction labeled coffee" (*U* 16.354–55). This judgment, this air of superiority, is a quality of the narrative, as if its language sought to transcend "common parlance": "Another little interesting point, the amours of whores and chummies, to put it in *common parlance*, reminded him Irish soldiers had as often fought for England as against her" (*U* 16,1040–42, my italics). To use the phrase "common parlance" is to separate oneself from the language, to quote it rather than to use it. Although Bloom's thoughts are described, "to put it in common parlance" is an idiom of the narrative. With its borrowed foreign and literary phrases and elegant variation, the narrative conveys a sense of striving for upward mobility, as if attempting to make "literature" out of common currency. Bloom's "bowing acquaintance" (*U* 16.340–41) with Italian provides a figure for the pretensions of the style, which evoke the gestures of a *bourgeois gentilhomme*. There is a further Irish twist here on the pretentiousness, however, for it suggests identification with specifically English bourgeois discourse and social categories, as exemplified in the phrase "the Thames embankment category" (*U* 16.123), which describes the indigent of Dublin with a stock phrase for the London poor. Indeed, the presence of comically *unidiomatic* phrases and slightly mistaken colloquialisms gives the sense that English phrases do not quite fit Irish narrative. (William Carlos Williams once wrote that "Joyce, Catholic Irishman, began with English, a full-dressed English which it must have been his delight to unenglish."[24]) Fine writing seems to be a struggle.

Thus, "cracks" and contradictions reveal themselves in the discourse of productivity and rationality. In *The Politics of Transgression*, Stallybrass and White show how the classical bourgeois body constructed its group identity by excluding the lower classes and separating itself as well from dirt and waste.[25] But in the Ireland of *Ulysses*, there exists no "self-confident national bourgeoisie with control over substantial wealth" (T. Brown 17), and the petite bourgeoisie feel the threat of a downward slide into the category of the "lumpen." In this Ireland, the attempt to separate oneself from dirt and waste has a certain desperation. "The system really needed toning up," Bloom thinks, regretfully, about Dublin's transportation system, and, in a chapter of puns, the word "system" suggests larger reference (*U* 16.341). Sanitation work goes on in the chapter—the street sweeper, the hypothetical worker who sweeps under the chairs in cafes that Stephen muses over, the "cleansing committee" which has "erected" male urinals "all over the place" (*U* 16.935), these are only some of the signs of the work of sanitation. To paraphrase Yeats, the language of the narrative, too, labors to be beautiful. But despite these attempts at beautification, sanitation, and productivity, we see much that is wasteful and non-productive in the chapter. Despite the narrative investment in the consolidation of bourgeois identity and its productive role in society, waste in the chapter suggests *both* the failure of this economy and a possible resistance to it. Gumley serves an emblematic function, here, as one who disturbs the calculus of productivity. The Dublin Corporation watchman, "evidently a glutton for work," Bloom surmises, "was having a quiet forty winks for all intents and purposes on his own private account while Dublin slept" (*U* 16.213–15). On the ledger of capitalism, Gumley's forty winks are put in the wrong column, in Gumley's "private account" rather than that of the Dublin corporation.

By a comic process of literalization in the language, bourgeois abstractions for the working classes are demystified and the "bottom" of the social body materializes:

Intellectual stimulation, as such, was, he felt, from time to time a first rate tonic for the mind. Added to which was the coincidence of meeting, discussion, dance, row, old salt of the here today and gone tomorrow type, night loafers, the whole galaxy of events, all went to make up a miniature cameo of the world we live in especially as the lives of the submerged tenth, viz. coalminers, divers, scavengers etc., were very much under the microscope lately. (*U* 16.1221–27)

Franco Moretti sees this passage as exemplifying the "petty-bourgeois philistine" voice, as represented by Bloom, who seems "unaware of the very reality of the workers, whose existence he must 'deduce' with an uproarious literal interpretation of the metaphor of the 'submerged tenth': 'coalminers, divers, scavengers'!" (Moretti 188–89). However, the comic literalization has a further effect. For, in Bloom's comic picturing of the lives of the "submerged," abstractions are demystified. We are made to see some of the absurdities of terms like "the underclass" and "the lower orders" (*U* 16.796), with all their subterranean and subhuman implications. If sociological abstractions like "submerged tenth" are meant to *sanitize* material conditions, the language play comically rematerializes the concept. (We might be reminded of the fact that "bathos" literally means depth.)

Throughout the chapter, one can say that the "bottom" of the social body returns in a number of guises, despite attempts at upward mobility and the sanitation of waste. This "bottom," of course, is felt most explicitly in the "three smoking globes of turds" of the horse (*U* 16.1876–77). If the horse is ubiquitous, the horse's ass receives special attention (and, again, we might return to *L'Asino*, the satirical paper Joyce read in Rome).[26] The bottom returns, that is, not only with the scavengers of the submerged tenth, but with references to anality, some of them punning. The salty "Lot's wife's arse" (*U* 16.980) in the song of the sailor is only one of a number of references to the bottom—like the reference to "buggers" (*U* 16.672), and to "Butt bridge" (*U* 16.9), to the knife in the "butt" (*U* 16.582) and the "end of the tether" (and, in view of the horse's deposits, a potential double entendre in Bloom's thought that Stephen will have "*heaps* of time to practise literature" [*U* 16.1860, my italics]).[27] According to Stallybrass and White, the repudiation of carnival "became a fundamental aspect of bourgeois cultural identity," and the state was "divided into the purified, legitimate body of people and the underworld of loafers, drunks, prostitutes." In "Eumaeus" the bottom returns.[28]

But this representation of waste, of all that is non-productive according to the system of bourgeois and capitalist value, is linked to a different kind of production—a production based on the notion of excess, superfluity, and accident. If one to way to look at the material inefficiency, verbal and otherwise, in the chapter is to speak of the failures of the system, one can also speak of the way that the extraneous and repetitious can suggest a possible crack or resistance in the bourgeois ideology of economy and value caused by something, like a parasite, both within the system and disruptive of it. If Bloom is focused on what is referred to as a kind of "capital opening" (*U* 16.1853) that is based on a model of good investments in the future, there is another potential hole or opening in the bourgeois system that suggests a different potential. One could say it is based on a pun on the notion of "filthy lucre" (*U* 16.1842), another clichéd phrase in the chapter, which suggests a kind of productive, messy "luck" or coincidence amidst the prostituted labor in the service of the economy. For waste of all kinds in the chapter suggests a kind of "expenditure," to use Bataille's word, which cannot be captured in the economy of utility and production. This thematic of waste pertains to language and meaning in the chapter, and conditions, I believe, a kind of receptivity of reading that may stretch the normal codes for making interpretive sense. If repetition and cliché in the language of the narrative mime the compulsive and determinate aspects of meaning, they can also suggest surprises and "striking coincidences" that function to show there are meanings in unexpected places. Despite the fact that there are all sorts of errors, mistakes, and, on the linguistic level, semantically vacuous connections, the chapter does produce unlikely doublings that create significances and breed a sense of motivation and an almost Bloomian faith in the meaning of randomness. What is viewed as waste—as non-productive repetition—from one point of view becomes an excess that produces meaning. Motivation re-enters not through some iconic idea of the signifier that suggests a *true* connection between the word and the thing, but through a more playful concept of representation that combines a sense of the aleatory and the necessary. It is as if coincidence, once discovered, seemed motivated all along, but motivated not by the past but by the not-yet, not by established meaning but by meaning that is in the process of coming into being.

This view of language (and the mode of reading it invites) suggests a similarity to Wittgenstein's idea of ordinary language. "There are here hugely many interrelated phenomena and possible concepts," he writes in the *Investigations*, "possibilities to which we are normally blind."[29] Wittgenstein's analysis of language, like Joyce's chapter, requires us to notice these possibilities. As Henry Staten paraphrases this analysis, "The investigation of meaning continually veers as aspect of a phenomenon suggest analogies and then the analogies suggest further aspects of their own, which also call for investigation."³⁰ In Joyce's "pedestrian" chapter, we veer from familiar paths of language and plot; we encounter surprising turns or tropes, and chance, yet meaningful, meetings. "You ought to eat more solid food," Bloom advises Stephen, "You would feel a different man" (*U* 16.814). Later Bloom again advises, "The only thing is to walk then you'll feel a different man" (*U* 16.1719). He passes his arm through Stephen's, "Yes, Stephen said uncertainly because he thought he felt a strange kind of flesh of a different man approach him, sinewless and wobbly and all that" (*U* 16.1723–24). Bloom's prudent advice, by virtue of the double meaning of the word "feel," becomes prophecy—Stephen does *feel* a different man, and that man is Bloom. Feeling here is physical and emotional; after tactfully maneuvering Stephen through street and conversation, Bloom moves and touches him.

This idea of meaning precipitates a different mode of reading. The element of chance and the "messy" expenditures in the chapter suggest a breakdown of the boundary between accident and purpose. "To groan at puns," Jonathan Culler says in an introduction to a collection of essays on puns, "is viscerally to reaffirm a distinction between essence and accident, between meaningful relations and coincidence, that has seemed fundamental to our thinking."³¹ But the wordplays of "Eumaeus" (including deliberately bad puns and puncepts) ultimately refuse us the security Culler describes. In a fine essay on Derrida's refashioning of the pun into the "philosopheme of a new cognition," Gregory Ulmer speaks of Derrida's debt to Joyce's language and describes Derrida's work in the following way:

> Against the emphasis on utterance as a performative *enunciation*, Derrida imagines comprehension in terms of the annunciation as it is couched in the apocalyptic mode, in the Biblical tradition of apocalyptic prophecy and forecasts. To perform writing in terms of annunciation, for a mind listening with a psychoanalytic or dialogical ear, requires a shift away from signifieds to tone . . . [w]hat is written, uttered as annunciation, comes to the receiver as a gift/ Gift. . . . (165–67)

By this concept, Ulmer argues, Derrida wants to ensure the sense that "the future of the text is never closed. . . . The pun is the philosopheme of this ear tuned to the other" (167–68). This kind of future-orientation works on the level of plot and language in "Eumaeus"—a certain "receptivity" develops out of the banality of the situation, a kind of "gift" that does not compute within the political economy of profits and investments. Derrida's metaphors are apposite here because they retain a kind of religious discourse in order to signify that which deconstructs the opposition between accident and purpose without signifying anything like religious faith.[32]

Thus, Joyce's economy of surprises arises from within, rather than transcends the banality of the "everyday." In the chapter's final tableau, a rear view of Stephen and Bloom silently watched by the driver of the sweeper car, we can see how the pedestrian pathways of ordinary language produce local connections, resolving the dilemmas of class represented in the chapter. "Side by side" and "*tête-à-tête*," Bloom and Stephen *walk out* of the chapter together in a kind of apotheosis of the pedestrian. Bloom has considered all the possible "walk[s] in life" that Stephen might take (*U* 16.1843), as well as "step[s] in the required direction" (*U* 16.1844–45), he has also considered upward mobility in terms of the way someone might force his way to the top "by the aid of [his] bootstraps" (*U* 16.1214). Finally, he "foot[s] the bill for the occasion" (*U* 16.1693). (Derrida has suggested that when Bloom and Stephen go "a step farther" [*U* 16.1633], we are meant to hear the echo of "stepfather," "a dream of legitimation through adoption."[33]) In the final tableau, their pedestrian connection is comically literalized even further, as the two step over obstacles—the horse's mire, the chain—*en route* to their destination (they passed "through the gap of the chains, divided by the upright, and, stepping over a strand of mire, went across towards Gardiner street lower, Stephen singing more boldly, but not loudly, the end of the ballad" [*U* 16.1881–83]). Far from transcending cliché, they themselves become one, a bourgeois couple, a "Bouvard et Pécuchet," to be married by Father Maher. (Perhaps the homoerotic implications of this "marriage" here suggest another kind of possibility, a connection that exists outside the classical economy of *reproduction*, which might provide another significance to the puns on anality in the chapter.) But Bloom and Stephen are produced as cliché *in the vision of the silent subaltern*, the driver who sees them as "two figures . . . both black, one full, one lean." Despite the comic patness of the tableau, we are left with the residue of the subaltern's alienated gaze. The music that might provide a "universal language" and charm the savage breast, of horse, of worker, of reader, is withheld from all but Bloom. In this pedestrian chapter, no one gets carried away.

Thus, although he dissects the ideology of the quotidian, Joyce posits no escape from banality, no false consciousness to be transcended. There is no pure platform, either Marxist or modernist, on which the artist can stand, from which to survey the wreckage of bourgeois society. At one point in the chapter Bloom thinks about an "all star Irish caste" of the "Tweedy-Flower grand open company" that Molly might be a part of (U 16.524–25), and there is a pun on the word "cast," spelled "c-a-s-t-e." In "Eumaeus" we see that the "nightmare of history" cannot be escaped; the ludic drama of language play is inseparable from social and political valences.

8

Legal Fiction or Pulp Fiction in "Lestrygonians"

"Real men eat beef": something like this flesh-eating virility is suggested in the first sentences in which we are introduced to Leopold Bloom: "Mr Leopold Bloom ate with relish the inner organs of beasts and fowls. He liked thick giblet soup, nutty gizzards, a stuffed roast heart, liverslices fried with crustcrumbs, fried hencods' roes" (*U* 4.01–3). We meet "Mr Leopold Bloom" at home in his kitchen. If the first sentence begins with a distanced and polite form of address to Bloom, it quickly plunges deep into his interior, where we see him, in turn, receiving the "inner organs" of animals.

Or do we? For one of the many miscues we encounter in *Ulysses* (like the conclusion of the "Lotus-Eaters" chapter, which we might erroneously read as a scene in which Bloom regards his own body in the bath) is this supposed scene of eating, which turns out instead to be a description of Bloom's habitual likes and dislikes, his "taste" ("most of all he liked . . ." [*U* 4.03]). We discover that this chunky, almost onomatopoetic description, is indeed a description of Bloom's *thoughts*: "Kidneys were in his mind as he moved about the kitchen softly" (*U* 4.06). This "real" man *imagines* himself eating flesh in his "real" kitchen—kidneys are *in* his mind as he putters around. This initial description gives substance to Bloom's interiority. It mimes for us the fullness of his inner life, a fullness and richness which the novel will increase in its pages. Although he subsequently *does* leave home to purchase a pork kidney at Dlugacz's, and is seen "chewing with discernment the toothsome pliant meat" (*U* 4.391), the initial culinary description pertains to his thoughts only.

The simulated dive inward—from third-person narration reminiscent of, say, "Emma Woodhouse, handsome, clever, and rich," to what feels like the *inside* of Bloom's gullet as he devours the inner organs of other creatures—extends the modernist project of the inward turn of narrative, extends it comically and corporeally, as if "fleshing out" the character from the inside out, an incarnation or embodiment of consciousness upon which fiction relies. Our surprise at finding ourselves in Bloom's *thoughts* reminds us that this graphic corporeality is, indeed, graphic—a representation in writing. The word made flesh is the flesh made word. Grammatically, the iterative narrative ("He ate with relish") emphasizes the fact that writing is made possible only through iterability, through the repeatability of the sign. Bloom first appears to us not in a particular scene of eating (an event) but under the sign of repeated and almost ritual feasting.

This first representation of Bloom in "Calypso" distinguishes his subjectivity from that of Stephen Dedalus, whose interaction with the world is ocularcentric ("thought through my eyes" [*U* 3.01–2]). Stephen takes in the world through what Kant calls the "objective" or mechanical sense of sight (not to be confused with "objectivity," but rather, signaling a distancing, a removal from the thing perceived).[1] His modality is the "ineluctable modality of the visible" (*U* 3.01). In contrast, despite the voyeurism in "Nausicaa," Bloom's prime modalities seem to be taste and smell, in Kantian terms the more "subjective" or chemical senses. With taste, unlike sight, the external object is transformed as well as taken in, through a process of liquefaction. "Lestrygonians" is the chapter in which Bloom is most clearly represented as taking in the world through his mouth and nose. The many puns and plays on food in the chapter construct a basic analogy between the processes of incorporating and digesting food in the stomach and the formation of the "self" through internalizing the environment. This analogy is structured as a kind of law of the chapter—"You are [or become] what you eat"—a law to which Bloom himself seems to subscribe. He looks at two Dublin theosophists and contrasts them with the beefy Irish policemen: "Dreamy, cloudy, symbolistic. Esthetes they are. I wouldn't be surprised if it was that kind of food you see produces the like waves of the brain the poetical. For example one of those policemen sweating Irish stew into their shirts you couldn't squeeze a line of poetry out of him" (*U* 8.543–47). Intake determines output. In "Lestrygonians," the chapter that derives its Homeric title from the cannibalistic tribe Odysseus and his men narrowly escape, Bloom recognizes the risks, even more than the pleasures, of incorporation. "Risky putting anything into your mouth" (*U* 8.859), he thinks, and, at the nadir of his experience in the Burton restaurant, his gorge rises in disgust at the sight of the beefy Irishmen who shovel food into their mouths like animals.

Orality in *Ulysses* culminates in "Lestrygonians," but it resonates throughout the novel, particularly in relation to the psychoanalytic concept of identification (a further twist on the idea that you are what you eat). For the figuring of mental processes as the bodily processes of ingestion or assimilation is crucial to the psychoanalytic discourse on the construction of the subject. The subject incorporates or ingests the "other" and is transformed, wholly or partially, after the model the other provides. The general name for this process is identification. "In Freud's works," Laplanche says, "the concept of identification comes little by little to have the central importance which makes it, not simply one psychical mechanism among others, but the operation itself whereby the human subject is constituted."[2] Originally, Freud seems to have thought of identification in terms of the oral or cannibalistic phase of libidinal development, and in *Totem and Taboo* (1912–1913), he relates it to the relationship between the father and sons in the primal horde, according to which the sons devour the body of the father in an act of possession and identification.[3] Derrida's term for the speculative idealism according to which the law of the father is interiorized through a process of ingestion is "*carno-phallogocentrism*." He speaks of an "idealizing interiorization of the phallus and the necessity of its passage through the mouth, whether it's a matter of words or of things, of sentences, of daily bread or wine, of the tongue, the lips, or the breast of the other."[4] In Joycean terms, this carno-phallogocentrism establishes paternity as *the* legal fiction. It is central as well to the rite of the Eucharist, the offering of Christ's body in the form of the wafer and his blood in the form of the wine. "Take, this is my body," Christ says in the Gospel of St. John; the Christian is he who eats and identifies with the ideal father.

In an immensely suggestive plenary speech at the Frankfurt Symposium in 1984, published subsequently in *James Joyce: The Augmented Ninth*, Julia Kristeva takes on Joyce's special relationship to the central symbol of the Eucharist and its implications for his fictional exploration of the process of identification. She writes:

> In his intense experience of Trinitarian religion, resulting in his subsequent derision of it, Joyce was confronted by its central ritual, the Eucharist, exemplary rite of identification with God's body, pivot of

all the other identifications, including the artistic and imaginary profusion favored by Catholicism. It is probable that this Catholic cultural context, profoundly assimilated by Joyce, met with a mechanism that was, in other respects, the motor of his fictional experience and which allowed him to concentrate his efforts of representation and elucidation upon the identificatory substratum of psychic function, so masterfully placed at the center of the ultimate of religions.[5]

From the first scene of the novel, in which the "wellfed voice" (*U* 1.107) of a "plump Buck Mulligan" (*U* 1.01) taunts Stephen Dedalus with the mock chalice containing the "body and soul and blood and ouns" of the "genuine christine" (*U* 1.21–22), both the general concept of hunger/nourishment and the specific oral ritual of the Catholic Mass, the Eucharist, are introduced as barometers of the way the characters partake of the world around them. "Personally I couldn't stomach that idea of a personal God" (*U* 1.623), Haines, the Englishman, says to Stephen. Haines's Protestant fastidiousness toward the rite of the Eucharist, his visceral disgust at the thought of Irish Catholics "stomaching" the body of Christ, demonstrates his refusal to risk any but the most intellectualized participation in the Irish culture around him. (Buck earlier refers to these "bloody English! Bursting with money and *indigestion*" [*U* 1.52–53, emphasis added]). On the other hand, the mocker, Mulligan, taunts Stephen with the thought of Christ's body and blood because his irony and thoroughgoing materialism neutralize the mystery of transubstantiation so that he sees only a wafer and a glass of wine, not the body and blood of Christ. In "Lestrygonians" Bloom thinks "that last pagan king of Ireland Cormac in the schoolpoem choked himself at Sletty southward of the Boyne. Wonder what he was eating. Something galoptious, Saint Patrick converted him to Christianity. Couldn't swallow it all however" (*U* 8.663–67). Bloom's "Jewish" view is one of empathy toward the pagan king force-fed the body of Christianity; transubstantiation fails in Bloom's rendition of conversion because the pagan king, unlike the Platonizing Christians, who idealize the process, cannot "swallow" Christ's body. It is immediately after this thought that the beefy smells of men make his gorge rise, suggesting a link in Bloom's mind between the cannibalism he associates with the Eucharist and the manly eating he witnesses in the Burton. Earlier, as Bloom watches the ritual of communion in All Hallows Church, he thinks, "*Corpus*: body. Corpse. Good idea the Latin. Stupefies them first. Hospice for the dying. They don't seem to chew it: only swallow it down. Rum idea: eating bits of a corpse. Why the cannibals cotton to it" (*U* 5.350–52). It is useful to remember that Catholic children are warned *not* to chew the host but to swallow it whole, a practice which avoids the implication of cannibalism and emphasizes Christ's spiritual incorporation in the communicant. Throughout *Ulysses* images of and attitudes toward the Eucharist put in high relief the question of identification; that is, of what one can assimilate or swallow and make part of one's being. Bloom, the twice-baptized Jew, is alternately fascinated and repelled by the ritual of the Eucharist. Bloom rejects both the triumph of idealization—the swallowing without chewing—and its materialist "manly" opposite, the chewing of dead meat.[6]

I want to trace the displacements and realizations of the topos of orality in the "Lestrygonians" chapter, where Bloom's food for thought is most dramatically represented. Here Bloom refuses a particular kind of virile communion and remembers, and mourns, a different kind of assimilation, a more vegetarian one, his reception of the half-chewed seedcake from Molly's mouth on Howth Hill. This erotic identification tells a "pulp fiction," different from the eat-and-be-eaten story in the Burton (all body and no spirit), different as well from the idealizing narrative of sacred communion through the host (all spirit and no body). The body of food Molly feeds Bloom is neither masticated brutally nor swallowed whole like medicine. This cherished memory of communion, savored in consciousness like Molly's photo in Bloom's pocket, is his weapon (a moly?) against the feeding frenzy that disgusts him in the Burton restaurant.[7]

In "Lestrygonians," it is lunchtime in Dublin. The Linati schema indicates that the technique of the chapter is peristalsis, the organ, the esophagus.[8] Lured by the smell of various foods, Bloom stops before several eating houses, debating about what he does or does not crave. He is hungry for lunch, and this hunger is intoned as general all over Ireland: he thinks of "the harp that once did starve us all" (*U* 8.606–7). Like the "famished ghosts" in the *Odyssey* who can come to life (and speech) only by drinking "hot fresh blood" (*U* 8.729–30), the Dubliners, including (non-kosher) Bloom, crave something to fill them up. "A barefoot arab stood over the grating," sniffing fumes from the nearby restaurant. "Deaden the gnaw of hunger that way. Pleasure or pain is it?" (*U* 8.235–37), Bloom thinks, speculating on strategies for dealing with unsatisfied desire. These are the musings of Bloom, the husband who has not had full intercourse with his wife for ten years and is about to be cuckolded, as he deliberately stays close enough to home and far enough away to experience the pain/pleasure of Molly's adultery.

What distinguishes the representation of orality in "Lestrygonians" from its appearance at Bloom's introduction in "Calypso" is Bloom's sense of victimization and loss of control. In "Calypso" eating is part of a domestic routine over which Bloom presides: he thinks about eating, feeds the cat and then Molly, and breakfasts on a tasty, slightly charred pork kidney—all are comforting components of a ritual ordering of domestic life. His morning collation, replete with "burnt offering" (*U* 17.2044), is a comic, domestic sacrifice. In "Lestrygonians" Bloom fails to exert the same control over how and what to eat and increasingly his senses are assaulted by the sights and smells of flesh that surround him. Early in the episode he remembers the unpleasant sensation of going down to the pantry to get Molly something at nighttime and suddenly encountering the odor of leftover codfish: "Don't like all the smells in it waiting to rush out" (*U* 8.23). He associates the phosphorus of the decomposing fish with the body of Christ on a luminous crucifix ("Our Saviour. Wake up in the dead of night and see him on the wall, hanging. Pepper's ghost idea. Iron Nails Ran In" [*U* 8.19–20]). In his kitchen he can more or less control the unpleasant smells; in "Lestrygonians," however, his thoughts about food keep triggering a recognition of his own mortality, as corpus and corpse continually collapse. If in "Hades" he takes comfort in the idea of the ecological efficiency of the food chain ("It's the blood sinking in the earth gives new life. . . . Well preserved fat corpse, gentleman, epicure, invaluable for fruit garden" [*U* 6.771–73]),[9] in "Lestrygonians" the vision becomes more personal—with horror he sees his own sacrificial place in the food chain. Bloom himself becomes the abjected, expelled body of food: "this is the very worst hour of the day. Vitality. Dull, gloomy: hate this hour. Feel as if I had been eaten and spewed" (*U* 8.494–95).[10] As he views the "men, men, men" chomping food in the Burton (*U* 8.653), Bloom is nauseated by his sense of their murderous cannibalism:

> Smells of men. Spaton sawdust, sweetish warmish cigarettesmoke, reek of plug, spilt beer, men's beery piss, the stale of ferment.
> His gorge rose.
> Couldn't eat a morsel here. . . .
> Every fellow for his own, tooth and nail. Gulp. Grub. Gulp. Gobstuff.

He came out into clearer air and turned back towards Grafton street. Eat or be eaten. Kill! Kill! (*U* 8.670–73, 8.701–3)[11]

Why is his reaction so violent? Why does the lover of inner organs of beasts and fowls, the man who likes the urinous tang of kidney, have such a strongly emetic response? In a provocative revisionary reading of Bloom's supposed nonviolence, Emer Nolan points out that earlier Bloom had accepted the joining of life and death in the food chain as an affirming part of life's process: "In the midst of death we are in life. Both ends meet. Tantalising for the poor dead. Smell of grilled beefsteaks to the starving" (*U* 6.759–61). Nolan says of Bloom's virulent reaction in the Burton: "However, in the face of actually existing human community and warm human bodies, this robust common man proves unable to imagine, for example, communal eating outside an economy of greed and selfishness." She sees the kill-or-be-killed rhetoric of Bloom's interior monologue as evidence that "his own appetite . . . inspires this appalling vision of endless gluttony and savagery."[12]

Nolan is right to question the complacency of humanistic accounts of Bloom as the heroic common man who rejects the violence and masculinism of the Dubliners around him. She is accurate about Bloom's hesitancy to participate in a masculine community (although I think it is more appropriate to speak of his ambivalence than fear), and she offers a corrective to the view that his outsider status is solely due to the anti-Semitism that surrounds him (in her view, as in Fredric Jameson's reading of the father-son relationship in *Ulysses* in "*Ulysses* in History," the oedipal plot so often stressed is itself a symptom of a lack of full social participation[13]). Indeed, Bloom's repulsion is even more puzzling in light of his earlier attraction to the social community that he recognizes is forged through the celebration of the Eucharist: "There's a big idea behind it, kind of kingdom of God is within you feel. First communicants. Hokypoky penny a lump. Then feel all like one family party, same in the theatre, all in the same swim. They do. I'm sure of that. Not so lonely. In our confraternity" (*U* 5.360–64). Given the strength of Bloom's nausea, however, the register of Nolan's analysis seems off the mark. Bloom doesn't merely reject "community" here, like a petulant child, as Nolan seems to suggest; rather, like Cormac, the pagan king, he "can't stomach" the idea of flesh as mere corpse. Despite Bloom's comic demystifications of the *idealization* operating in the rite of the Eucharist, he has trouble facing the nonsublimated version of incorporation, the atavistic image of the body wholly devoid of spirit. The food chain, a once comforting image of death providing nourishment for new life, is now "frozen" in Bloom's horrific vision of male meeting and meat-eating. At all costs Bloom attempts to avoid the taste of death.

It is possible to relate Bloom's repulsion here to the traditions that cling to this fallen-away Jew. In her essay on abjection, Kristeva reminds us that for Jews, the corpse is "a body without soul . . . it must not be displayed but immediately buried so as not to pollute the divine earth." In the Burton, Bloom confronts the unredeemed and unredeemable corpse, a vision exacerbated by his recent experience in the cemetery. As Kristeva puts it,

> The corpse (or cadaver: *cadere*, to fall), that which has irremediably come a cropper, is cesspool, and death; it upsets even more violently the one who confronts it as fragile and fallacious chance. A wound with blood and pus, or the sickly, acrid smell of sweat, of decay, does not *signify* death. In the presence of signified death—a flat encephalograph, for instance—I would understand, react, or accept. No, as in true theater, without makeup or masks, refuse and corpses *show me* what I permanently thrust aside in order to live. These body fluids, this defilement, this shit are what life withstands, hardly and with difficulty, on the part of death. There, I am at the border of my condition as a living being. My body extricates itself, as being alive, from that border. Such wastes drop so that I might live, until, from loss to loss, nothing remains in me and my entire body falls beyond the limit—*cadere*, cadaver. [Think of Bloom's pleasure in defecation.] If dung signifies the other side of the border, the place where I am not and which permits me to be, the corpse, the most sickening of wastes, is a border that has encroached upon everything. It is no longer I who expel, "I" is expelled. . . . The corpse, seen without God and outside science, is the utmost of abjection. It is death infecting life. Abject . . . it is thus not lack of cleanliness or health that causes abjection but what disturbs identity, system, order.[14]

The corpse—seen without God (or love/agape) and outside of science—this is the vision Bloom has in the Burton.

As James McMichael points out in *"Ulysses" and Justice*, thoughts of food and sex overlap in Bloom's mind in "Lestrygonians." In a very suggestive discussion of Bloom's hunger in the episode, he notes that Bloom puts off satisfaction of his hunger, rejecting the frenzied activity of "bolting to get it over" (*U* 8.661) that he sees: "As his continuing to say both 'yes' and 'no' to sex is, his thinking of food to say 'no' to it is Bloom's resistance to the time it takes for bad things to happen."[15] McMichael sees deferral—deferral of sleeping with Molly and deferral of the satisfaction of his hunger—as Bloom's strategy of delay, a way of resisting time (McMichael links this to his idea that it is Bloom rather than Molly who resists "full carnal intercourse," out of fear of conceiving another child like Rudy). "Because his thoughts about food and sex collapse into one another, Bloom thinks of the progeny that come from lovemaking not as persons the body engenders so that they might live but rather as what the body passes and disposes of as vile. The stillborn, for Bloom, are 'trouble for nothing' (*U* 8.389–90), waste, as Rudy is waste"(McMichael, 181). This remark is particularly suggestive in light of Kristeva's description of the corpse as "the most sickening of wastes."

This vision of Rudy as dead matter, like the vision of the host as dead meat, prevents the idealization of mourning. The "cannibalism" in the Burton is an image of corpse-eating without both the idealization of mourning and the space of deferral. Like Blazes "Boylan with impatience" (*U* 11.426), these men satisfy their urges immediately. Constantly thinking about Blazes and Molly's impending assignation, Bloom is himself stalling so as not to go home. As McMichael points out, this stretching out of time is Bloom's strategy; it is his means of feeling in control. He checks his watch throughout the chapter: "Time going on. Hands moving. Two. Not yet. / His midriff yearned then upward, sank within him, yearned more longly, longingly. / Wine" (*U* 8.791–94). The image of the men eating in the Burton is an image of blood-lust immediately gratified. The opposite of love, as Bloom states it in "Cyclops," is not only hatred, but force. Plot is a suspension of consumption, a refusal to force the moment to a crisis. The moment in the Burton seems to end the suspension of time in a vision of animalistic gratification.

In contrast, Bloom is an incorrigible savorer and planner, a man who lives between past and projected satisfactions, perpetually in mourning and anticipation. As reciprocal and prolonged hungers, food, and sex are played off one another in the chapter, beginning with Bloom's entrance into the Burton to escape sexual temptation, the smell of food replaces that other smell that rushes out at him in the chapter, the perfume of female bodies. It is as if the body of the world presses in on Bloom's interiority, massaging his own cravings; yet he resists succumbing wholeheartedly to this lure:

"A warm human plumpness settled down on his brain. His brain yielded. Perfume of embraces all him assailed. With hungered flesh obscurely, he mutely craved to adore" (*U* 8.637–39). This "warm human plumpness" is, of course, associated throughout the novel with Molly's body; the plumpness on Bloom's brain displaces his desire for Molly onto a general eroticization, as if diffusing her particular perfume ("what kind of perfume does your wife use" [*U* 5.258]) into the atmosphere. It is this threat of satisfaction that propels him into the Burton, as if he is choosing the lesser of hungers to satisfy. "He turned Combridge's corner, still pursued. Jingling, hoofthuds. Perfumed bodies, warm, full. All kissed, yielded. . . . His heart astir he pushed in the door of the Burton restaurant. Stink gripped his trembling breath: pungent meatjuice, slush of greens" (*U* 8.641–51). But in the Burton he finds that the smells of men are more dangerous than the scent of a woman.

As a temporary stay against hunger, Bloom does make a culinary choice—a cheese sandwich and wine. Tellingly, his meal is later dubbed "the unsubstantial lunch" (*U* 17.2047), a chosen alternative to meat as both substance and symbol (transubstantiated matter). Indeed, before choosing cheese, he mentally catalogs the various ways in which he can protect himself from unholy meat, through prescriptions both kosher and vegetarian. "Kosher. No meat and milk together" (*U* 8.751), he thinks, again relying on Jewish traditions. Momentarily, he mulls over Jewish dietary exclusions and taboos which function as a purification—less violent than abjection, they are alternative forms of protecting oneself from the taste of death ("I hate dirty eaters" [*U* 8.696], he thinks as he witnesses the carnivorous orgy of men). Bloom's uncharacteristic fastidiousness further leads him to thoughts of the ritual fast of atonement at Yom Kippur, a "spring cleaning of inside" (*U* 8.752) as he puts it, that replaces the murderous sacrifice with rules of atonement. Vegetarian traditions also cross his mind: "After all there's a lot in that vegetarian fine flavour of things from the earth garlic of course it stinks after Italian organgrinders crisp of onions mushrooms truffles" (*U* 8.720–22). Of course, we know that Bloom is no vegetarian; indeed, he ridicules the dreamy theosophist vegetarians like a "real man" regarding a flower child eating tofu. And even the pacific cheese sandwich cannot wholly free him from thoughts of death. In "Hades," only hours earlier, he thinks, "A corpse is meat gone bad. Well and what's cheese? Corpse of milk" (*U* 6.981–82). Cheese, too, reminds him of the food chain: "Cheese digests all but itself" (*U* 8.755), Bloom thinks before he eats his sandwich, projecting cheese, surprisingly enough, as the victor in the food chain, like paper winning over rock in the children's game. But the cheese and wine he chooses to eat suggest a different kind of ritual than either Catholic communion or cannibalistic frenzy. In "Ithaca," the "unsubstantial lunch" is linked, parenthetically, to the "rite of Melchisedek" (*U* 17.2047). Melchisedek is the archetypal priest of the Old Testament.[16] Ransacking various possible identificatory roles for himself, Bloom casts himself as a Jewish priest, engaging in a rite different from both the transubstantiation of the host in the Eucharist and the nontransubstantiation of the food in the Burton.

The cheese and wine he eats represent a kinder, gentler form of organic breakdown, the chemical process of fermentation.

> Wine soaked and softened rolled pith of bread mustard a moment mawkish cheese. Nice wine it is. Taste it better because I'm not thirsty. Bath of course does that. Just a bite or two. Then about six o'clock I can. Six. Six. Time will be gone then. She.
> Mild fire of wine kindled in his veins. I wanted that badly.
> (*U* 8.850–54)

The wine Bloom drinks is distinctly *not* the symbol of the blood of Christ, not, that is, the idealization of the divine body. It is a fermented drink that liquefies the bodies of food so that they achieve a consubstantiality. Furthermore, this is food that mixes rather than separates according to strict dietary code. Parts of speech liquefy in imitation of the process of transcorporeality occurring in Bloom's mouth, as he tongues the soft pulpy mixture. No brutal mastication, this softening in the mouth replaces force with enzymatic transformation. This image of satisfaction, represented in a kind of indolence of the lotus-eaters sort, fills up Bloom *and* the time it takes for Boylan to make his way to Molly: this "glowing wine on his palate lingered swallowed" (*U* 8.897). This image of ingestion links fermentation with the very action of memory: "Glowing wine on his palate lingered swallowed. Crushing in the winepress grapes of Burgundy. Sun's heat it is. Seems to a secret touch telling me memory. Touched his sense moistened remembered" (*U* 8.897–99). The present pulpy mixture evokes the remains of an earlier day. A ripening ("Sun's heat it is"), a pressure ("Crushing in the winepress grapes"), a liquefaction, produce a pulp fiction in the brain, a sweet, moist memory different from Molly's brand of pulp fiction, her "sweets of sin." Bloom's senses are lubricated; a softening and yielding in his brain produces Molly herself and her seedcake, the metonymy for Molly as mollification.

> Softly she gave me in my mouth the seedcake warm and chewed. Mawkish pulp her mouth had mumbled sweetsour of her spittle. Joy: I ate it: joy. Young life, her lips that gave me pouting. Soft warm sticky gumjelly lips. . . . Kissed, she kissed me. (*U* 8.907-16)[17]

It is the woman who begins the process of transformation and sexual exchange. As Frank Budgen records it, Joyce told him:

> "Fermented drink must have had a sexual origin . . . In a woman's mouth, probably. I have made Bloom eat Molly's chewed seed cake."
> I told [Joyce] I had just read a German book in which was described a tribal orgy on a South Sea island. The drink was prepared by the women of the tribe. They chewed a certain herb and spat the pulp into a huge crock out of which the men then drank.[18]

This is Molly's Eucharist; in the gift of the seedcake she offers her transubstantiated body ("Take, this is my body") in a sacred rite. This identification through orality does not sublimate the body in pursuit of idealism, the kind of sublimation that is troped in Bloom's thoughts of the coldness of the Greek statues in the library, who have no anuses, no holes for food to enter or exit the body, or the coldness of the nymph in the picture, *The Bath of the Nymph*, above the Blooms' conjugal bed. This Eucharist is *warm*, tasted, an already chewed body that offers an exchange of sexual eros. But it is not the gross, material body eaten in the Burton, the profaned body of matter without spirit. It is, instead, a counterpart to the Eucharist, a symbolic satiation that makes of Molly a nourishing, yet not devouring, mother. This erotic identification through the transfer of pulp from Molly's mouth to Bloom's, between her "sticky gumjelly lips," contrasts with the terrifyingly vampiric "mouth to her mouth" kiss in Stephen's poem."[19]

Yet immediately Bloom thinks, "Me. And me now," then watches two copulating flies "stuck" on the windowpane, the antithesis of the erotic moment he has just remembered. It is shortly after this that we lose Bloom's interior monologue for a while as he goes to the urinal ("Dribbling a quiet message from his bladder came to go do not to do there to do. A man and ready he drained his glass to the lees and walked" [*U* 8.933–34]). The narrative pulls back to a dialogue between Nosey Flynn and Davy Byrne about Bloom, and it is as if he were robbed of his full, richly nourished interior, metaphorically to be replaced by his own full bladder. Nosey and Davy discuss Bloom, "—I noticed he was in mourning" (*U* 8.944), Davy says; this suddenly externalized view reminds us of the fact that the moment of oral exchange is a memory only, made more vivid and painful because of the ten years that have elapsed since full carnal intercourse has occurred between the Blooms—it is, indeed, a kind of mourning for a love already lost. The constant pressure of Molly's impending adultery and the reminder of the Blooms' less than full carnal relationship reveal the "incertitude and evasion of the love object," as Kristeva puts it in another context.[20] The tone of the chapter is indeed elegiac—"I was happier then. Or was that I?" (*U* 8.608). Despite the numerous feedings and eatings in which Bloom participates in the chapter, his yearnings go unsatisfied, a sense of the mourning of his lost self and love pervades. This memory of amorous communion, so vividly *re-presented* (and also remembered in Molly's monologue), captures the elegiac quality of the sacrament of the Eucharist—a ritual that, through iteration, attempts to conserve an essence (the love of Christ), that simultaneously preserves the full sense of the loss of that love object. If Christ's sacrament is one way of getting at the problem of identification through incorporation, Molly's pulp fiction provides an alternative image of communion not constructed in the carno-phallogocentric mode, a communion culminating in the substance of Molly's words incorporated, as it were, on the final pages of *Ulysses*.

The mollification of the seedcake stands as the symbol of the fluidity and liquidity of identifications that mark Joyce's text. By thematizing and enacting moments of oral assimilation, present and remembered, the "Lestrygonians" chapter focuses our attention on the way in which texts are transubstantiations, marriages of body and meaning. Dominated by the "subjective" senses of taste and smell, "Lestrygonians" is, at the same time, one of the most metatextual of chapters, for it reminds us of the process of identification through assimilation that underwrites all fiction amid the superfluidity of such identifications that mark Joyce's protean *Ulysses*.

9

"Twenty Pockets Arent Enough For Their Lies"

Pocketed Objects as Props of Bloom's Masculinity in *Ulysses*

We are all familiar with the famous photograph of Joyce taken by C. P. Curran when Joyce was twenty-two.[1] Joyce adopts a stance of studied casualness: hips slightly forward, hands in pockets, head cocked slightly to one side, he mildly challenges the camera with an expression that gives nothing away. The gesture of the hands in the pockets is an integral part of the stance of self-containment, composing the subject in a closed circuit. His hands and his thoughts are hidden from view. The pose teased the photographer into asking what was on Joyce's mind. A viewer might wonder what is in his pockets.

As we all know from Richard Ellmann, Joyce was reported to have replied to the photographer's question, "I was wondering would he lend me five shillings" (caption under plate VIII, *JJII*), suggesting that the mind may be full of schemes but the pockets are almost empty. In the hypothetical afterlife of the photograph, Joyce will attempt to con the photographer. His wits will have to compensate for his empty pockets. In contrast, the mock-priest, Mulligan, does perform a coin trick in the first chapter of *Ulysses*. The old woman delivering tea to the tower needs to be paid, Haines reminds them. The cost of the tea is two shillings twopence.

> Buck Mulligan sighed and, having filled his mouth with a crust thickly buttered on both sides, stretched forth his legs and began to search his trouser pockets.
> —Pay up and look pleasant, Haines said to him, smiling.
> Stephen filled a third cup, a spoonful of tea colouring faintly the thick

rich milk. Buck Mulligan brought up a florin, twisted it round in his
fingers and cried:
—A miracle! (*U* 1.446–53)

Mulligan is a magician, a miracle maker who can pull a rabbit out of a hat, a florin from a habitually empty Irish trouser pocket. As we know, much is made in *Ulysses* of what is not found in men's trouser pockets. Money, especially, is scarce. Latchkeys, too, are absent or misplaced: Bloom begins his day by remembering that he left his latchkey in the pocket of another pair of trousers; Stephen begins his day by momentarily pocketing the "huge key" to the tower (*U* 1.530), only to relinquish it soon after. Money and keys, of course, signify one's stake in society's property and one's claim to a proper share of its commodities. Mulligan's sleight of hand allows him to mystify the origins of money in colonial labor in a show of shamanistic powers.[2] In contrast, Stephen eschews Mulligan's pretense of magical powers. After pocketing the coins he has been paid by Mr. Deasy, he thinks: "A lump in my pocket: symbols soiled by greed and misery" (*U* 2.227–28). The telltale bulge in the trouser pocket only *seems* to symbolize the potency of possession; indeed, shortly after this Stephen emphasizes his sense of impotence, with a phrase that resonates beyond its specific reference in the chapter: "The lump I have is useless" (*U* 2.259).

A whole performance of "to have and to have not," of bulging pockets and useless lumps, pervades the multiple references to pockets in *Ulysses*. The novel is full of ritualized performances in which all sorts of everyday objects are hoarded, relinquished, exchanged, and transferred via male pockets. Mulligan's magic act underscores the way pockets function as repositories of props for the performance of character in general and masculinity in particular, props that are invested with magical powers. The "20 pockets" in the male suit, suspiciously viewed by Molly as not enough "for their lies" (*U* 18.1236–37), contain resources for charming the world. Yet Mulligan's hocus pocus disguises the phallic anxiety attached to the performance of the self and the characters' nagging suspicions that the lumps in their trousers are indeed useless.

Fetishism provides the link between everyday objects and the magical investments of desire; it provides as well a clue to the compensatory functions of material objects for the characters that circulate through Dublin in *Ulysses*. In an essay in *Fetishism as Cultural Discourse*, an excellent collection co-edited with Emily Apter, William Pietz explains that the word "fetishism" originally referred to the primitive religious practice of worshipping "terrestrial, material objects."[3] Through Marx and Freud, the older anthropological discourse came to highlight the investments of desire in objects that circulate and are exchanged in modern society, with Marx focusing on the collectively valued commodity and Freud on the more personal and idiosyncratic projections of desire. In both Marxist and Freudian discourse, however, "[o]bjects are revealed as provocations to desire and possession," as Apter puts it.[4] It is, of course, in classical psychoanalysis that the fetish object is viewed as a substitute phallus, revealing and concealing the "fact" of maternal castration. Yet, as revisionary work on fetishism has shown, "the idea stipulated by classical psychoanalysis that virtually any object—fur, velvet, chair legs, shoelaces, apron strings, hatbands, feather boas, etc.—can become a candidate for fetishization once it is placed on the great metonymic chain of phallic substitutions ultimately undermines the presupposition of a phallic *ur*-form, or *objet*-type."[5]

Bloom's thought, "no key, but potato," captures the way he props up his sagging masculinity with the magic charms in his pockets. An updated version of Odysseus's moly, the potato is associated with Bloom's mother. It is his talisman, the fetish object that he endows with all the powers of possession that he lacks. "Potato I have," he reassures himself, as he embarks on his circulation through Dublin (*U* 4.73), and in "Circe," after a near miss with the sandstrewer, the stage directions tell us that Bloom "feels his trouser pocket" for comfort in "poor mamma's panacea" (*U* 15.201–2). In the same chapter, Zoe asks Bloom, "How's the nuts?" (*U* 15.1299), and puts her hand in his pocket and feels instead the potato, which she calls a "hard chancre" (*U* 15.1304), bawdily linking the tuber and syphilitic phallus.[6] Although he lacks the patriarchal keys to Dublin society, most of the day Bloom gains authority and confidence from his protective amulet. In his classic study *The Psychology of Clothes*, J. C. Flugel describes the carrying of amulets on the person to ward off evil spirits: "it is extremely convenient," he says, "to carry about some amulet which can be trusted to ward off the evil influences without the necessity of active intervention. For this purpose various objects, supposed to possess magical properties, were hung or otherwise attached to the body."[7] "Without the necessity of active intervention," Bloom arms himself for passive combat, one could say; in the modern suit, however, the amulet is pocketed conveniently rather than hung on the body. In returning magical properties to things, the fetishist locates a potency that he otherwise lacks.

In a way, all the small objects that Bloom carries in his pockets are amulets, for pockets in *Ulysses* are reservoirs of possessions and self-possession, the daily arsenals with which the male characters leave their houses, armed for circulation in society ("A potato, don't leave home without it," one might say). Pockets are temporary havens for the characters' private property as they navigate their way through city streets. We might think of pockets as the material counterparts of the interior monologue, containers that harbor and construct the domain of the private. In being temporary and portable, pockets contain objects that contrast with the more official and societal "secrets" of the drawer inventoried in the "Ithaca" chapter of *Ulysses*. Birth certificate, bank passbook, stock certificate, insurance policy, graveplot purchase document, and official records of a name change—these contents of Bloom's second drawer establish the more permanent record of Bloom as a stakeholder in society. Coins, rather than bankbooks; cards with pseudonyms, rather than official records; daily newspapers and advertisements of paradisal communities; food and soap—these are the more perishable and vulnerable commodities protected in the portable pouches of the pockets. As Flugel puts it, "[C]lothes, like the house, are protective; but, being nearer the body and actually supported on it, they are (unlike the house) portable. With their help, we carry—like snails and tortoises—a sort of home upon our backs, and enjoy the advantages of shelter without the disadvantage of becoming sessile."[8]

According to Anne Hollander in *Sex and Suits*, the man's suit—Bloom's suit, with waistcoat, trousers and vest—consolidated the "modern masculine image," consolidation virtually in place by 1820. In contrast to women's fashion, the masculine suit, she says, "suggests probity and restraint, prudence and detachment."[9] The image of prudence and self-possession is an important part of Bloom's self-representation of his bourgeois masculine image; pockets allow for the careful arrangement and concealment of one's personal effects (think of Bloom's self-conscious gesture of "prudently pocketing" Molly's photo in the cabman's shelter [*U* 16.1644]). Pockets provide cover for Bloom's elaborately constructed rituals of docking imports and exports momentarily on his person—elaborate shell games in which he receives, fondles, transfers, and replaces objects. Things virtually appear and disappear into the separate compartments of Bloom's "inner pocket," "handkerchief pocket," "sidepocket," "heart pocket," and "trouser pocket." These pockets provide ordering and circulating spaces in a private economy under Bloom's control. Martha's flower and Molly's soap are punctiliously rearranged and separated on Bloom's person, allowing for the literal compartmentalizing, one might say, rationalizing, of his desires ("Change that soap now. Mr Bloom's hand unbuttoned his hip pocket swiftly and transferred the paperstuck soap to his inner handkerchief pocket" [*U* 6.494–96]). Indeed, Molly herself focuses on the number of secret chambers enabling male deception: "Ill see if he has that French letter still in his pocketbook I suppose he thinks I dont know deceitful men all their 20 pockets arent enough for their lies" (*U* 18.1235–37). Slipping Martha's letter and his own Henry Flower card into his sidepocket, Bloom carefully arranges an alibi, a screen, for his deflowering of Martha's letter: "His hand went into his pocket and a forefinger felt its way under the flap of the envelope, ripping it open in jerks" (*U* 5.77–78). Martha's letter is a kind of prophylactic (or French letter); the penetration of the envelope in the pocket is safe and prudent sex, a honeymoon in the hidden hand.

Yet if they harbor the domain of the private, Bloom's pockets house as well his passports to the public sphere. As a middleman between the economic base and the superstructure, as Jennifer Wicke has put it in describing Bloom's job as an ad canvasser, Bloom is a willing and active participant in the circulation of commodities.[10] Unlike Stephen, he welcomes commercial exchanges. Indeed, his pleasure in the accumulation and manipulation of the objects in his pockets distinguishes him from the more critical and parsimonious Stephen, whose gestures include divestment more than inventory. This commerce with the world is crucial to constructing Bloom's bourgeois masculinity, his participation in the public sphere.

Thus, as way stations between private and societal domains, pockets are portable spaces that facilitate Bloom's illusion of controlling the exchanges in which he participates. He buys a kidney—"His hand accepted the moist tender gland and slid it into a sidepocket. Then it fetched up three coins from his trousers' pocket and laid them on the rubber prickles. They lay, were read quickly and quickly slid, disc by disc, into the till" (*U* 4.181–84). The sensuous symmetry between the gland sliding into his pocket and his own coins sliding quickly into the till conveys the tactile, even sexual, pleasure that Bloom derives from his role in commodity culture, in the rituals of buying and selling. We might remember Apter's idea that all sorts of objects can function as fetishes if they exist on the metonymic chain of phallic substitutions, as "moist glands" are wont to do. Yet, what the tactile pleasure of the fetish suggests in the above example is the way in which pockets are the spaces where characters struggle to personalize commodity culture, to invest the objects in circulation with their particular desires and magical projections. As Pietz observes, Marx saw the fetish-worshipper as deceived into believing that an inanimate object would "comply with his desires" (Pietz 136). Joyce seems to have a more fluid view of the flow of desire between an individual and society's commodities and represents a more mysterious process in which subjectivity is constructed amid commodity exchange.[11]

So Bloom's private rituals depend on and attempt to refashion commodities, for example, as when the daily newspaper—a symbol of the urban everyday—serves Bloom as a detachable phallus, his own fetish object for masculine display. To gird himself for his trip to the post office to see if Martha Clifford has responded to him, Bloom draws the *Freeman* from his sidepocket, in a bravura show of his masculinity: "As he walked he took the folded *Freeman* from his sidepocket, unfolded it, rolled it lengthwise in a baton and tapped it at each sauntering step against his trouserleg" (*U* 5.48–50). Imitating the wide-hipped sauntering girl who purchased sausages, no less, in Dlugacz's earlier in the morning, Bloom orchestrates his performance of masculinity with the prop of his "baton," wearing the phallus on the outside. As with Martha's unpocketed letter, the unpocketed *Freeman* shows how Bloom commandeers circulating language, fetishizing textual objects, investing them with his own desire.

Yet Bloom's ritual management of masculine props cannot protect him from exposure and humiliation. Such exposure comes when M'Coy interrupts him and asks, "How's the body?" (*U* 5.86), and "Who's getting it up?" (*U* 5.153), questions that remind us of the lack the fetish object is deployed to conceal. Another moment comes when Bloom, unexpectedly spying Boylan, desperately inventories his ammunition, like a turtle who retreats into its shell:

Look for something I.
His hasty hand went quickly into a pocket, took out, read unfolded Agendath Netaim. Where did I?
Busy looking.
He thrust back quick Agendath.
Afternoon she said.

> I am looking for that. Yes, that. Try all pockets. Handker. *Freeman.*
> Where did I? Ah, yes. Trousers. Potato. Purse. Where?
> Hurry. Walk quietly. Moment more. My heart.
> His hand looking for the where did I put found in his hip pocket
> soap lotion have to call tepid paper stuck. Ah soap there I yes.
> Gate.
> Safe! (*U* 8.1182–93)

The analogy between pockets and consciousness is never clearer than here; Bloom's anxious thoughts and his things spill willy-nilly about, the syntax unable to compartmentalize effectively the disparate contents of and on his person. "Try all pockets," Bloom vainly instructs himself. In this passage, Bloom anticipates Beckett's Molloy, who performs the most famous pocket ritual in modern literature—the distribution into four pockets of sixteen sucking stones, individually sucked and deposited.[12] Molloy's stripped-down version of appropriation and self-possession seems a far cry from Bloom's bourgeois delight, yet the futility of trying to control the placements, replacements, and displacements of desire is poignant in both cases—and comic.

It is in "Circe" that this futility is dramatized in theatrical spectacle as Bloom's inner pockets are picked, his privacy anything but inviolate: "Beware of pickpockets" (*U* 15.245), Bloom warns early in the chapter. The objects prudently pocketed or relinquished now speak their own desires rebelliously, like Molly's soap or the watch which Bloom has earlier drawn from his pocket in embarrassment, caught in the act of masturbation by Cissy Caffrey. It is emphasized in "Circe" that Bloom's pocketed objects are mostly fetishes associated with women: Molly's "wandering soap," his mother's "potato preservative," Molly's *Sweets of Sin*.[13] These commodity fetishes, in Marxist fashion, literally take on a life of their own, refusing to sit still for Bloom's displacements. Indeed, the metonymic "slide" of phallic substitutions reaches its apotheosis as sticks, "stiff" legs, a "stiff walk" (*U* 15.207), and "stiffpointed" tails (*U* 15.1252) abound in the chapter. The prosthetic baton Bloom has made of the *Freeman* is now replaced by Cissy Caffrey's "the leg of the duck," which she distributes to Molly and to Nelly to strap on wherever they please. The phallic mothers have their revenge. Indeed, the sexual differentiation that pockets signify—women carry their objects in their purses, men carry them in their pockets—is itself undermined. After Tommy and Jacky run into Bloom at the beginning of the chapter, Bloom "pats with parcelled hands, watchfob, pocketbookpocket, pursepoke, sweets of sin, potatosoap" (*U* 15.242–43), trying to remain in possession of his possessions, which form unnerving combinations and substitutions within his pouches. The pocket is now a "pocketbookpocket"; "purse" and phallic "poke" are combined in "pursepoke." It is in "Circe" most of all that the "thing itself," the phallus, is revealed as a prop. The pocket, by day associated with the masculine suit, by night reveals its female properties, specifically, its pouchlike, womblike function. The props of masculinity and femininity circulate and combine in the heated compression of the chapter. The fetishes, provocations to desire and possession, reveal the way desire is an errant thing not possessed or pocketed, but always misplaced and displaced. Finally, for all Bloom's intimate and fond contact with the possessions he harbors, his elaborate pocket rituals can neither conceal his sense of lack nor make commodities conform to his own desires. The comic animism of the fetish in "Circe" signals the slippery slope of substitution, once the metonymic chain of displacement begins.

It stages as well a certain demystification of the artist's conjuring act, a resistance to his magical powers. There is a link between the talismanic potency of the fetish and the seduction of details that contribute to realism's power. It is a connection implicit in the following description in Hugh Kenner's *The Stoic Comedians*: "But Joyce tended to fondle data which comes in finite sets, and to enumerate these sets, and when the data is as protean as the life of a great city, he avails himself of various delimiting devices—a single day, a city directory, a newspaper—to give at least the appearance of a finite set."[14]

In *Ulysses* the narrative fondles, invests, and inventories data in the manner of Bloom. In the narration of *Ulysses* we are made to see the sleight of hand performed in all representation—the conjuring of the "things" of the world, "the hidden hand . . . again at its old game" (*U* 15.975). Watch carefully as the baton waves—take your mind off the narration and a scene has been moved, objects magically appear without being properly introduced. Anti-realism and realism merge in this fiat, this performance. But if we are careful, we must see through the deliberate mystifications of pulling rabbits out of hats, that is, the aesthetic of art's autonomous creation out of the "deep pocket" of the author's mind. For if the fetish reminds us of the mysterious workings of fantasy and desire, it also reminds us of the material object and its putative value in circulation. The fondling of data and the investment of everyday objects with desire provide a corrective to the view that art is cut off from the world.

10

Bloom in Circulation

Who's He When He's Not at Home?

> By lorries along sir John Rogerson's quay Mr Bloom walked soberly, past Windmill lane, Leask's the linseed crusher, the postal telegraph office. (*U* 5.1–2)
> He walked back along Dorset street, reading gravely. (*U* 4.191)
> Stephen went down Bedford row, the handle of the ash clacking against his shoulderblade. (*U* 10.830–31)
> Almidano Artifoni walked past Holles street, past Sewell's yard. (*U* 10.1101)

Joyce's *Ulysses* is a novel of walking. In its peripatetic passings, early twentieth-century Dublin is documented. Critics have claimed that city walking characterizes the modernist city novel, constituting its "idiosyncratic features."[1]

Baudelaire's "flaneur" has provided a particularly popular conceptual model for interpreting modern city novels, including *Ulysses*, despite the flaneur's pre-twentieth-century origin. Walter Benjamin's reading of Baudelaire is highly influential. According to Benjamin, Baudelaire's flaneur is a reader of modern urban spaces, an observer of the city who feels himself out of place in it. Like Baudelaire himself, the flaneur is a "lyric poet in the era of high capitalism."[2] He "demanded elbow room and was unwilling to forgo the life of the gentleman of leisure. Let the many attend to their daily affairs; the man of leisure can indulge in the perambulations of the *flâneur* only if as such he is already out of place."[3] Anke Gleber's *The Art of Taking a Walk: Flanerie, Literature, and Film in Weimar Culture* establishes a "theory of literary flânerie" that draws heavily on Benjamin's *The Arcades Project* and his essays on Baudelaire. She regards flanerie as "a privileged mode of perceiving modernity and its many realities."[4]

In these discussions the flaneur is a figure both out of place and out of date, a nineteenth-century gentleman who observes rather than participates in the modern urban experience. A number of Joyce critics have focused on Joyce's revisionary use of the figure of the flaneur. At the 2000 International James Joyce Symposium, two entire panels on Benjamin and Joyce were devoted to the relevance of the figure of the flaneur for interpreting Joyce's city walkers, Leopold Bloom in particular. Enda Duffy, Luke Gibbons, and Patrick McGee all located a postcolonial counter-tradition of flanerie in Joyce's Irish translation of the continental concept.[5] In his more sustained exploration of the figure of the flaneur in *The Subaltern "Ulysses,"* Duffy views the continental model as a regressive, nostalgic figure. However, he finds it fruitful to consider Bloom as an "enlivened, reborn flaneur" (63). In his continental and English versions, according to Duffy, the flaneur "exists in metropolitan modernist works as the last hostage of realism whom the modernists (Döblin in *Berlin Alexanderplatz*, Woolf in *Mrs. Dalloway*) could not bear to let go" (67). Duffy says that the modernist flaneur operates as a "nexus" for "nostalgic desires" (67). In contrast, Bloom is the flaneur as subaltern subject. The figure of the flaneur thus becomes a progressive, rather than regressive trope.

In this essay, I, too, consider the art of walking in *Ulysses*, particularly as practiced by Leopold Bloom, in relation to the figure of the flaneur; however, I read it within, rather than against, the conceptual framework of nostalgia. I agree that flanerie is a kind of hand-me-down garment for both Leopold Bloom and Stephen Dedalus, one that fits and does not fit in revealing ways. But rather than dismissing nostalgia as a rearguard impulse jettisoned by the new postcolonial subject, I will argue that on many levels, Joyce exploited "nostalgia" of time and place in his representation of Dublin and Dublin walkers. Considering the role of nostalgia helps generate an image of Bloom's city walking that is not ideologically fixed in the subaltern position. After briefly considering Stephen Dedalus as a would-be flaneur, I will focus on Joyce's use of nostalgia in the Homeric sense of a longing for "home," as it applies to both Bloom's minicirculation through Dublin and the representation of Dublin in *Ulysses*.

The European flaneur provides a model for Stephen as he wanders through Dublin streets attempting to read the signatures of the city. In *Stephen Hero* and *A Portrait*, in particular, Stephen is an emulator of Baudelaire's flanerie, an estranged walker in the city who desperately seeks to become its lyric poet. Baudelairean flanerie introduced a new aesthetic of perception, a connection between the flaneur and the artist as reader of the city text that Stephen exploits:[6] "As he walked thus through the ways of the city he had his ears and eyes ever prompt to receive impressions" (*SH* 30). It is in the streets that he composes his essay: "His forty days were consumed in aimless solitary walks during which he forged out his sentences" (*SH* 69). In his conversations with Maurice, he comes closest to the model of peripatetic philosopher and flaneur, who combines "rambling, thinking, observing and talking" (Barta xiii). Baudelaire's flaneur is a man of leisure; Stephen, in contrast, is a struggling Dubliner frustrated in a depressed colonial economy. One can read his departure for Paris between *A Portrait* and *Ulysses* as his trip to the capital of the nineteenth century to become the Baudelairean poet he finds it hard to be in his native Dublin. We learn in *Ulysses* that Stephen walked through the streets of Baudelaire's Paris collecting observations: "Proudly walking. Whom were you trying to walk like?" (*U* 3.184). Adapting the European stance of the flaneur in the earlier novels is one way that Stephen prepares himself to leave Ireland and fly by the colonial nets that entangle him. Stephen's mother's death cuts short this continental adaptation. Stephen returns to Ireland only to suffer the humiliations of displacement once again ("He has the key. I will not sleep there when this night comes" [*U* 3.276]). Back in Dublin, Stephen continues to link his mental and physical "tropings": "Turning his back to the sun he bent over far to a table of rock and scribbled words" (*U* 3.406–7). He vacillates between desiring to be Dublin's lyric poet and escaping the city altogether.

Just as romantic nostalgia fuels Stephen's recourse to a nineteenth-century peripatetic model, it is a commonplace of *Ulysses* criticism that nostalgia also underwrites the Homeric structure of *Ulysses*. As in the *Odyssey*, nostalgia—a kind of homesickness and longing for home—fuels Ulysses/Bloom's journeys. A major difference between the forays of the European flaneur and Bloom's comings and goings in *Ulysses* is Bloom's mental homeward turning throughout the day, and his eventual *nostos*. Unlike the quintessential flaneur, Bloom is a traveling homebody, a petit bourgeois who worships household gods despite the pain they also bring. Bloom's minijourneys can be regarded as "tactics," as Michel de Certeau uses the term in *The Practice of Everyday Life*, artful ways of navigating the "cityful" of objects, people, and memories as he strategically waits to return home at day's end.[7]

Who's he when he's not at home? we might ask of Bloom, whose mini-epic travels through Dublin are almost always conducted in relation to 7 Eccles Street, betraying tactics of either approach or avoidance. "Longest way round is the shortest way home" (*U* 13.1110–11), Bloom thinks to himself as he visits Sandymount Strand to meditate (and, it turns out, to masturbate) at the end of the day, before visiting Mrs. Purefoy. If epic always "takes the long way round," Joyce's rendition of Odysseus's voyage makes delay strategic, a tactic of avoidance and a way to keep desire alive. "At four she" (*U* 11.309, 352) and "At four" (*U* 11.305, 392) are refrains that echo in Bloom's mind, referring to the time that Molly presumably told him Blazes Boylan was coming to rehearse (*U* 11.305, 308, 309). "Funny my watch stopped at half past four" (*U* 13.846–47), he realizes after his voyeurism of Gerty MacDowell. Home is a figure longed for *because* it is "incomplete"; narrative wanderings are prolonged in the process of Bloom's wanting and not wanting to return home.

Bloom's ambivalence is most poignantly represented in "Lestrygonians," where desire manifests itself as a general hunger:

> He raised his eyes and met the stare of a bilious clock. Two. Pub clock five minutes fast. Time going on. Hands moving. Two. Not yet.
> His midriff yearned then upward, sank within him, yearned more longly, longingly. (*U* 8.790–93)

Two pages later we read, "Just a bite or two. Then about six o'clock I can. Six. Six. Time will be gone then. She" (*U* 8.852–53). Bloom is killing time rather than killing suitors. The eighteen miles he covers on June 16 (eight on foot and ten by tram, horse-drawn carriage, and train[8]) are fueled by a nostalgia that keeps desire going as it defers his actual return. This narrative tropism, the repeated turnings toward and away from home, is an integral part of Bloom's modus operandi as city walker—his pedestrian wanderings serve the function of passing time as he passes through the city anticipating and deferring his return.

One of Bloom's strategies to maintain his emotional connection with home and protect himself on his journeys is never to leave 7 Eccles Street without little bits of home accompanying him. Since the days of Louis-Philippe, Benjamin says, "the bourgeoisie has endeavoured to compensate itself for the inconsequential nature of private life in the big city. It seeks such compensation within its four walls. Even if a bourgeois is unable to give his earthly being permanence, it seems to be a matter of honour with him to preserve the traces of his articles and requisites of daily use in perpetuity."[9] The inventory of favorite possessions in the "Ithaca" chapter supports this idea of compensation within the four walls of home. But equally important is the way in which the domestic is at least partly portable. Souvenir objects play a significant role in helping Bloom survive his mini-journeys on June 16th. He leaves home with his moly (his potato) and his money in the pockets of his suit (see the previous essay, "Twenty Pockets"). Compartmentalizing the components of his desire and nostalgia in his pockets—Martha's flower, Molly's picture, his mother's talismanic potato, and his money, Bloom circulates throughout Dublin, his tactics and deferrals depending upon the nostalgic image of Penelope at home, however compromised he knows that home to be. As in the *Odyssey*, home depends upon a woman in place as the man journeys, with her image accompanying him as a souvenir.

These souvenir objects help counteract Bloom's sense of conjugal displacement from home and bed. But his displacement is part of a more general structure of displacement and longing underlying the urban experience. Discussing the general plight of the pedestrian within urban geography, Certeau sees city walking in relation to a longing for "the proper," or home, that is never satisfied:

> To walk is to lack a place. It is the indefinite process of being absent and in search of a proper. The moving about that the city multiplies and concentrates makes the city itself an immense social experience of lacking a place—an experience that is, to be sure, broken up into countless tiny deportations (displacements and walks), compensated for by the relationships and intersections of these exoduses that intertwine and create an urban fabric, and placed under the sign of what ought to be, ultimately, the place but is only a name, the City.... [T]here is only a pullulation of passers-by, a network of residences temporarily appropriated by pedestrian traffic, a shuffling among pretenses of the proper, a universe of rented spaces haunted by a nowhere or by dreamed-of places. (103)

Certeau's description of this "shuffling among pretenses of the proper" has increased resonance for Dubliners, in a country where the landlord is likely to be English or Anglo-Irish. As he circulates through Dublin, Bloom is triply displaced—as cuckold, Jewish outsider, and Irish renter. As Duffy, Gibbons, and McGee rightly observe, the colonial walker is situated in a different relation to the monuments of the city and its mapped-out spaces than to his European counterpart, the flaneur. But in reading Bloom's Irish form of flanerie, as "aggressive, emancipatory, and the blueprint for a potential version of new postcolonial subjectivity" (63), Duffy seems to freeze Bloom into the static position of subaltern. Certeau's model affords a more hybrid and improvisational pattern of comings and goings, constraints and liberations—emotional, ideological, novelistic.

Certeau's framework provides a useful apparatus for analyzing the way "ordinary practitioners of the city" (93) create specific and defining trajectories through the city according to the "tactics" that they deploy. With particular resonance for analyzing Joyce's novel, Certeau explicitly links the work of tactics to the *metis* of Odysseus. He regards "the proper" as a victory of space over time. On the contrary, because it does not have a place, a tactic depends on time—it is always on the watch for opportunities that must be seized "on the wing" (xix). In Certeau's schema, pedestrians use tactics as they walk through the city, "jerry-built" trajectories taken amidst the spatial constraints and interdictions of the city (102). The walker "actualizes possibilities," pursuing his particular crossings, drifting, improvisations, and detours, some consciously, some not. The bodies of these city walkers "follow the thicks and thins of an urban 'text' they write without being able to read it. These practitioners make use of spaces that cannot be seen; their knowledge of them is as blind as that of lovers in each other's arms" (93). Displaced from the home he both longs for and avoids, nostalgic and crafty Odysseus/Bloom fills the time with compensatory exchanges, movements, errands, little comings and goings, departures and returns that occupy his attention. In constructing his daily itinerary, avoidance and activity are in artful blend.

Take his first foray at 8:00 on the morning of June 16. From the moment he leaves 7 Eccles Street, Bloom's circulation involves knowing what to avoid as much as what to engage. In his first trip of the day, "He crossed to the bright side, avoiding the loose cellarflap of number seventyfive" (*U* 4.77–78). This is avoidance born of familiarity, the act of a wily commuter who knows how to take detours for purposes of both efficiency and safety. Just as he avoids his neighbor's cellarflap, he avoids his acquaintances in the street. This act of avoidance is emblematic of Bloom's general avoidance of the "phatic" function, that is, an avoidance of the "effort to ensure communication" (Certeau 99). Yet Bloom is not wholly successful. As he seeks the privacy of his own pocket in which to deflower the letter from Martha Clifford he has just received, M'Coy intrudes. "Take me out of my way," Bloom thinks (*U* 5.82). Although Bloom is often cast as an outsider, a stranger amongst the other Dubliners, in fact, he is adept at avoidance because he knows the terrain of the familiar.

This familiarity is yet one more aspect of Bloom's difference from the continental flaneur. Unlike metropolitan cities such as Paris and Berlin, in which the European flaneur reads the new semiotics of modernity, Dublin is a place at once alienating and yet too cozy. "I wonder," Joyce said to Budgen about Dublin, "if there is another [city] like it. Everybody has time to hail a friend and start a conversation about a third party."[10] The circulation of unwanted parties and unwanted stories dogs Bloom's steps throughout the day and night. On a typical day, he seeks to maintain his distance from much of the hailing and saluting that goes on in "Wandering Rocks." If the European flaneur of the metropole passes as observer amid the anonymous crowd, Bloom passes through city streets where he is all too often recognized, necessitating new reactive strategies. This sense of domesticity and knowledge bred of familiarity separates Bloom from the flaneur. And Bloom's willing participation in commodity exchanges should be mentioned alongside his forms of resistance.

Certeau's point is that individual walkers through the city often imaginatively navigate around the obstacles and monoliths the city presents to them. He views the deployment of tactics in the everyday practice of walking as a sign of freedom within constraint, a "discreteness" of statement (98) in what he calls the rhetoric of walking. He says that the walker "condemns certain places to inertia or disappearance and composes with others spatial 'turns of phrase' that are 'rare,' 'accidental,' or illegitimate" (99). Like Duffy and Gibbons in their discussions of the colonial flaneur, Certeau sees the rhetoric of walking as potentially emancipatory, a way to evade the totalizing, bureaucratic plan of the city. Although I find Certeau's model useful and more flexible than Duffy's, I want to illustrate, with three short examples, how multivalenced is Joyce's depiction of the rhetoric of walking, so that one cannot assign a particular ideological weight to the activity of walking. First, the "Wandering Rocks" chapter illustrates how everyday practices like walking can be consistent with social conformity as easily as social subversion. Walking in this chapter of perambulation concludes in gestures of obeisance to the "cavalcade" of power. The ubiquitous and mindless salutes throughout the chapter, parodied in the final line in which even Almidano Artifoni's "sturdy trousers" salute the viceregal procession, reveal how "rare male walkers" subscribe to colonial ideology (*U* 10.1282, 1278–79).

The second example, from "Eumaeus," is meant to question further Duffy's view of Bloom as subaltern flaneur. Such a view effaces the ways in which Bloom attempts to distinguish himself from many of his fellow travelers. In "Eumaeus," where economic exploitation is represented in the itinerancy of Dubliners whose "leisure" derives from being out of work or underemployed, Bloom struggles to distinguish his own travels from theirs. Despite the sympathies with workers, peasants, and tenants he demonstrates in the chapter, he takes pains to separate the "peaceable pedestrians" like himself from the "famished loiterers" (*U* 16.121–22, 123). The discourse of bourgeois rationality and regulation woven throughout the chapter establishes Bloom's self-congratulatory distance from the "submerged tenth" he encounters (*U* 16.1226).[11]

My final counterexample to a reading that flatly associates movement with liberation in *Ulysses* involves women walkers, figured differently in relation to movement through the city. The obvious example is the prostitute. As Gleber points out in *The Art of Taking a Walk*, women are in a wholly different relation to flanerie, for when they circulate, like the prostitute in the straw hat in *Ulysses*, their mobility is read as promiscuity. In this case, movement signifies economic constraint. But a more interesting counterexample to movement as the positive sign of freedom is Gerty MacDowell, whose physical disability is revealed precisely at the moment she moves in "Nausicaa":

> Slowly, without looking back she went down the uneven strand to Cissy, to Edy, to Jacky and Tommy Caffrey, to little baby Boardman. It was darker now and there were stones and bits of wood on the strand and slippy seaweed. She walked with a certain quiet dignity characteristic of her but with care and very slowly because—because Gerty MacDowell was . . .
> Tight boots? No. She's lame! O!" (*U* 13.766–71)

As Susan Stewart points out in a brilliant reading of "Nausicaa," it is only when Gerty moves that the perfect pornographic tableau of desire, which depends upon stasis, is fractured.[12] What's missing or lacking becomes visible only then, disturbing Bloom's fixated gaze. Like Molly's picture "prudently pocketed" in Bloom's suit built for traveling, Gerty's fetishized image is appropriated by the male traveler and is disturbed only in her movement.

Thus, Joyce represents the tactics of male walkers alternately succeeding and failing to compensate for the displacements they suffer. In a larger sense, Joyce exploited nostalgia in constructing *Ulysses* as itself a testament to a home always incomplete. Like Bloom with Molly's image in his pocket, Joyce created the seven-hundred-odd pages of the novel as a kind of souvenir of the city that has passed out of existence.

"I want . . . to give a picture of Dublin so complete that if the city one day suddenly disappeared from the earth it could be reconstructed out of my book"—these are some of the most quotable lines in Budgen's *James Joyce and the Making of "Ulysses"* (67–68). When Joyce made this statement to Budgen in Zurich in 1918, the Dublin of 1904 was already gone. As Susan de Sola Rodstein has pointed out in her excellent essay, "Back to 1904: Joyce, Ireland, and Nationalism," the "back-dating" of *Ulysses* betrays a desire to preserve a Dublin already altered in a decade of radical political change, coupled with "a post-Rising sense of the city's actual perishability."[13] My point is not that Joyce regretted the decade of revolutionary activity between the setting and the writing of *Ulysses*, but that in the complex archaeological layering of political landscapes, he creates a souvenir of a time and place passing and gone. The city is arrested, dated, in its premodern phase. The spatial and temporal distance between the city and its novelistic image, between "home" and Joyce, is captured in Joyce's signature at the end of the novel, which records his migration away from the city of his origin—"Trieste-Zurich-Paris, 1914–1921" (*U* 18.1610–11).

At what point would a picture, a souvenir photograph, be "complete" enough to replace the original? The answer, of course, is never. Susan Stewart points out that the souvenir is always incomplete: it is metonymic, substituting a part for the whole, a sample. As Stewart puts it, the souvenir "both mourns and celebrates the gap between object and context of origin" (164). *Ulysses* is such a miniature and souvenir in two senses: in a general way, it partakes of a kind of nostalgia that could be said to mark all narrative: "The souvenir may be seen as emblematic of the nostalgia that all narrative reveals—the longing for its place of origin" (Stewart xii). But the back-dating of *Ulysses* heightens the sense of nostalgia and remembrance, making *Ulysses* a historical novel. Dublin is dated—both documented at a specific time and out of date by the time of the novel's publication (a point that is emphasized in the meta-dating of the novel itself when Miss

Dunne types "16 June 1904" in the "Wandering Rocks" chapter [*U* 10.376]). Furthermore, the particular date Joyce chose, June 16, 1904, had personal resonance for him, functioning commemoratively. For superstitious Joyce it was significant that June 16 was the day he and Nora went walking together.[14] A souvenir, Stewart says, "moves history into private time. Hence the absolute appropriateness of the souvenir as *calendar*" (138). *Ulysses*, then, functions as both historical novel and anniversary celebration, the textual souvenir of a moment and experience. Stewart points out that the souvenir "contracts the world in order to expand the personal" (xii), the world cut down to size. Via *Ulysses*, the Dublin of June 16, 1904, is immortalized as *James Joyce's* Dublin. The spate of books with such titles as *James Joyce's Dublin*, *James Joyce's Ireland*, and *James Joyce's Odyssey: A Guide to the Dublin of "Ulysses"* make us suspect that Dublin, and Ireland by proxy, indeed "belonged" to him.[15]

But, as we know, June 16th has come to be identified as Bloomsday, not Joyce day. The personalization, the nostalgia, to which Stewart refers is invested most clearly by Joyce (and, I would contend, by most readers of *Ulysses*) in Leopold Bloom. On Bloomsday Dublin travels are commemorated in anniversary performances in European cities that, at least at the beginning, duplicated Joyce's own migrations.[16] Desmond Fennell's *Bloomsway: A Day in the Life of Dublin*[17] is only the most recent fictional update of Bloom's itinerary.[18]

In the acts and arts of walking in *Ulysses*, particularly Leopold Bloom's, spatial and temporal "passings" coalesce, so that the data of the real, accumulated as the city is traversed, commemorate a home perpetually desired but already lost. A careful reading of the pedestrian travel in *Ulysses* reveals a constant refrain of "passing" that doubles the sense of movement in space and time. The temporal aspect is muted in narrative phrases cited earlier, such as "By lorries along sir John Rogerson's quay Mr Bloom walked soberly, past Windmill lane" (*U* 5.1–2) or "They went past the bleak pulpit of saint Mark's, under the railway bridge, past the Queen's theatre: in silence" (*U* 6.183–84). But the sense of a city past and passing is sometimes foregrounded explicitly, as in "Lestrygonians" when Bloom's "smile fade[s] as he walked" (*U* 8.475), and he thinks,

> Cityful passing away, other cityful coming, passing away too: other coming on, passing on. Houses, lines of houses, streets, miles of pavements, piledup bricks, stones. Changing hands. This owner, that.

> Landlord never dies they say. Other steps into his shoes when he gets his notice to quit. (*U* 8.484–87)

In *Epic Geography: James Joyce's "Ulysses,"* Michael Seidel speaks of the "mapping impulse" evident in the representation of the wanderings in *Ulysses*, an impulse toward "the realization of place names."[19] Yet, although the picture of Dublin is denoted monument by monument and street by street, the refrain of passing creates a spectral urban landscape. The city is a haunted landscape and the scene of multiple displacements. The documentation of place is punctilious because it is always partial.

In representing Bloom's nostalgic journey through a Dublin already vanished, Joyce reenacted what Stewart calls the "very desire of part for whole which both animates narrative and, in fact, creates the illusion of the real" (xii). The tactics of walking and the tactics of representation, Bloom's and Joyce's *metis*, overlap in a city novel that conjoins flanerie and nostalgia, modernity and epic return. In documenting the "cityful passing," Joyce represented narrative *and* domestic longing in action, with their losses and compensations on display.

IV

Close Encounters

Hospitality and the Other

Consolidating the domain of the proper and venturing into the world—the previous section explores these sometimes competing desires of the characters in *Ulysses*, particularly Leopold Bloom. As he navigates his home and his hometown, Bloom displays his strategies and tactics for opening himself up to others inhabiting the landscape and consolidating his possessions and self-possession. As we have seen, the address to the other in welcome occurs not only on the road, but also at home, most resonantly in the "mass" celebrated by Stephen and Bloom in the kitchen of 7 Eccles Street. It is figured as well in the seedcake, and its moist memory, that Bloom shares with Molly. The address to the other occurs at the level of both conscious and unconscious processes. Despite Bloom's *metis* in calibrating and controlling this address, the other cannot be safely circumscribed in time or in space, tactically or strategically, to use de Certeau's terms. For, although hospitality has its rituals, the close encounters with others and with the "other" in *Ulysses* destabilize the boundaries between the familiar and the foreign for both host and guest (think of Stephen's reaction to Bloom in "Ithaca": "—Yes, Stephen said uncertainly, because he thought he felt a strange kind of flesh of a different man approach him, sinewless and wobbly and all that (*U* 16.1723–24).

The thematic of hospitality runs throughout Joyce's oeuvre, from *Dubliners* to *Finnegans Wake*. It is also a matter of form—of boundaries drawn and breached narratively, generically, formally. The next essay, "Close Encounters," explores hospitality not only thematically but also formally, as a kind of "geometry" that creates an inside and outside of the text. As a prelude to the discussion of hospitality in Joyce's work, it focuses first on modern and modernist fiction more generally, including the example of E.M. Forster. Both Forster's last novel, *A Passage to India*, and his posthumously published short stories are instructive for our discussion of hospitality as both theme and formal boundary.

Close Encounters

How do modernist texts create distinctions between what is included within, and what is excluded from, their pages? This question involves, but is not confined to, the question of hospitality. Hospitality is a subject of particular currency in theory, criticism, and, indeed, politics today, for it is a discourse of how a society regulates its interactions with its others: immigrants, aliens, enemies, animals. It is a question of homeland security. Hospitality involves conventions of welcoming the other into the sanctuary of the home under certain laws and understood pacts. I am interested in the way modernist texts stage and enact hospitality through close encounters with the other—the foreign, the strange, and the "queer."

Yet, what I wish to address with this notion of modernist inclusions and exclusions is not only a question of theme, of the way this fiction does or does not include certain strangers. I am concerned with these issues of social and psychic inclusion, but I want to try to get at these questions of community and hospitality through the issue of form. Here, "form" is neither the opposite of content or matter, nor the spatial form in Joseph Frank's classic discussion of modern literature that located the structure of a novel in the totality of its symbolic patterns.[1] Borrowing from Niklas Luhmann in *Theories of Distinction: Redescribing the Descriptions of Modernity*, I am defining form as an operation that creates a distinction; it marks a difference between the inside and the outside. Relying on the work of the logician G. Spencer Brown, Luhmann says, "Drawing a distinction severs an unmarked space to construct a form with a marked and unmarked side."[2] In *Laws of Form*, Spencer Brown puts it this way: "The theme of this book is that a universe comes into being when a space is severed or taken apart. The skin of a living organism cuts off an outside from an inside. So does the circumference of a circle in a plane."[3] The circumference of the circle is a boundary. Although we normally think of form as the shape within the circumference of the line, in Luhmann's and Brown's terms, the form is two-sided. Luhmann's is a theory about observation, of observing where the cut of form has been placed. Observation is regarded as a "formal device, a device that brings a world into being."[4] What are the epistemological limits inscribed with this cut? What knowledge is relegated to the outside and upon what distinction does the cut rely?

I want to see how productive this concept of form can be for discussing modernist texts as formal operations of inclusion and exclusion in which boundaries are drawn and, yet, the limits of these boundaries are exposed. This attention to form is, of course, one of the primary features of modernist texts themselves. In the preface to his novel, *Roderick Hudson*, Henry James acknowledges: "Really, universally, relations stop nowhere, and the exquisite problem of the artist is eternally but to draw, by a geometry of his own, the circle within which they should happily *appear* to do so."[5] Compare this statement by James with Luhmann's statement:

> No one can see everything, and one gathers possibilities of observation only by engaging in distinctions that are functioning blindly at the moment of observation because they take the place of, and must hide, the unobservable unity of the world. Distinctions serve as two-sided forms that direct the operations of designating, referring, and connecting.... Knowledge serves—as does, in a different way, art—to render the world invisible as the "unmarked slate." (74)

I want to extrapolate from this idea of form, with some help from discourses on hospitality, to rethink the production of meaning in modernist texts. Like all texts, modernist fiction formally encodes "theories of distinction." Modernist writers, however, make the cut with varying degrees of ironic self-consciousness and an acknowledgment of limitations. The nodal points for this acknowledgment are multiple, but I am particularly interested in how exclusions of a threatening, yet seductive, other inform and deform the text. In these modernist texts, multiple strategies—of telescoping, interchanging, and interpenetrating marked and unmarked spaces reveal the wall drawn between inside and outside to be permeable, the excluded other already within the gates. In linking formal exclusions and inclusions with social and psychic infiltration, I also invoke a concept drawn from Jacques Derrida's work on hospitality, specifically, his description of "absolute hospitality" as a welcoming of "the uninvited guest."[6] The other is an agency that broods over the host, deconstructing the "at-home."

Even before Derrida turned to the explicit theme and figure of hospitality, one could say that the project of deconstruction revealed how "the uninvited guest" dwells within the walls of textual enclosure. In *Of Grammatology*, for example, Derrida shows how Western metaphysical philosophy has attempted to keep the alien at bay.[7] The foundational texts of Western philosophy create a totality that excludes what philosophy cannot master. Yet deconstruction reveals that the alien is already within the walls of the enclosure. Writing is found to be already within the supposed plenitude of speech and presence. In other paradigmatic examples, Derrida performs the same operation. In his essay on Franz Kafka's "Before the Law," for example, he describes the way in which literature and narrative are the uninvited guests at philosophy's table.[8] Through his reading of Kafka, Derrida deconstructs Immanuel Kant's definition of moral law. Kafka's parable shows that in Kant's formulation, even as the law purports to be universal and to precede any particular example of it, the law is contaminated by the very instances, or idioms, it attempts to exclude. Derrida shows that fiction is at the core of legal thought: "Though the authority of the law seems to exclude all historicity and empirical narrativity, and this at the moment when its rationality seems alien to all fiction and imagination—even the transcendental imagination—it still seems *a priori* to shelter these parasites" ("Law" 190). For Derrida, Kafka's fiction rejects the universalizing law of the Kantian categorical imperative and emphasizes, instead, the singular, the particular, that precedes the law in its abstract formulation. Temporally and spatially, the idiom, or literature, is "before the law," already there within it and not a supplement to it.

In "Modernism and Imperialism," his influential treatment of the colonial geography of modernism, Fredric Jameson focuses on the formal deformations engendered by the operations of exclusion in metropolitan modernist fiction. In his reading of such texts, the "unmarked space" takes its revenge. Arguing that modernist texts betray absences or "holes" in them because they are warped by a denial of their imperialist foundations, Jameson puts it this way: "Colonialism means that a significant structural segment of the economic system as a whole is now located elsewhere, beyond the metropolis, outside of the daily life and existential experience of the home country."[9] He points to the *formal* absences in the text that signal this "strategy of containment" (50): "As artistic content it will now henceforth always have something missing about it, but in the sense of a privation that can never be restored or made whole simply by adding back in the missing component: its lack is rather comparable to another dimension, an *outside* like the other face of a mirror, which it constitutively lacks, and which can never be made up or made good" (51, my italics).[10] Jameson's analysis is fruitful for focusing on the way the "outside" signifies textually. However, his provocative analysis has two shortcomings: 1) it fails to account for modernism's ironic or self-deconstructive relation to its own formal geometries of inclusion and exclusion, hospitality and defense, and 2) his rather static view of the mechanisms of the repression of the other in the colonial situation inhibits a more nuanced reading of particular political and psychic variations of the drama of form. For example, he regards *Ulysses* as exempt from the symptomatic deformations of English metropolitan fiction, with their symbolic gaps. In his view, *Ulysses* is a text *adequate* to representing totality because the city of Dublin is both colonial (and thus the colonial is not found "elsewhere") and provincial (everyone knows everyone else). In his strangely naturalistic reading of the Dublin of *Ulysses*, Jameson ignores the way Joyce's semicoloniality complicates, rather than precludes, the deformation of the text.[11]

Before proceeding to focus on geometries of inclusion and exclusion in the first and last stories in Joyce's *Dubliners*, "The Sisters" and "The Dead," I want to illustrate my discussion of modernist form with the example of E. M. Forster's final novel, *A Passage to India*.[12] The novel tests the limits of the form of the English novel as it thematizes and formalizes acts of hospitality between East and West. The form of the English novel Forster inherited could no longer accommodate the things he wanted to say, as he tested the limits of the liberalism of his own injunction, "only connect," from *Howards End*.[13] If the early sections of *A Passage* begin with confident sentences about friendship and loyalty, the traumatic colonial encounter threatens to disrupt what Edward Said has called the "dynastic" form of the nineteenth-century novel.[14] The rhetoric of hospitality, of invitations extended to Indians by the English and to the English by Indians, is threatened by a more radical and disruptive hospitality. As Sara Suleri says in *The Rhetoric of English India*, "even as the narrative assumes descriptive power over the symbolic geography that it maps out, it equally questions the limits of its own claims to comprehensiveness."[15]

This questioning, however, is enacted as a drama of inclusion and exclusion with multiple formal operations. Literary genres, by definition, enact laws of belonging and inclusion. In *A Passage to India*, the "unmarked" and the "marked" no longer remain distinct, as the very distinction between inside and outside teeters. The novel begins by bracketing the extraordinary from the ordinary: "Except for the Marabar Caves—and they are twenty miles off—the city of Chandrapore presents nothing extraordinary" (7). The distinction between the norm and its exception, the city and the Caves, is one that the sane and decent Englishman, Fielding, struggles to maintain. Progressively in the novel, however, mystery refuses to remain within erected enclosures—either in the category of the extraordinary, as is suggested at the beginning, or neatly sandwiched, in a section entitled "Caves," between two other structural demarcations, "Mosque" and "Temple." If initially the Caves figure an impenetrable otherness, the "unmarked" space for the English colonists, the final section of the novel lifts the boundaries between marked and unmarked space, turning hospitality into an uncontrollable event. The result is a challenge to the categories of distinctions upon which humanism itself depends.

Dr. Aziz, the Moslem doctor who desperately seeks friendship with the Englishman, Fielding, voices the idea that friendship itself depends upon its opposite, exclusion, and that acts of hospitality must be controlled: "We must exclude someone from our gathering, or we shall be left with nothing," he says early in the book (38). Yet *A Passage to India* stages the collapse of this geometry of exclusion. While the incident in the cave is the event that does violence to the regulated behaviors of host and guest, it is in the final section of the novel, "Temple," that there emerges a more radical challenge to the distinctions upon which liberal humanism is based. In the thought experiments of the Hindu, Narayan Godbole, in which he tries to stretch the geometry of inclusion beyond its normal humanist categories, Forster reaches toward a philosophy of radical hospitality. In the figure of Hindu inclusiveness, the novel extends Forster's previous novelistic stagings of the encounter with otherness that occurred wholly within a European context (in effect, the "other" is German in *Howards End* and Italian in *A Room with a View* and *Where Angels Fear to Tread*[16]). The final section of the novel, "Temple," represents a breach of both the Western and Eastern forms that have attempted to contain the reach of hospitality and restrict the disruptive effects of the extraordinary:

> Thus Godbole, though she was not important to him, remembered an old woman he had met in Chandrapore days. Chance brought her into his mind while it was in this heated state, he did not select her; she happened to occur among the throng of soliciting images, a tiny

splinter, and he impelled her by his spiritual force to that place where completeness can be found. Completeness, not reconstruction. His senses grew thinner, he remembered a wasp seen he forgot where, perhaps on a stone. He loved the wasp equally, he impelled it likewise, he was imitating God. And the stone where the wasp clung—could he ... no, he could not, he had been wrong to attempt the stone, logic and conscious effort had seduced, he came back to the strip of red carpet and discovered that he was dancing upon it. (286)

Mysteriously, Godbole has not experienced the moment with the wasp; it is Mrs. Moore's memory of the creature that transmits itself to him. The wasp is seen by Mrs. Moore in the first section of the novel when she reaches to hang up her cloak on a peg. She thinks, "Perhaps he mistook the peg for a branch—no Indian animal has any sense of an interior" (35). On the one hand, this sentence can be taken as an instance of the Western projection of intransigence and irrationality onto the colonial landscape. Yet, on the other hand, the wasp becomes a symbol of the puncturing of the membrane separating private memories as well as the ethical difference between the human and the animal. In his thought experiment, Godbole attempts to stretch inclusiveness to encompass the stone, but he reaches his limit—his act of inclusion cannot extend to the inanimate world. "One old Englishwoman and one little, little wasp," Godbole thinks to himself, and then goes on to reflect, "It does not seem much, still it is more than I am myself" (291). Forster's novel tests the myths of shared sympathies and secure superiorities, what S. P. Mohanty has called "the ambiguous imperial-humanist myth of our shared human attributes which are supposed to distinguish us from animals."[17] Godbole attempts to challenge the sentimentality and chauvinism of this basic humanism. He tries to imagine the consciousness of the other in his own thoughts and manages to include the wasp, another living thing, but his hospitality founders on the inclusion of inanimate stone. Indeed, at the end of the novel, the inanimate landscape functions as an impasse to colonial friendship. As Suleri points out, human impasse is displaced onto the physical landscape of India—"'No, not yet,' and the sky said, 'No, not there'" (144).

Yet, Hinduism and the Indian landscape themselves feel strangely like surrogates for some alterity beyond the geometry of inclusion the text constructs and tests. In drawing the operative distinction between colonialist and colonial subject, in creating a drama of interchange between marked and unmarked space, Forster allows the distinction between heterosexuality and homosexuality to be occluded. Homoeroticism within *A Passage to India* goes for the most part unacknowledged, along with its contribution to the volatility of the colonial encounter. In his posthumously published short-story collection, including "The Other Boat," written in 1957–1958, and "The Life to Come" (the one story in his collection written before *A Passage to India* was completed), Forster explores new categories of distinctions within the previously "unmarked" side of homoeroticism.[18] In these stories, the "ordinary" and "extraordinary" are reversed: "I shall never write another novel after [*A Passage to India*]," Forster wrote to Siegfried Sassoon in 1923, "my patience with ordinary people has given out. But I shall go on writing. I don't feel any decline in my 'powers.'"[19] As early as 1911, Forster wrote of his "sterility" and "weariness . . . of the only subject that I both can and may treat—the love of men for women & vice versa" ("Introduction" xiv). Although Suleri cautions against explaining the silences in *A Passage to India* by invoking Forster's own homosexuality, she nonetheless admits that the novel is "both an engagement with and a denial of a colonial homoerotic imperative" (147). The posthumously published stories, in contrast, are hospitable to the knowledge of the eroticism and violence that inform the colonial encounter. If *A Passage to India* tests the limits of the liberal fiction of Indians and Englishmen being in the same boat, the short story yokes together by violence the partners in colonial encounter in an "Other Boat" entirely. In this fictional vessel, interpenetration, not interchange, is the rule, as the orifices of the text (but only implicitly, the body) admit the other. The admission of this other knowledge still operates covertly; indeed, the sexual act of sodomy is euphemistically represented in the novel. But knowledge comes from beyond or behind the boundary. As Mark C. Taylor points out in a discussion of alterity in Emmanuel Levinas, "There are at least two things the subject never sees, or never sees directly: his face and his backside. Bodily orifices like eyes, ears, nostrils, mouth, and anus elude the specular gaze. Nor can the thetic subject 'see' itself constituting itself in acts intended to establish its identity by repressing everything that defiles the body proper."[20] In the more truncated "cut" of the short story, Forster represents the ambiguous dominations, subjections, and interpenetrations in the colonial encounter.[21]

For Joyce, too, the formal brevity of the short story aptly telescopes the process in which regulated forms of hospitality erupt into stranger, more queer and disruptive encounters with the other. In the two stories that frame *Dubliners*, "The Sisters" and "The Dead," boundaries are established and then breached with violence—the boundary between the living and the dead and the boundary between host and guest. What Joyce called the "style of scrupulous meanness" (*Letters II* 134) works to police the borders, titrating the role of the other and regulating encounters with the dead. The "scrupulous meanness" of the writing of these stories in a sense mirrors the "scrupulous[ness]" of Father Flynn and Gabriel Conroy, who seek to regulate and master their responsibility to the other (*D* 17). In the rituals of the mass and confession in the case of Father Flynn, and in rituals of hosting and cosmopolitan generosity in the case of Gabriel Conroy, the other is invited to the table. Communion is offered in the expected places. Yet the controlled and legislated forms of communion and hospitality between "the living and the dead" and the self and the other give way to something queerer (*D* 224). In both stories, more radical eruptions of hospitality and encounter mark the text indelibly by including that which form and style have sought to repress. What is missing becomes a palpable absence, as the very brevity of the narrative form exerts a kind of pressure. The "cut" of form that mostly passes unnoticed finds its emblem in the "*gnomon*," the incomplete form cited in the first story, "The Sisters" (*D* 9).

In these stories, the dead brood over the living until an uncanny visitation occurs. In "The Sisters," a deeply disturbing annunciation is staged as the dead Father Flynn invades the dreams of the narrator as a young boy, alarmingly reversing the roles of guest and host. In "The Dead," the civilized hospitality that Gabriel Conroy praises gives way to a more radical kind of visitation that shatters his identity. In this radical hospitality to the ghosts of the dead, Gabriel is forced to rethink hospitality under what Anne Dufourmantelle has called "the threat of finitude and love" (*Hospitality* 148). In both stories, language and form are marked by this alterity.

"There was no hope for him this time: it was the third stroke" (*D* 9). When we come upon the first sentence of "The Sisters," the word "stroke" is ambiguous—is it a cardiovascular episode or the sound of the clock? And who is the "he" for whom it is too late—the narrator or someone else? We learn that the stroke is the paralytic episode Father Flynn has already suffered when the story begins, the stroke that has already ended his life. Yet it is also the stroke that at once begins the story and cuts us off from the encounter so central to the narrative: the encounter between the priest and the young boy. Both the boy, arriving at the house, and the reader, coming to the story's beginning, arrive belatedly, after Father Flynn takes his mysteries to the grave. In conventional terms, the most important events in the story have already occurred: the breaking of the chalice and the development of the relationship between the priest and the boy. We begin the story with the sense of having missed something; the present is like an incision between past and future. If most narratives naturalize their Jamesian task of drawing a geometry of inclusion, Joyce, instead, makes us aware of the "cut" of form. When the word "*gnomon*" surfaces in the boy's consciousness, it provides a geometrical figure for the incompletion we experience.

In his essay "Before the Law," Derrida writes that the law "figures itself as a kind of place, a *topos* and a taking place" ("Law" 200). This definition highlights both the spatial aspect of law, its topography, and its aspect as event, as a "taking place." "The Sisters" opens Joyce's collection so powerfully because it is a story in which the boy's and the reader's exclusion from the law of the father is represented as cryptic and encrypted both temporally and spatially. We stand at the gates of the law, like Kafka's protagonist, attracted to and excluded from the mystery of Father Flynn. In barring us from the crucial dramatic events preceding the priest's death—the dropping of the chalice and encounters between priest and boy—the narrative establishes a screen. Writing of Kafka, Derrida says, "The inaccessible incites from its place of hiding" ("Law" 191). Although "The Sisters" begins with ambiguity about the priest's death (the boy looks for the sign of the two candles in the window to confirm his suspicions), once the death is established, the boy longs to enter the priest's inner chamber, to view death's work, but has "not the courage to knock" (*D* 12). The eponymous sisters encourage the boy's desire to enter the room of death, but the adults do not encourage him to probe its cryptic knowledge. Indeed, the formal barring of our access to the law is heightened by the euphemism and cliché the adults employ to block the boy's access to this deeply unsettling queerness of the priest. Like the understated phrase "idle chalice" (*D* 18), a term that masks the depth of the priest's disappointment in his failed priesthood, the idle words work to contain, in ordinary language, the significant, but deeply unsettling, tutorials that have taken place. The sisters struggle to name and yet not to name this queerness: "—He was too scrupulous always," and "—Mind you, I noticed there was something queer coming over him latterly" (*D* 17, 16). The women go about their business of overseeing the house of mourning. The men have a more disturbing sense of the priest's relationship with the boy. They more actively defend against the knowledge of the priest's queerness, as evidenced by the ellipses in their sentences: "—No, I wouldn't say he was exactly... but there was something queer... there was something uncanny about him" (*D* 9–10). "Queer" is not just the word the adults use to name their sense of the danger in the close encounter between the priest and the boy. "Queer" is the distortion of language into ellipses; "queer" is the odd displacement of the title; "queer" is the gnomon, a truncated form.[22]

As the narrator struggles to make sense of his relationship with Father Flynn, he too seeks refuge in the ordinary. If he is drawn to the house, almost fatefully ("Night after night I had passed the house" [*D* 9]), the normalcy of his explanation—"(it was vacation time)" (*D* 9)—is meant to deflect the disturbing suggestion of compulsion. He remembers those "ordinary days" at the drapery store where the priest and sisters live, days when a notice "used to hang in the window, saying: *Umbrellas Re-covered*" (*D* 12), and he minimizes the impact of the priest's death (he finds it "strange" that neither he nor the day is in mourning [*D* 12]). Umbrellas and language recovered, however, are not sufficiently prophylactic to protect the boy from the emerging effects of his encounters with the priest. In the orientalized eroticism of his dream, the drapery of the everyday returns as the "long velvet curtains" of Persia (*D* 13). The dream intrudes on the boy's awareness, representing his unstable identification with, and responsibility toward, the priest. As he does in Hosty's Ballad in *Finnegans Wake* (*FW* 44–45), Joyce mines the reversals and paradoxes implicit in the act of hospitality that are present etymologically in the Latin word from which "host" derives, *hostia*, meaning sacrifice and victim.[23] In the dream, the two figures change roles, as the priest seems to summon the boy to hear his confession: "[T]he grey face still followed me. It murmured, and I understood that it desired to confess something. . . . I felt that I too was smiling feebly as if to absolve the simoniac of his sin" (*D* 11). Taylor points out that in writing of the responsibility to the other, Levinas speaks of the Infinite which comes to pass in the face of the neighbor, who "summons" the subject (211). Taylor says that Levinas likens this summons to a citation or a "susception," meaning a "taking (of holy orders)" (211). In the frightening encounter enacted in the dream, the boy identifies with the infinite responsibility that overwhelmed the priest in his office. "The duties of the priesthood was too much for him," Eliza says in characteristic understatement (*D* 17). The breaking of the chalice is the outward sign of this breach that occurred long before the priest's death.

In the strange and foreign words "simony" and "simoniac" (*D* 9, 11), the perversion of responsibility to the Infinite is introduced, for sacred hospitality is a gift and not a sale. In the pact between them, the boy senses an unsavory bribe of some sort, an erotic exchange that accompanies tutelage in the mysteries of priestly ritual. In *Joyce and the Politics of Egoism*, Jean-Michel Rabaté suggests that "sodomy" is the repressed term in the story, the fourth or missing corner of the "gnomon."[24] Indeed, in an important discussion of hospitality that focuses on *Ulysses*, he says that "sodomy" might appear "as the arch-sin" in the short-story collection, "precisely because in its inception it just describes a city in which human relations are perverted, without bringing a clear accusation against male homoeroticism" (168). Yet the move from "simony," the word that mesmerizes the boy, to "sodomy," a word and concept not presented in the text, must be carefully described. On the one hand, this suggested link captures the erotic penetration of the boy's psyche that goes unacknowledged by the narrator. Through one of the many examples of substitution and displacement in the story, the boy's fascination and disgust with the fluids in the priest's mouth and his habit of letting "his tongue lie upon his lower lip" suggest a different kind of exchange (*D* 13). In calling it the "arch-sin," Rabaté appears to relegate this attraction to the realm of criminality, whereas the story remains far more ambiguous in its presentation of the eroticism of the priesthood's mysteries and responsibilities to the other.

In commenting on "An Encounter," Margot Norris has pointed out that there is a contradiction between Joyce's description of these stories as from the point of view of a young boy and the sense of the language and perception of an adult.[25] In "The Sisters," too, the meaning of the close encounter is never rationalized in a coherent perspective. But the apostolic attraction of the priesthood makes "The Sisters" a queerer story with which to begin the collection than the more explicit story of "An Encounter." For unlike the accidental meeting between pedophile and boy in "An Encounter," the inaugural story of the collection locates the queerness at the very heart of the cryptic law of the father. What remains outside the story proper, the blind spot still beyond the circle of its form, is the value of the story's telling: Is this a narrative of trauma, the demand for which comes from the necessity of repeating and working through (like the ancient mariner doomed to stop the wedding guest)? Or is the narrative an act of conflicted rescue, a recognition that, within the life of a young boy, secret knowledge has been transferred to the apostle? In this inaugural story of Joyce's collection, Dublin is a place where the dead brood over the living, haunting the home front and estranging it from itself.

In "The Dead," as in "The Sisters," an attempt is made to contain openness to the other in ritual forms of hospitality, most prominently in the event at the story's center; the party. At the party, an inner circle of friends is welcomed, while strangers are kept on the outside looking in at the warmth and welcome around the table. The prose of "The Dead" enacts a careful geometry of inclusion and exclusion, a party of its own that catalogues the welcomed items and just as carefully excludes others. The lavish and loving inclusion of the details of the dinner amid its presentation, their paratactic listing and savoring, echo the preparations of the hosts. The prose, like the planning of the party, is a means of controlling the admitted guests.

As the favorite nephew and privileged guest, Gabriel Conroy is the would-be host, the male spokesperson for the female acts of hospitality. Like a good hostess with a checklist for a perfect party, Gabriel begins with both his speech and his life-script more or less intact, in conformity with a cosmopolitan narrative of tolerance, generosity, and acceptance. Helping with bad guests like Freddy Malins and parasites like Mr. Browne, he is the sovereign presence in the story, the host who presides. Gabriel believes in the laws of hospitality that govern the Greeks, laws that insure certain rights and privileges for the guests as they sit at table. Such classic hospitality depends upon power and mastery, the sovereignty of the host that allows him to exclude an improper guest and, conversely, to say who is welcomed to sit at the table. Indeed, Gabriel explicitly takes hospitality for his after-dinner subject, juxtaposing the hospitality of the past with the more modern refusals that rattle him from a woman like Miss Ivors. Against what he perceives as the narrowness of her Irish chauvinism, he proposes an urbane, European cosmopolitanism. As Rabaté and other critics have pointed out, Gabriel's view of hospitality is "fissured" first when Lily, then Miss Ivors, then Gretta puncture his carefully composed view of the pact between guest and host and his evocation of the stability of "home" (158).

Yet I would argue that the story challenges the concept of old-fashioned hospitality even more radically than Rabaté suggests and ascribes a deeper, more threatening, and potentially more valuable openness to the unexpected guest. The appearance of the alien in what Rabaté refers to as the "fake universality" of hospitality is both more disturbing and radical than mere exposure of the limits of a too-facile humanism (157). Gabriel's namesake is the Archangel who brings to Mary the news of the Holy Ghost's visitation. Gabriel Conroy faces the disruptive annunciation of Michael Furey, a ghost who disrupts his identity. As Anne Dufourmantelle points out in her dialogue with Derrida in *Of Hospitality*, death is the final visitor: "Death carries off what it touches, it precisely does not 'visit.' The hospitality it gives is definitive and cannot be reciprocated. It is Orpheus in search of Eurydice: in wanting to take her back from death, it is he who will be carried off" (*Hospitality* 150). Although Michael Furey is literally "carried off" by death, Gabriel, the host, is himself taken hostage by the same visitor, as he feels himself approach "that region where dwell the vast hosts of the dead" (D 223). In trying to reach Gretta/Eurydice and bring her back from her memories, he himself is carried away. The story ends outside of the geometry of responsibility Gabriel has so carefully tried to draw. Host and guest dissolve as the (g)host of Michael Furey haunts the place from which he has been excluded by Gretta's silence and Gabriel's complacency.

This unconditional hospitality is mediated by a prior moment, during which Gabriel looks at Gretta with "a strange friendly pity" (D 222). Although this look is often read as one more instance of control that Gabriel exercises over his wife, it can be read otherwise. Here, the *xenia*, the pact between the host and the stranger, comes in the unusual guise of friendship, a friendship between husband and wife. As opposed to the case of colonial friendship straining the liberal framework of *A Passage to India*, Gabriel's "strange friendly pity" is a form of hospitality that marks a disruption of the familiar and formulaic. In place of the lust that he hoped would rekindle the old relationship between Gretta and himself is a new feeling, a feeling so strange that its only translation is in terms of a familiar word, "friendship," one that had never entered the conjugal relationship before. This change, in a quiet and undramatic register, stretches the familiar to include the "strange."

But what of the lyricism that ends the story? This prose factors into a discussion of hospitality because it has presented an interpretive crux precisely around the issue of inclusiveness. Critics have posed the question: do the lyrical rhythms signal Gabriel's retrenchment into self-absorption, a shrinking of capacity in which the self only masquerades as engaged in community? Or do these rhythms represent a fading out of boundaries, a place where the self fuses with the living and the dead? In "Dead Ends: Joyce's Finest Moments," Seamus Deane critiques Joyce's style in *Dubliners* as an *exclusionary* device; he claims that Joyce's lyricism "excludes ethics by the intensification of repetitive rhythms that betoken morbid self-obsession. It is the opposite of an ethical condition."[26] Speaking of the end of "A Painful Case," Deane says that "the fleeting prospect [of an ethical condition] ... disappears as the serried ranks of final sentences close up in their neat, neurotic repetitions" (25). Deane acknowledges that, in this example, Joyce's purpose is to betray the character's paralysis, to show him in a state that is the opposite of active engagement with the other. However, Deane's more sweeping and damaging claim in his essay is that Joyce's own fine writing in "The Dead," in particular, reveals that he succumbs to his own lyricism. Deane accuses Joyce himself of maintaining exclusion and thereby relinquishing the possibility of either an ethics (an encounter with a single other) or a politics (an encounter with a group of third persons in solidarity).

I would argue that Deane's equation between style and politics ignores the way that the lyricism concluding "The Dead" opens up to the anonymous third person through Gabriel's unexpected response to Gretta. The abstraction in the phrase "the living and the dead" enters the text *after* the dead are brought nearer the living through the narration of Gretta's experience, that is, after the boundary between the two is breached in the singular. The anonymous third person, the other, is thus instantiated in the singularity of a particular person, a second person singular, that is, the "you" of Gretta.[27]

The newspaper account that snow is "general over Ireland" (*D* 223) is, on the one hand, the media's creation of an imagined community that elides the fissures we know to exist between Celtic and English and between the West and East of Ireland. Yet alongside this fantasy of national unity, alongside the pseudo-unity created by the weather, is a hospitality to the other that passes through the particular, the idiomatic; in this case, Gretta is transformed from Gabriel's view of the symbolic woman hearing "distant music" to a haggard and very particular sleeping face (*D* 210).

It is just this encounter between abstraction and particularity, law and singularity that occurs in *Ulysses*, a text in which the idiomatic mediates fictions of totality. If "Jewgreek is greekjew. Extremes meet" (*U* 15.2098–99), the significance of encounter in *Ulysses* does not remain within abstractions but involves the graphic inscription of the smell and touch and feel of a particular other. The opening of the text is enacted in "Calypso," where the novel begins anew, replaying its own narrative time: "Mr Bloom ate with relish the inner organs of beasts and fowls" (*U* 4.01–2). Bloom puts the organs in the organization of the novel (in the Linati and Gilbert schemas, Stephen's episodes have no "organs" assigned to them[28]). If it is first in Stephen's dream that a Bloom-like figure makes a gesture of hospitality

("In. Come. Red carpet spread" [*U* 3.368–69]), in beginning itself again with Bloom this time around, the novel enacts hospitality to a different kind of flesh, perceived most intimately by Stephen in "Eumaeus": "Yes, Stephen said uncertainly, because he thought he felt a strange kind of flesh of a different man approach him, sinewless and wobbly and all that" (*U* 16.1723–24).

12

Joyce in Transit

> Besides how could you remember everybody? Eyes, walk voice. Well, the voice, yes: gramophone. Have a gramophone in every grave or keep it in the house. After dinner on a Sunday. Put on poor old great-grandfather. Kraahraark! Hellohellohello amawfullyglad kraark awfullygladaseeagain hellohello amawf krpthsth. (*U* 6.962–66)
>
> —What is a ghost? Stephen said with tingling energy. One who has faded into impalpability through death, through absence, through change of manners. (*U* 9.147–49)

Like his characters Leopold Bloom and Stephen Dedalus, Joyce was obsessed by the haunting voices of the dead. While Bloom fantasizes about the technological voiceprint of "greatgrandfather," Stephen, always more abstract in approach, defines a ghost in terms of "impalpability" and "absence": "A ghost," he says in the library chapter, is "one who has faded into impalpability through death, through absence, through change of manners."[1] As Maria DiBattista has remarked, one might take Stephen's definition as a description of the way literary influence works across generations and cultural boundaries, a kind of "transculturation": "Metempsychosis, the resubstantiation of ghosts that Joyce took for his literary model in *Ulysses*, is always a transcultural act, since the summoned and reincarnated spirit inevitably returns to different times, altered ways of living."[2]

In their afterlife, Joyce and his texts are carried metempsychotically across cultural, linguistic, national, and gender divides to undergo a "change of manners." Post-Joycean writers and translators engage in what Plato called anamnesis, recollection or an act of recovery, which can be refigured as an inner listening to the voices of the dead. This notion of a text's afterlife, which underwrites both Stephen's and, to a lesser extent, Bloom's metaphoric descriptions of inheritance, applies to translation as well as imitation. "The Platonic doctrine of the divine inspiration of poetry clearly had repercussions for the translator, in that it was deemed possible for the 'spirit' or 'tone' of the original to be recreated in another cultural context. The translator, therefore, is seeking to bring about a 'transmigration' of the original text, which he approaches on both a technical and metaphysical level, as a skilled equal with duties and responsibilities both to the original author and the audience," writes Susan Bassnett-McGuire in her book on translation.[3] The inheritors of Joyce, writers and translators alike, work this territory, between Stephen's impalpable ghost and Bloom's voiceprint, between inspiration and *techné*.

Yet both post-structuralism and cultural studies (particularly postcolonial studies) have taught us to interrogate this Platonic vocabulary of origin and presence, the idea that an "essence of Joyce" can be bottled for posterity. Post-structuralism forces us to explore how the literary icon "Joyce" is *constructed* by the inheritors who need him. In his emblematic reading of how Socrates and Plato appear in Matthew Paris's postcard (Socrates seated at a writing desk, with Plato standing behind), Derrida says that it is the son and inheritor who dictates the legacy he wants to receive: "The presumptive heir, Plato, of whom it is said that he writes, has never written, he receives the inheritance but as the legitimate addressee he has dictated it, has had it written and has sent it to himself."[4] This Joycean "inversion," the son fathering the father, suggests that anamnesis and projection are intertwined, that writers construct what they can use from cultural icons such as "Joyce" and wrestle with or discard what they cannot. "Put on poor old greatgrandfather," Bloom thinks, and there is a double entendre in the phrase "put on," insinuating that listening to the dead may involve a "doing" of their voices in ventriloquy (like that of Shakespeare in "Circe").

If Derrida's remark subverts the notion of a pure original bequeathed to inheritors, cultural and postcolonial studies further remind us of the political overtones of any ghosting of one writer by another. One cannot describe the transmission of an essence or spirit from the "beyond" *without* considering the materiality of language, culture, and history that clings in the process. The admonitions of postcolonial theory, in particular, remind us that a nonhierarchical coexistence of cultures is a myth; the international importation and exportation of cultural icons is a politically loaded project. Hospitality across borders involves ambivalence. These reminders are particularly germane to the concept of a transcultural Joyce. The dominant view of Joyce's greatness has encouraged his portrayal as an internationalist: either, as he functioned for Richard Ellmann and Hugh Kenner, in the role of defining figure of modernism, bricoleur of European literature and languages, or as he functioned for Franco Moretti, in the role of a pathologist who conducts "a monumental autopsy of an entire social formation," that of liberal capitalism.[5] Instead, it is important to place "Joyce" and his afterlife in a context at once more local and more global than his previous European designation—that is, presenting him as at once more particularly "Irish" *and* more postcolonial, in a literary mapping that includes other formally colonized states. This is not to say that the European context is eschewed here, only that "international modernism" is recognized as a particular positioning on a scale of affiliations and cultural encounters. "To revise the problem of global space from the postcolonial perspective," Homi Bhabha writes in *The Location of Culture,* "is to move the location of cultural difference away from the space of demographic *plurality* to the borderline negotiations of cultural translation."[6] In focusing on the way Joyce is translated, rewritten, and reread across different cultures and languages, one can attempt to engage the local dynamics of "borderline negotiations" considered in a transnational context.

Joyce as cultural icon provides a particularly interesting case for such an investigation, since he himself can be said to occupy a special borderline position—both canonical modernist and Irish writer of colonial and postcolonial periods, or, as Fredric Jameson and others have described him, a "First World, Third World" artist. Jameson conceives of Joyce in the "exceptional situation" of "overlap and coexistence" between two incommensurable realities of the metropolis and of the colony simultaneously. He reads *Ulysses* as the product of such a situation "which reproduces the appearance of First World social reality and social relationships . . . but whose underlying structure is in fact much closer to that of the Third World or of colonized daily life."[7] Seamus Deane, Terry Eagleton, Emer Nolan, and Declan Kiberd, as well as Jameson, have restored the significance of Joyce's position as an Irish writer writing in the first half of the twentieth century. As Kiberd says of Ireland, "The country was, and still is, one of those areas where two codes most vividly meet: and, as such, its culture offers itself as an analytical tool at the very twilight of European artistic history. . . . Radical modernism, as practised by a Joyce or a Rushdie, has been a prolonged attempt to render this accounting, [that is] to write a narrative of the colonizers and colonized, in which the symbiotic relation between the two becomes manifest."[8] This recent criticism has restored the discussion of Joyce to the colonial politics of its production, reconceiving the aesthetics of modernism in relation to the colonial past and the postcolonial present.

The repositioning of Joyce as an *Irish* writer in contemporary criticism might seem to militate against his consideration in more global and transcultural terms. On the contrary, recent explorations of the scope of Joyce's community affiliations—metropolitan, national, and international—till the field for such discussion, examining Joyce's own "transcultural" position on the border. For the question of Joyce's Irishness is itself vexed by the issue of representation and address: How does one speak of the "constituency" Joyce represents? Dublin, Ireland, Europe? In what sense does he speak to and even for the postcolonial position? Indeed, "Irishness" itself cannot be taken for granted. Transculturality operates within Ireland itself. Joyce as a particular cultural icon has been "useful" to writers within Ireland and of Irish descent, for whom he comes across divides other than national, such as the divide of gender, in the case of Eavan Boland, the Irish poet, for example. Boland has discussed the mystery of influence even within a national culture: "The fact is that I began my writing life learning the categories of Irishness and identity which he had spent all his resisting."[9] For one writer or translator to make "use" of a predecessor involves a complex process of selection, misuse, and misreading. Boland has discussed why Joyce has not been more influential on Irish women writers, particularly poets. She highlights the multiple cultures within Irish society as well as lines that connect and separate based on geography and gender. In pondering the mysteries of influence, Boland asks why Joyce was both "the most present of Irish writers . . . [and] one of the least available." She says, "The Dublin I began to write in was a divided city and a conflicted poetic culture."[10]

A product of an English mother and Irish father who grew up mainly in England, Brigid Brophy apostrophizes Joyce in her novel *In Transit: An Heroi-Cyclic Novel*. A self-entitled "misprinted mistranslated overestimated sadomasturbatory pornofantasy-narrative,"[11] the novel both salutes and critiques the Irish patriarch. For Brophy, as for Stephen Dedalus before her, the father's voiceprint is so powerful that she can "hear" him only by making a rebellious gesture of tuning him out: "Old Father Finnegan Go-and-don'tsinagain . . . I can't hear you, ex-father. I've switched me deaf-aid off" (228).

In the *Dictionary of Literary Biography*, S. J. Newman calls Brigid Brophy "one of the oddest, most brilliant, and most enduring of . . . 1960s symptoms."[12] Brophy describes her own work as a "howl for tolerance" (*Dictionary* 138), and in that expression she aligns her fiction and essays with the disruptive cry for liberation that the sixties have come to represent. If *In Transit*, published in 1969, is a "symptom" of the sixties, it is a distinctly *post-1968* sensibility also represented in such works as Deleuze and Guattari's *Anti-Oedipus: Capitalism and Schizophrenia* (published in French in 1972), as well as Kristeva's essays during the sixties and seventies (collected in *Desire in Language: A Semiotic Approach to Literature and Art*).[13] *In Transit's* indeterminately sexed and multiply-split narrator declares at one point: "Our programme:—Undo the Normative Conquest" (27).

Indeed, the wickedly satiric narrative skewers shibboleths of "mainstream" culture, staging various countercultural uprisings—sexual, political, linguistic. Lyotard's account of how postmodernism welcomes the collapse of master narratives is predicted in the novel.

However, in staging its own version of the "revolution of the word," Brophy's novel acknowledges what is often repressed in discussions of postmodernism—its profound debt to, and anxiety of influence toward, modernism. Specifically, Brophy's anarchic text exposes its own underpinnings, one might call it, in Joyce's work—"Pardon me, ma'am," the narrative voice says to its self-created "interlocutor," "your mollibloomers is shewin'" (35). Brophy's is a postmodern text that explores its own origins in an Irish-inflected modernism. Anticipating Jameson's work, her metacritical narrative suggests that Ireland's colonial history makes Joyce's fiction both postcolonial and modernist. On the one hand, Brophy's novel presents the Irish as linked to other colonial groups in their experience of "transculturation" as "disculturation," to use Fernando Ortiz's term.[14] "We speak English as a foreign language, even when we have no other. (This is my foster-mother-tongue, since when I have used no other.) . . . Imperialism gave us Irish/Indians/West Indians its vocabulary, but the idiom wouldn't travel. Imperialism steeped us in its pan-citizenship and receded, leaving us the first non-citizens" (*In Transit* 34–35).

On the other hand, the Irish are represented as a special case of the colonial legacy—particularly inventive foster children:

We Irish had the right word on the tip of our tongue, but the imperialist got at that. What should trip off it we trip over. . . . What begins as endemic lapsus linguae we peddle as precious lapis, with which we illuminate our Book of Sells (an early Book of Ours). We are never knowingly underbold. We are in the grips of compunsion. Youlysses have fore-suffered all. (35)

Both the pain and benefit of this linguistic lapse are exacerbated in the condition of Irish expatriation: "Transplant us further, who are unrooted in the first place, banish us from growth and home, banshe banhe, and we will astonish you by how we run to riot in false flowerings of double-headed counterfeit coinages" (35). "Compunsion" is both compulsion and compensation, and out of this mixture of necessity and invention comes a distinctly Irish (and Joycean) contribution to modernist linguistic experiment. Aside from a few stray phrases in Latin and other languages, the language of *In Transit* exemplifies this compunsion, composed, as it is, in a Joycean English of rhyme, pun, and rebus. Indeed, early on in the novel, the narrator fantasizes that he/she grabs a mike ("mike" is both a microphone and an allusion to the Irish) and announces a debt to his/her famous compatriot: "My fantasy steps tiptoed up on that ever-tempting serpent, my compatriot, mike. Should I snatch it and announce to all In Transit my tribute to my great Triestine compalien, the comedichameleon, the old pun gent himself? I could loose on the Lounge his obituary: I am the voyce of one crying in the wilderness; reJoyce with me" (35–36). The narrator "does" Joyce's transcultural voices; it is Joyce's possessive mastery in dispossession that informs the undoing of "Normative" Conquests.

Yet if the novel names Joyce as transcultural forefather, it nevertheless also treats him as a father who must be outgrown. For the "Triestine compalien" is, after all, both *compatriot* and *alien*. At the end of the novel, Pat (one of the main narrators, who also doubles as Patrice) renounces Joyce's legacy in an apostrophe that ironically echoes Stephen Dedalus's address to his mythical namesake in *A Portrait of the Artist as a Young Man*: "Old Father Finnegan Go-and-don'tsinagain . . . Well, I saw through you, you old pro-facade, before I was out of my boyhood or girlhood . . . I can't hear you, ex-father. I've switched me deaf-aid off" (228). In this passage, which also evokes the deaf-eared dialogue of the washerwomen in the *Wake*, Brophy suggests both allegiance to and rejection of the law of the father. For in her exploration of a postgendered position for her protagonist, Brophy both draws on and trumps the gender instabilities in Joyce's texts. Like Boland, Brophy suggests that the Joycean revolution of the word works its disruptions still within a certain phallic framework. Brophy's central metaphors of circulation and transit attempt to figure more radical indeterminacies of sexual identity, even as they pay homage to Joycean (and, by way of Joyce, Odyssean) exile.

The "in transit" of Brophy's title refers most literally to the setting of the novel and situation of its main protagonist. The "action" takes place in a European airport lounge, in which the adult protagonist, an Irish orphan whose two sets of parents, natural and foster, have been killed in plane crashes, decides not to take his or her scheduled flight. While this would-be traveler circulates within the airport transit lounge, planes take off unpredictably and, for a while, not at all. Indeed, for much of the time, all scheduled flights are canceled, a cancellation which suggests that detour and digression have replaced purposeful trajectory. "Within this pocket," the first-person narrator says in the first of four sections: "within this fully accounted-for, justified and sewn-up detour in my life, I can be simultaneously relaxed and efficient. I am on my way yet free to stray" (23). He/she muses on the emblematic quality of the transit lounge which is a "droplet of the twentieth century; pure, isolated, rare twentieth century" (22). The narrator conducts "a sit-in on the present tense" (29).

This suspended present is likened by the narrator to "a free-ranging womb," a vessel of transformation, in which stable identities are unbound, including the narrator's. By the end of the novel, the narrator concludes: "out of that egg, ego too am re-hatched. It no longer matters a damn of course whether 'I' is masc. or fem. or whether 'you' is sing. or plur." (228). The narrator ponders, "Suppose the structure which, like an organic conveyor belt, has been *transporting* [my italics] all my thoughts and experiences all these years is but an arbitrary convention?" (217). Such a realization about the arbitrariness of structures, including the linguistic and narrative syntax that keeps subjects and objects in their places, requires a deconstruction of sorts.

In section II, the first-person narrator/traveler, realizing he/she has forgotten his/her sex and sexual orientation, hilariously careens from one position to another in a Beckett-like journey. Sitting in the lounge, the narrator tries subtly, and unsuccessfully, to ascertain his/her sex and gender. For example, he/she seeks the privacy of the lavatory to "see for himself/herself," but realizes (à la Lacan) that knowledge of his/her sex must precede an entrance into the men's or ladies' room. The fact that most of the first two sections of the novel are cast in the first person is important, since the first-person pronoun is ungendered, leaving the reader as well as the narrator with no clue as to the narrator's gender. The narrator tries to arrive at "an exhaustive tabulation of the sexual ways in which I could, and in one of which I must, be related to my fellow beings": "I am a man/I am a woman/I am a homosexual man/I am a homosexual woman" (89). But this strict parsing of possibilities fails to solve the problem and the repeated grammatical structure of the sentence—subject verb complement—seems to reify fixed cultural assumptions and to preclude more fluid permutations of sexual possibilities. ("I noticed," the speaker tells us, "I had unconsciously compared being a woman to negativeness and being homosexual to partialness" [89]). The novel becomes a detective novel and a hunt for the possibly missing (and probably stolen) phallus. (The second section is entitled "Sexshuntwo the Case of the Missing (Re)Member.") In section III, the narrator splits into a double character called "Unruly" and "O'Hooligan" (72) on the one hand and O'Rooly on the other. Both mischief maker and detective, the agonistic protagonist alternates between pleasure in free circulation and an attempt to maintain order and curb errant behavior:

> Hooligan, I accused myself, o hooligan O'Hooligan: you're the hooligan who by night crept into the hall of sculpture (glided into the gliptotek, you did, hooligan) and vandalised the exhibits by chopping 'em all in two across the waistline, after which you hooligamused yourself by re-assorting the demi-torsos and putting the from-the-waist-up of the Venus de Milo on top of the from-the-waist-down of the Hermes of Praxiteles.
> A grand old mutilation of the sperms, *that* was. WellI'llbeciades (72).[15]

The absence of the "member" and of "memory" launches a fantastic, punning linguistic journey, in which Brophy parodies the myth of the phallus as transcendental signifier, the Hermes myth that props up paradigms of the journey that underwrite Western culture. One is reminded of another "sixties" text, Norman O. Brown's *Love's Body*, which postulates Hermes's journey in the following terms:

> The wandering heroes are phallic heroes, in a permanent state of erection; pricking o'er the plain. The word coition represents genital sexuality as walking, but the converse is also true: all walking, or wandering in the labyrinth, is genital-sexual. All movement is phallic, all intercourse sexual. Hermes, the phallus, is the god of roads, of doorways, of all goings-in and comings-out; all goings-on.[16]

Brophy's comic and feminist fantasy of the wandering phallus seems like a cross between Norman O. Brown and Luce Irigaray, a "pricking" of the myth of the mobile phallus and parodic deflation of phallogocentric theories of circulation. In a final passage that is one of many self-described "ALIENATING INTERLUDE"s in the narrative addressed to the reader, we read "The management trussts [sic] the clientele has by now observed that at least one of the hero(in)es immolated throughout these pages is language" (*In Transit* 214). In a parody of castration, the multilingual narrator "loses" French and then German during an episode of "linguistic leprosy": "my languages gave their first dowser's-twig twitch and I conceived they might be going to fall off" (12). The transcendental signified anchoring language is exposed as "trussed-up" fiction.

The "hero(in)e immolated . . . is language": indeed, one piece of the narrative is a pornographic tale called "L'HISTOIRE DE LA LANGUE D'OC (THE STORY OF OC'S TONGUE)" (98), the mother tongue, who alternately is bound by and then escapes from various masters of language. "'And did you suppose, Och,' enquired the Maestro Hugh Bris in his accustomed courteous tones . . . 'that puns such as yours could go unpunished?'" (214). But such prideful masters of language cannot stop its errancy and detours. The "story of the tongue of Oc" (141) is a tongue-in-cheek critique of preemptive bindings and mappings, of priestly critical practices that seek to fix meanings, including the meaning of gender. In Joycean fashion, one of the narrators refers to the narrative of *In Transit* as a "juicifixion" (217) which repeatedly and deliberately stages a failure to nail the body of language down. Transculturality seems a metaphor for the freedom of border crossings, a mode of evading customs control.

Brophy's Irish traveler owes his/her greatest debt to two previous exilic wanderers: Joyce and his Ulysses, and this pair of exiles represents as well the anarchic circulation of the signifier that refuses to stabilize in a linguistic "home." Indeed, "Unruly's" etymological roots are traced back to "Oruleus," a name, we are told, that is "latinised as Ulrix and thence rather quaintly englished as Unruly" (175). "Youlysses have fore-suffered all. Before the Jew wandered, jew did. Is that another of your dog-headed Irish slips?" (35). Before Joyce's wandering Jew was Homer's Greek, with the suggestion, through the pun on the French verb "lire," to read, that the reader, the "you" of the text, is a fellow sufferer and traveler as well. The narrator says at one point, Ulysses is "the hero who can never accomplish the return of the native, because he isn't one" (35). This Greek wanderer is the quintessential exile, the emblem for the condition of language as always already fallen from a "home" or origin, the post-structuralist position. Odysseus is Latinized, updated, and "Irished" by way of Joyce's Dublin Jew; it is through the figure of Joyce that Brophy's narrator remarks the peculiar relevance of Irish displacements to the pains and pleasures of modernism's internationalism and postmodernism's decenterings:

> Look what became of my distinguished compatriot when, making, with the Irish predisposition to internationalism, for the first handy free port, he was transplanted to windy Trieste, that evocative Avoca where three streams of vocables meet, where everyone is a foreigner and most are anarchist. The wind in Trieste's steep streets lifts the anarchist's soft hat clean off his hard-boiled head. And who compatpats after I, pounding louder than the Triestine tram, pom-pom-ing more reliably than the anarchist's soft-boiled bomb? Ulysses, the hero who can never accomplish the return of the native, because he isn't one. (35)

Trieste, Joyce's adopted home, emblematizes language as always already riotous and dislocated, and transcultural Joyce and his Ulysses (complete with Bloomian acts of hat retrieval) its resident aliens. Yet, curiously, the Irish forefather who tries to enlist Pat in his "holy atheistic crusade whose object will be to de-convert the natives" (204) is ultimately rejected: "Sorry, ex-father. I'm a lapsed pat" (204). Near the end of *In Transit*, the hero/heroine Pat/Patrice climbs out on a ledge over the transit lounge and contemplates suicide. Several persons below try to get him/her to speak with his/her father. "Quit codding," Pat says, "I killed him off," referring to the two sets of Irish parents killed in plane crashes in the novel. "'No, Pat, hold on. It's me. They got the idiom wrong, that's all.' 'O, it's *thou*. Old Father Finnegan Go-and-don'tsinagain. Father Irefish Finn . . . Belt up, ex-father. Will you clear the line for some more urgent interlocutor?' . . . And I look down into the crowd again. I recognise them as, indeed, my very close kin. I think that is why I want to suicide" (228).

This enigmatic passage suggests the painful position of Pat, the Irish orphan, who feels both a kinship with her Joycean heritage and the sense of an ending, the possibility that that heritage no longer sustains her circulations. The narrator says earlier: "The only plausible item in Irish legend is that Saint Patrick banished the phallic symbols from Ireland. (Avaunt, I conjure, eyeing that rose-crowned hose-pipe, Mike, from beside my martello tower of pastcards)" (31). Joyce's postings are figured as a collapsing martello tower of "pastcards," a phallic, Irish fortification that might of necessity be relegated to the past.

Indeed, the narrative's own ancestry is problematic, suggesting that even the metaphor of parentage, with its secure roles for male and female, does not suffice to represent the foster, mixed, and transcultural ancestry of the sex-changing narrative. The cross-dressings and castrati of baroque opera figure prominently in the history of the instability of sex and gender, but no definitive source can be found: Irish opera, Old French, Sterne, are just some of the overdetermined intertexts. "For we are not at all sure it was you, after all, o Irish O'Pera, who initially set this sexchange in train. It may quite well have been you, O.Fr. (=Old French [signed Scholiast One]), you sly old wench, with your already remarked habit of being coy about what's girl and what's boy and your vicious officious imparting of misinformation about the sex of objects possexed" (143).

In an interview Brophy comments on her bending of gender and sexual identity in her novel:

> The whole purpose of fiction is that the writer (and thereby the reader) is transported into some form of life which is absolutely different from his own; and to be transported, if one is female, to a male character, and vice versa, is a terribly light transposition: this is a very small flight, compared to what the imagination *can* do. Consequently, I feel a certain obligation to insist on the mental interchangeability of the sexes, as well as believing that this is basically true.[17]

In this view, Molly Bloom's soliloquy would be a step, but a tame one; Bella/Bello in "Circe" would be closer to what Brophy suggests here, but the chapter's bracketed status in the plot (what is *really* happening?) complicates the significance of the "mutilation of the herms" to which Brophy alludes.

In fact, it is a different literary tradition that Brophy credits for the most imaginative work in the area of gender-bending, a lineage traced from Irish Oscar Wilde to English Ronald Firbank (and, presumably, to half-and-half Brophy, not coincidentally the author of an excellent biography of Firbank). In the biography she says, "Firbank . . . bound himself in tacit apprenticeship to Oscar Wilde: in the subjects of aestheticism and homosexuality."[18] Later in the biography she opines, "[Firbank] fused his own identity with Wilde's on the points of grotesqueness and 'eccentricities'—all of which are metaphors of the sexual eccentricity Firbank shared with Wilde" (*Pranc-*

ing Novelist 564). "Like James and Wilde," she writes elsewhere, "Firbank seems to have virtually made himself French."[19] Aligning herself with this "enfrenched" English tradition of aestheticism and homosexuality more strongly even than with that "pun gent" Irish "compalien," Brophy makes a telling statement in her list of the "three greatest novels" of the twentieth century: *The Golden Bowl*, *A la recherche du temps perdu*, and Firbank's *Concerning the Eccentricities of Cardinal Pirelli*.[20] *Ulysses* and *Finnegans Wake* are conspicuously absent.

At the very end of *In Transit*, the narrator's words echo Anna Livia's concluding address to her father in *Finnegans Wake*: Anna Livia says, "I go back to you, my cold father, my cold mad father, my cold mad feary father, till the near sight of the mere size of him, the moyles and moyles of it, moananoaning, makes me seasilt saltsick and I rush, my only, into your arms" (FW 628). This final reunion takes a less soothing and lyrical form in Brophy's version:

> Aphrodite is re-sea-born of the sperm and spume bubble-and-squeaking about her da's off-torn, projectiled, sea-crashed virile member and drifts to the foamrubbed shore chanting an old, enchanting mermaidshanty or ariaphrodisiacavatina to me. I am not so daft as to try to back out the way I came. I shall take the longer but infinitely safer route forward, knee after cumbrous knee. (230)

Brophy ends with the birth of desire—Aphrodite, sprung from the foam which gathers about the genitals of Uranus, the daughter rising from the "sperm" and "spume" of the dead phallus of the Greek/Irish father ("da" is, of course, an Irish appellation). There is both homage and disaffiliation in the lines, an acknowledgment that however important Joyce is as a precursor, the way forward is not the same as the way back. Eavan Boland speaks of the mysteries of influence that complicate any neat version of the way tradition is passed on, even within what would seem to be a national culture. In her novel, Brophy's eccentric transpositions and border crossings—of language, nationality, and sexuality—borrow, and, at the same time, add a turn of the screw to the "double-headed counterfeit coinages" of the wily Irish "comedichameleon," that already transcultural James Joyce.

V

Return to Dublin

13

Reopening "A Painful Case"

KAREN R. LAWRENCE AND PAUL K. SAINT-AMOUR

How stands the case with the eleventh story in *Dubliners*? Is it a case for a detective, a judge, a physician, a psychoanalyst, or a social worker? What exactly is the case the title names as painful? And is that case open or closed? On the face of things, "A Painful Case" seems to be as decisively sealed as the inquest into Emily Sinico's death, with its diagnosis of "shock and sudden failure of the heart's action" and its verdict that "No blame attached to anyone" (*D* 114–15). James Duffy's journey from isolation to entanglement back to isolation ends with a paragraph of decelerating repetitions—eight sentences beginning with "He," each sentence a hammer blow on a coffin nail—the last of which is the most unlyrically terminal of *Dubliners*' last lines: "He felt that he was alone" (*D* 117). But already the cases have multiplied: are we talking about the case of Duffy's entanglement or that of his isolation? About the medico-legal case made necessary by Mrs Sinico's death, taking shape as an inquest that also reveals her case of alcoholism? Or are we talking about the text itself, a story that appears to be signed, sealed, and delivered?

In the tradition of the most generative scholarship on "A Painful Case," our essay insistently reopens the extravagantly closed case—or rather cases—of Joyce's story. We understand Joyce's story as itself revisiting a case—as reactivating a series of past conditions and events in order to learn or exhibit something. We ask: why is this case worth reopening? What kinds of attention does it ask us to pay to someone else's predicament? And how have previous readings of the story replicated its vexed status as a case? Our responses to these questions challenge Joyce's own dismissal of the story as one of the two weakest in *Dubliners* (*SL* 127); "A Painful Case," we suggest, is indispensable, and not only in its role as an etude for "The Dead," whose more explicit engagement with problems of hospitality, politics, and ethics it anticipates. Insofar as it dramatizes a risk run by all the *Dubliners* stories—the risk of diagnosing or sentencing their subjects as if they were cases—"A Painful Case" is the most formally and ethically self-reflexive story in a sequence known for its self-reflexivity. As a snare that anatomizes its own lures and springs, "A Painful Case" may be the paradigmatic story in *Dubliners*.

Let's begin, then, with the word "case" itself.[1] Joyce's original title for the story was "A Painful Incident," and his decision to alter it suggests a more than casual investment in the word that prevailed in the final title. "Case" in its many senses of an example or circumstance or action derives from the Latin *cadere*, "to fall," and suggests some condition or event that has befallen. ("Incident," though less multiple in its definitions, descends from the same verb.) "Case" means "a state of matters pertaining to a particular person or thing," that is, a specific rather than a general set of conditions or circumstances. In law, a "case" pertains to "the state of facts juridically considered" as well as "the case as presented or 'put' to the court by one of the parties in a suit; hence the sum of the grounds on which he rests his claim." The word squints both at the content of the matter at hand—its facts, exhibits, and testimonies—and at the rhetorically charged staging of that content in the theater of the courtroom. In considering the cases put to us by Joyce's story, we will need to ask where propositional content ends and staging begins, as well as what happens when these dimensions in the story fuse together.

In contrast to this first semantic cluster, the word "case" in the sense of a container or receptacle comes from the Latin *capsa*, "box," from the verb *capere*, "to hold." Thus when we speak of opening or closing a case we are, in a sense, conflating two etymologies, imagining an instance or situation or set of arguments as if it were an enclosed space. This imagined closure, we might add, is one of the ideological functions of a "case" in the medical, forensic, legal, and bureaucratic sense. The production of imaginary closure is also among the aesthetic functions of a work of fiction. But if Joyce's story foregrounds the notion of a "case," it may be in order to question the continence and the ethical viability of that very notion. This is a story, after all, in which one putatively closed case encloses another: Mrs Sinico's death, adjudicated at inquest and encased in cold print, is embedded in Mr Duffy's case history, which is in turn enclosed within a short story written by James Joyce. What if these embedded cases were all prematurely closed? What work would be accomplished by their foreclosure? What violence?

And what would it mean to reopen, and to hold open, these cases? In order to address these questions, we begin by tracking the language and logic of case through the story, attending to how the text narrates its several cases while also exhibiting tendencies to close, foreclose, diagnose, fix, and adjudicate. We also pay close attention to what interrupts or troubles these tendencies—namely, *invitation, voice,* and *touch*. These terms, we suggest, converge in a thematics of hospitality that is not only ethically and politically charged but also historically inflected by Dublin's status as an occupied city. In our closing discussion of the story's critical reception, we argue that the story's theme of hospitality has implications for its readers: this is a story whose prospect of radical hospitality and litany of failed invitations ask us to read and to encounter the Other with a widened aperture of welcome.

"A Painful Case" putatively takes its title from that of the *Dublin Evening Mail* account of Mrs Sinico's death, "DEATH OF A LADY AT SYDNEY PARADE: A PAINFUL CASE" (*D* 113). But this subtitle is itself a reference to a bit of indirect speech in the body of the article: "The Deputy Coroner said it was a most painful case" (*D* 115). The identity of the speaker here is significant: a coroner is a public official charged with investigating the deaths of those who have died by non-natural causes such as accident or violence. Such a person's duties straddle the boundary between medicine and law, combining the work of diagnosis with that of legal adjudication. The coroner's title comes from the phrase *custos placitorum coronae* or "guardian of the crown's pleas"—a phrase attached to the medieval origins of the coroner as an "officer of the royal household responsible for safeguarding the property of the Crown." It is a reminder of the intimate connections between colonialism and bureaucracy in turn-of-the-century Dublin. But whereas colonialism seems to be only an element of the story's background, urban infrastructure is, in a sense, a shadow protagonist of "A Painful Case." While composing the story, Joyce wrote to his brother Stanislaus with the following questions: "A Painful Case—Are the police at Sydney Parade of the D division? Would the city ambulance be called out to Sydney Parade for an accident? Would an accident at Sydney Parade be treated at Vincent's Hospital?" (*SL* 75). Although Joyce made similar sorts of informational queries about other *Dubliners* stories, none of them is as densely populated with urban officialdom and other infrastructural figures as "A Painful Case." These figures congregate most thickly in the newspaper account of the inquest—a fully quoted article that takes up a fifth of the story's length—in which an assistant house surgeon of the City of Dublin Hospital, a sergeant and constable of the police, two railway employees, and a representative of the railway company appear alongside the Deputy Coroner and the husband and daughter of the deceased in establishing the cause of Mrs Sinico's death. As if to confirm the link between governmentality and the varieties of "case" in play here, the story's title phrase recurs in *Ulysses*' "Cyclops" episode in a hangman's letter to the High Sheriff of Dublin: "*Honoured sir i beg to offer my services in the abovementioned painful case i hanged Joe Gann in Bootle jail on the 12 of Febuary 1900 and i hanged. . . .*" (*U* 12.419–20; original emphasis and spelling).

If the title of "A Painful Case" is a third-order quotation—a title quoting a subtitle quoting an article quoting a witness—it seems to have emanated from the mind of its protagonist, who, we are told, has pasted the headline of a patent medicine ad onto the first page of his collection of epigrams (*D* 108). But in many respects Mr Duffy is less the origin than the object of the narration, which provides the reader with a record of his existence. That "A Painful Case" begins with the words "Mr James Duffy" identifies the story itself as a case-file bearing the name of its subject as if on a folder's protruding tab; it is, notably, the only *Dubliners* story that begins in this manner, with the title and full name of a protagonist who thus appears to be the sum of his file. An aphorist, bibliophile, and would-be translator who lives "at a little distance from his body" and "read[s] the evening paper for dessert," Mr Duffy is a testament to the victory of word over flesh (*D* 108, 112); he is, as R. B. Kershner puts it, "a man made of words."[2] The opening paragraph, whose catalogue of Mr Duffy's things seems to mimic the purple-inked stage directions he has written in his translation of Hauptmann's *Michael Kramer*, threatens to set a stage on which no actor will appear: the paragraph's last nine sentences avoid mentioning Mr Duffy in name or pronoun, replacing the man with a roster of objects. Thanks to a series of passive verbs, even his writing seems to proliferate without him: we are told that "stage directions . . . were written," "a sentence was inscribed," "a headline . . . had been pasted" (*D* 108); but we are never told explicitly *by whom*.[3] Eerily, this subtraction of agency extends beyond Mr Duffy to the reader. Just as we become aware that the narrative has enlisted us in conducting a warrantless search of the protagonist's room—that we have been casing the joint—the syntax of the paragraph's final sentence describes a trespass *with no agent*: "On lifting the lid of the desk a faint fragrance escaped—the fragrance of new cedarwood pencils or of a bottle of gum or of an over-ripe apple which might have been left there and forgotten" (*D* 108).⁴ By starting with a misplaced modifier (surely "a faint fragrance" is not what lifts the lid of the desk), this sentence revolves around an absent figure—an agent dissolved in the details of the case. The uncanny implication: that cases are not built by invasive agents but are self-made, self-compiling. We are not casing the joint after all; the joint is self-casing. What's more, we learn a paragraph later that the suspect, with his habits of dispassionate self-description, has understood himself as a case from the start: "He had an odd autobiographical habit which led him to compose in his mind from time to time a short sentence about himself containing a subject in the third person and a predicate in the past tense" (*D* 108).

When the narration finally turns from the room back to its inhabitant, it does so in a diagnostic rather than a forensic manner, as if the foregoing inventory of his personal effects were a document in his medical file: "Mr Duffy abhorred anything which betokened physical or mental disorder. A mediæval doctor would have called him saturnine." The whiff of archaism in the prose accords with Mr Duffy's habit of living "at a little distance from his own body, regarding his own acts with doubtful side-glances" (*D* 108). By enumerating his distinguishing features, his habits, his movements, and his associates, the ensuing paragraphs continue to build the case of Duffy, although it is difficult to know whether we are reading a brief for the prosecution or for the defense. Even where they describe Mr Duffy's isolation and rage for order, the aphorisms in the prose also radiate something of his self-satisfaction, as if they shared Duffy's pleasure in neatly dismissing the company and predicaments of other people: "He never gave alms to beggars and walked firmly, carrying a stout hazel"; "He had neither companions nor friends, church nor creed" (*D* 104, 105). These epitomes of Duffy's likes and dislikes defend and insulate him, allowing his life to unfold without incident, painful or otherwise. His one early dalliance with thoughts of transgression ("He allowed himself to think that in certain circumstances he would rob his bank but, as these circumstances never arose, his life rolled out evenly—an adventureless tale" [*D* 109]) is carefully controlled, a moment of mental permissiveness. In "A Painful Case," sentences *sentence*—they judge the case summarily—but they collude with Duffy too, providing a stay against eventfulness and singularity.

The "adventureless tale" of Mr Duffy's routine becomes a narratable "adventure" (*D* 110) with the introduction of Mrs Sinico, whose voice breaks the protective spell of iteration and aphorism. Having sat down in a sparsely attended concert hall, Mr Duffy is addressed by the woman sitting next to him: "—What a pity there is such a poor house to-night! It's so hard on people to have to sing to empty benches" (*D* 109). Her remark, the only line of direct discourse in the main narrative, is the first event in a story that has so far described only conditions. Even more remarkably, it is the first intersubjective act that suggests a reciprocity not born of duty; prior to it, Mr Duffy has "lived his spiritual life without any communion with others, visiting his relatives at Christmas and escorting them to the cemetery when they died." The neat symmetry of the sentence levels the holiday and funeral accompaniments, both of which Mr Duffy regards as "social duties [performed] for old dignity'[s] sake" (*D* 109): living and dead relatives, before his friend's arrival, were indistinguishable repositories of social principle.

Even direct discourse in a text is mediated, but Mrs Sinico's comment departs multiply from what precedes it—as speech rather than narration, as exclamation rather than description, as an address to a particular listener (Duffy) rather than to an implied general one (the reader). Duffy takes her utterance as an "invitation to talk," and his acceptance of that invitation seems to shunt the story away from its opening profile, or profiling, of Mr Duffy onto a narrative track that promises that something will happen. Nonetheless, his eventual withdrawal from Emily's life—his final refusal of her invitation—is already legible in this first exchange: the conversation her speech opens gets entirely drowned out in the narrative by a description of Mr Duffy's scrutinizing her for future recollection's sake: "While they talked he tried to fix her permanently in his memory." He learns that the young lady who accompanies her is her daughter, he judges the mother's age accordingly, then he studies her face:

> Her face, which must have been handsome, had remained intelligent. It was an oval face with strongly marked features. The eyes were very dark blue and steady. Their gaze began with a defiant note but was confused by what seemed a deliberate swoon of the pupil into the iris, revealing for an instant a temperament of great sensibility. The pupil reasserted itself quickly, this half-disclosed nature fell again under the reign of prudence... (*D* 109–10)

So detailed a description might suggest a deep attentiveness on Mr Duffy's part to his interlocutor, an attentiveness that takes in her facial features, her eyes, the temporality of her gaze, and what that gaze appears to reveal about her conflicted temperament. Yet Mr Duffy's scrutiny, we should remember, is driven by a desire to "fix her permanently in his memory"—to immobilize, master, and possess rather than to listen, understand, or respond. He no sooner hears the first strains of Mrs Sinico's call—her appeal as a fellow being—than he begins transforming that appeal into an inventory; Mr Duffy cannot shut down his writing machine.[5] As philosopher Emmanuel Levinas has argued, the stakes of face-to-face encounters, and of their failure, are by no means trivial. For Levinas, such encounters are the fundamental scenes of ethics, scenes that bid us respond to the Other not as an object but as a subject, however unlike ourselves. Levinas comments that

> ... access to the face is straightaway ethical. You turn yourself toward the Other as toward an object when you see a nose, eyes, a forehead, a chin, and you can describe them. The best way of encountering the Other is not even to notice the color of his eyes! When one observes the color of the eyes one is not in social relationship with the Other. . . . the face is meaning all by itself. You are you. In this sense one can say that the face is not 'seen.' It is what cannot become a content, which your thought would embrace; it is uncontainable, it leads you beyond.[6]

In stark contrast to Levinas's ethical encounter with the uncontainable face of the Other, Mr Duffy's gaze reduces Mrs Sinico's face to a list of appurtenances and a story about their owner's divided temperament—in other words, to a content, another closed case study. This encasement begins to look like the story's master gesture: every opening is foreclosed, every "invitation" refused, every swoon recovered from. With each reassertion of the "fixing" logic of case, the possibility of an ethically vital relationship—of a radical attentiveness, of a listening without limit—withers away.

We will return in a moment to the case of Mr Duffy and Mrs Sinico, but here it is worth glancing at the politics that this story about a failure of face-to-face ethics keeps in its peripheral vision. As Levinas points out, one cannot extrapolate in any simple way from the ethical relation to the political, from the second-person to the third-person; even if the Other can demand an infinite attentiveness of me, how do I square that potentially limitless demand with the presence of *other* others—with their aggregate demand upon me or with my responsibility to relations of solidarity or justice with individual third parties? Yet "A Painful Case" attempts to describe one hinge between the ethical and the political. As Mrs Sinico becomes his "confessor," Mr Duffy tells her about his past association with the Irish Socialist Party. "The workmen's discussions, he said, were too timorous; the interest they took in the question of wages was inordinate. He felt that they were hard-featured realists and that they resented an exactitude which was the product of a leisure not within their reach. No social revolution, he told her, would be likely to strike Dublin for some centuries" (*D* 111). Four years later, as he sits in the public-house at Chapelizod Bridge thinking over her death (he has learned of it in the Tory, anti-nationalist *Mail*), five or six working-men nearby discuss the value of a gentleman's estate in County Kildare. Sipping his punch, "Mr Duffy sat on his stool and gazed at them, without seeing or hearing them." Although his gazing without apprehension presumably results from the "shock which . . . was now attacking his nerves" (*D* 116), the moment is symptomatic of Mr Duffy's more general incomprehension of the working classes, and it brings his relinquished political life within the radius of the ethical question of attending to the Other. If such an attention is insufficient to account for the political, it is nonetheless indispensable to the formation of solidarity with other political subjects, particularly with members of another social class. Mr Duffy's observation that "no social revolution . . . would be likely to strike Dublin for some centuries" is rhetorically self-serving, casting him in the role of a radical intellectual who is disappointed by the unrigorous pragmatism of the working classes and therefore qualified to prophesy the failure of their movements. But whereas Mr Duffy's prophecy is offered as a detached observation about someone else's revolutionary ambitions, it indicts the prophet more than it glorifies him. By connecting Mr Duffy's failure to listen in his face-to-face encounters with Emily and his failure to see or hear the working classes, the story implies that his inability to attend to the Other makes him partly responsible for the very political conditions that disgust him. If an educated and politically sympathetic member of the clerkly class cannot attend to the workers deeply enough to see why they might be apprehensive, concerned with the question of wages, or resentful of his "exactitude" when it is underwritten by his leisure, it is no wonder that the prospects for social revolution seem so remote.[7]

The story of Mr Duffy's aborted political involvement surfaces as a testament to the power of Mrs Sinico's invitation to talk. For unlike Mr Duffy, Mrs Sinico has the capacity to hear the Other, and it is this capacity—her role as his confessor—that momentarily invades the defenses Mr Duffy has erected against face-to-face encounters. Before the glimmer of "adventure" is extinguished by routine, the pair's thoughts become entangled through conversation indirectly reported. Phrases like "for many years" and "every morning" give way to adverbial markers such as "little by little" and "sometimes" that hasten toward the singularity of scene. "Little by little, as their thoughts entangled, they spoke of subjects less remote" (*D* 107). The vibrating music unites them as they experience the sensation of hearing together. "Sometimes he caught himself listening to the sound of his own voice. He thought that in her eyes he would ascend to an angelical stature; and, as he attached the fervent nature of his companion more and more closely to him, he heard the strange impersonal voice which he recognised as his own, insisting on the soul's incurable loneliness. We cannot give ourselves, it said. We are our own" (*D* 107). Although this seems like Mr Duffy's typical work of self-alienation, akin to his "odd autobiographical habit," we might also read it as a kind of empathy through hearing, as if he heard his own voice with her ears instead of his own. This momentary opening, this accelerating pace of intimacy, however, leads to a singular encounter that ruptures the relationship: "one night . . . Mrs Sinico caught up his hand passionately and pressed it to her cheek." Mr Duffy reacts with surprise. "Her interpretation of his words disillusioned him. He did not visit her for a week." The steel trap of aphorism swallows the moment: "They agreed to break off their intercourse; every bond, he said, is a bond to sorrow" (*D* 107–8).

Along with Mr Duffy's life, the narrative returns to the comfort of habit and summary, reporting events with so little affect or emphasis that they are barely distinguishable from routine: "His father died; the junior partner of the bank retired. And still every morning he went into the city . . ." (*D* 112). We learn that two months after his last meeting with Mrs Sinico, Mr Duffy sentences their relationship once again: "Love between man and man is impossible because there must not be sexual intercourse and friendship between man and woman is impossible because there must be sexual intercourse" (*D* 108). The aphoristic law according to Mr Duffy obliterates the face-to-face encounter. The second person, like Mr Duffy's "I," disappears into the third persons of man and man or man and woman.

The drive to "fix" the Other permanently in a summary judgment finds its correlate in the newspaper account of an event—the inquest—that reduces the circumstances of a life and death to the question of blame for the latter. This fixation happens partly through the name's relationship to the case. Whereas we have previously known only the last name of the deceased, the *Mail* names her fully as "Mrs Emily Sinico," as if the native climate of the name were the juridical setting in which its bearer becomes a case or file. (The full name of "Mr James Duffy," remember, was duly stated for the record at the story's outset; "A Painful Case" has been a mock-inquest from the start.) Given the constraints of social codes and of his own nature, Mr Duffy was, during their "intercourse," no more able to address Emily by her Christian name than to invite her back to his room, and the narrative has observed the same distance. But although her full name never explicitly reappears in the story, it is invoked toward the end, when Mr Duffy hears it in the noise of a goods train: "It passed slowly out of sight; but still he heard in his ears the laborious drone of the engine reiterating the syllables of her name" (*D* 117). The manuscript of "A Painful Case" spelled out those chugging syllables: "Emily Sinico. Emily Sinico."[8] By invoking her name—sans title, significantly—without putting it on the page, Joyce's revisions gesture toward the unutterable nature of a male-female intimacy that was neither polite friendship nor publicly acknowledged marriage. In its ghostliness, the deceased friend's intimate name, heard but not written, also resembles the spectral "touch of her hand" Mr Duffy is shocked to feel while he is alone in his rooms; it resembles, too, the kinesthetic "touch" of the dead woman's voice on his ear (*D* 116, 117). As he retraces the steps of their last extended walk together, he again experiences her annunciation: "she seemed to be near him in the darkness. At moments he seemed to feel her voice touch his ear, her hand touch his. He stood still to listen" (*D* 117). Still, as shocked as he is by her voice and touch, their mutual disappearance in the story's final paragraph proves even more terrible. Haunting is at least a form of accompaniment, the touch and voice of even some ghostly Other testifying to the presence of a second person, of a "you." The end of such a haunting marks the final death of that "you" and the arrival of a world in which the self is truly alone. Fittingly, it seems to be the locomotive's incantatory repetition of Emily's full name, linked as her name is to the closed case of her inquest, that drives away the impression and the ethical appeal of her presence; the legalities and generalities of the *case* banish *voice* and *touch*, the experience of the second person.

Before we turn to the story's final paragraph, we need to attend to what enters the text alongside the sense of Emily's nearness. Her visitation, while it lasts, suffuses the narrative with the language of hospitality, a language—and with it, an ethic—that until now has been repeatedly warped or warded off. Early on in an intercourse initiated by his friend's "invitation to talk,"

Mr Duffy hastened to deform the scene of invitation into one of coercion: having "a distaste for underhand ways and, finding that they were compelled to meet stealthily, he forced her to ask him to her house" (*D* 110). No one in "A Painful Case" is both unconditionally welcomed (think of the warrantless search in which the story's opening paragraph enlists the reader) and able to accept such a welcome—to come in. As if in recognition of this impasse, nearly all of "A Painful Case" is set on peripheries: Duffy lives "as far as possible from the city of which he [is] a citizen," spends his evenings "roaming the outskirts of the city," later visits the Sinico cottage "outside Dublin," and at long last, walking in Phoenix Park to the west of the city proper, "turn[s] his eyes to the grey, gleaming river, winding along towards Dublin" (*D* 107, 109, 111, 117). But by the time Mr Duffy gazes for the last time from the outskirts to the center, that gaze has altered: whereas the story's first sentence records his contempt for the city from which he has distanced himself, now, with Emily's voice and touch drawn near, Dublin's lights "burned redly and hospitably in the cold night." The sight of those lights, and of lovers entwined at the base of the park's wall, prompts Mr Duffy's realization that he is "outcast from life's feast," a phrase that chimes twice (*D* 117). The feast he has refused is partly the feast of eros and partly, as a scriptural reverberation reminds us, what the narrator earlier called "any communion with others" in his spiritual life (*D* 109).[9] But the story's social geography also identifies the foregone feast as that of the civic—of that scorned city center and the "civic life" (*D* 109) to whose conventions Duffy made only grudging concessions. Duffy's double refusal of hospitality and of the civic might make us hear even the inert institutional name "City of Dublin Hospital" a little differently: this setting of the inquest into Mrs Sinico's death is haunted by an alternate narrative path in which the City of Dublin had been a site of hospitality rather than a swarming ground of "case"—of investigation, judgment, and reportage.

In its opening profile of Mr Duffy, the narrative voice caught its subject's scorn for "the conventions which regulate the civic life," but we should remember that his occasional nods to those conventions—"visiting his relatives at Christmas and escorting them to the cemetery when they died"— were the only moments prior to his "adventure" with Mrs Sinico when he veered from his righteous solitude. Thus the "civic" was set up early on as a matrix of social reciprocity, and thus as a foil to those institutional structures (court, hospital, press, police) that would later preside over the painful case of Mrs Sinico's death. By then figuring the city as the locus of hospitality and of the vital feast from which Mr Duffy is outcast, the story's penultimate paragraph suggests that the civic might be more than a bourgeois social code: it might be that which welcomes the outcast. Mr Duffy is a disaffected citizen of Dublin rather than its outcast, but his figurative self-description invites us to imagine a literal counterpart: the true outcast, the asylum-seeker, the non-citizen who wants to come in. Such a figure haunts the story's last page alongside Mrs Sinico and briefly recasts Dublin, its lights burning hospitably in the cold night, as a city of refuge.

The hospitality granted the outcast by such a city would be radical, unbounded by pact or by the expectation that the city would benefit economically or politically from the welcome it proffers; it would be the very kind of unconditional hospitality that Mr Duffy can neither accept from Mrs Sinico nor extend to her.[10] That these two varieties of hospitality—the intimate and the civic—can be thought in tandem here points up, again, the story's interest in considering the political stakes of the face-to-face relation. But we should note that this consideration does not lead to an easy cosmopolitanism, as an echo of contemporary political oratory in the story attests. On the day of Edward VII's coronation in 1902, John Edward Redmond, then head of Ireland's Nationalist Party, gave a speech on the steps of Dublin City Hall protesting the festivities taking place in London. Addressing England, Redmond said, "You cannot hide from your guests the skeleton at your feast." That skeleton was the fact that Ireland "lies at your very heart oppressed, impoverished, manacled, and disloyal, a reproach to your civilization, and a disgrace to your name."[11] Joyce's echo of Redmond's words situates the problem of hospitality in respect to the history of British colonialism. It insists that acts and failures of hospitality, both individual and civic, might have an altogether different meaning and being in an occupied colonial capital; that Mr Duffy's rejections of solidarity and intimacy might allegorize the colony's stunted political powers of initiative, welcome, accord, and reciprocity in domestic and international registers; that the skeleton at one feast might understandably fail to preside as host over another. For all that the lights of Dublin burn hospitably toward the story's end, a certain historical skepticism keeps them distant: the city of refuge is a prospect, not yet a present space of asylum.

The final paragraph of "A Painful Case" performs a feat of subtraction: the train with its dactylic cargo ("Emily Sinico. Emily Sinico") has passed out of sight, its rhythm ebbing from Mr Duffy's ears and with it the sound of Emily's name and his sense of her nearness—his short-lived impression of her voice and her touch. Element by element the once-detailed world of the story is pared away, leaving a nullity in which Mr Duffy's listening is a call that elicits no response but perfect silence.

> He turned back the way he had come, the rhythm of the engine pounding in his ears. He began to doubt the reality of what memory told him. He halted under a tree and allowed the rhythm to die away. He could not feel her near him in the darkness nor her voice touch his ear. He waited for some minutes listening. He could hear nothing: the night was perfectly silent. He listened again: perfectly silent. He felt that he was alone. (D 117)

This is Joyce's prose at its most elemental or skeletal, as shorn of ornament as Mr Duffy's room. If Duffy's habit has been "to compose in his mind from time to time a short sentence about himself containing a subject in the third person and a predicate in the past tense," then the paragraph marks that habit's reassertion, suggesting that Mr Duffy has "turned back the way he had come" in mental routine as well as in space. The language describing his self-portraiture—technicalities about sentence parts, person, and tense—should draw our attention to the grammar of this final paragraph, which is the crowning instance of his "autobiographical habit." Here, alongside the dwindling of Mr Duffy's world, the resources of language seem to have narrowed to a lone kind of declarative sentence. The proper nouns whose specificities of place, name, title, institution, and season are so important both to the rest of "A Painful Case" and to the logic of "case" in general have all been deducted, leaving a spare archipelago of pronouns. Looking more closely at these, one discovers that the story's final closing down of "case" is grammatical. In the first half of the paragraph, the masculine pronoun that stands in for Mr Duffy appears in the subjective, objective, and possessive cases—*he*, *him*, and *his* respectively—as if the possibility were still open that he could enter into reciprocal relations with others, be the object to another's subject, be claimed, or claim another as his own. In the fourth sentence the masculine and feminine pronouns are still found entangled, if only to declare "her" vanishing: "*He* could not feel *her* near *him* in the darkness nor *her* voice touch *his* ear" (emphasis added). But if an intimacy lingers in those pronouns even as they describe the withdrawal of Emily's ghost, the elimination of "her" in the last four sentences closes the masculine pronoun down to the subjective case alone, to the "he" that tolls five times before the full stop. No longer haunted by her, he seems to lose even the solace of his own self-division. The benches are empty: Duffy is a listener in a vacant hall.

How do we understand the subtractions of this final paragraph—its repetitions, its loss or renunciation of variety and specificity, its listening without response? Do these moves signal Mr Duffy's entrapment in a solitude from which no one will rescue him? Or his willful retreat to a solitude on which no one, thankfully, will impinge? Are they the culmination of the logic of "case" as general law rather than case as particular instance? Or do they enact the supersession of that logic, with its love of specifics, by something else? Do they make us want to convict and sentence Mr Duffy? To exonerate him? To damn or absolve him? To diagnose and treat him? And if they strand the reader in a space of radical undecidability, to what end do they do so?

One thing is clear: the story's final paragraph tends to function as a decision-space for its readers. The paragraph practically impels us to take an interpretive stand about it and, by extension, about its protagonist's final status. Many of those who have written on "A Painful Case" have found a kind of tragic epiphany in its final lines, where the blows of the previous paragraphs land fully: Mr Duffy realizes that he has missed his chance at intimacy; that he has brought about the death of the one person who offered it to him; that he will be unremembered when he dies; that he is absolutely alone. This way of reading sees Mr Duffy as a figure of pity and terror and his readers as experiencing both instruction and relief at the hands of Duffy's chastening example. By contrast, several recent commentators have viewed "A Painful Case" as ending *happily* insofar as its protagonist gets what he wants—what he has, in fact, engineered: a life so sealed off from desire, vulnerability, and responsibility that what would be self-incriminating utterances for less walled-off people ("He had sentenced her to ignominy, a death of shame.... No one wanted him; he was outcast from life's feast" [D 117]) are self-congratulatory ones for Mr Duffy. Such a reading is advanced by Garry Leonard, who traces Duffy's rage for isolation to a condition of primary narcissism, one that compels him to uphold the fiction that he has an integrated ego and to do so without even minimal recourse to others.[12] Seamus Deane makes a similar diagnosis, although with an emphasis on ethics rather than the psyche: "The closed, repetitive structure of Mr Duffy's inhuman life has resumed. There is no other in his world, no responsibility for the other. This is a style that excludes ethics, by the intensification of repetitive rhythms that betoken morbid self-obsession. It is the opposite of an ethical condition, the fleeting prospect of which disappears as the serried ranks of final sentences close up in their neat, neurotic repetitions."[13] Deane goes further than Leonard in claiming that the style of Joyce's story is complicit in its protagonist's inhumanity, neurosis, and ethical nullity, its repetitions ratifying Mr Duffy's choice of routine over Mrs Sinico's posthumous appeal to him. For Deane, the text itself plays silent partner to its protagonist, doubling his ethically closed self-regard.

These readings vary from one another in obvious ways, but they also have something crucial in common: a moment at which Mr Duffy's psycho-sexual and/or ethical state is decisively adjudicated. In this, they are strangely faithful to "A Painful Case," most obedient to its immanent logic precisely where they are most critical of that logic's outcome (as in Deane's reading). The story's self-presentation as a "case"—as the case of Mrs Emily Sinico nested within the case of Mr James Duffy—has reproduced itself, that is, in a tendency among its commentators either to diagnose Mr Duffy or to certify his moral condition as if for sentencing. As we have seen, the text invites such critical gestures by staging diagnoses, verdicts, and sentencings of its own ("A mediæval doctor would have called him saturnine"; "Death . . . had been due to sudden failure of the heart's action"; "No blame attached to anyone"; "he had sentenced her to ignominy"; "he was outcast from life's feast"). Not all of the critical verdicts are as unsparing as Leonard's judgment of Mr Duffy or Deane's of the text itself, but even those readings that plead Duffy's case remain within the narrow thumbs-up-or-thumbs-down option embedded within the story's medico-legal settings and architecture. If "A Painful Case" invites such judgments, however, its theme of hospitality issues a counter-invitation to its readers—an invitation to extend a hospitality of our own, one that does not (as no truly radical hospitality does) depend on the health, innocence, normality, or ethical receptivity of the guest. This would be to chart a third way through the story, neither condemning nor recuperating Mr Duffy but instead offering him precisely the kind of welcome he refuses Mrs Sinico, the "hobbling wretches" and other "wrecks on which civilisation has been reared," the working classes, and finally all humankind (*D* 115). This would also be the kind of welcome that no one, in the wake of Mrs Sinico's death, will extend to him in the world of the story—again, a welcome beyond diagnosis or verdict, a hospitality that takes neither his wellness nor his illness, neither his culpability nor his pitiability, as its precondition.

Such a hospitality would knit closely with the queer readings that have lately quickened the story's critical reception; it might also draw us past the binarisms that have at moments characterized these readings. Roberta Jackson criticizes the medicalization of same-sex desire by turn-of-the-century criminal and sexological discourses, adding that this process led to unacceptably confining and essentialist models of homosexuality. Yet she concludes, with a certainty the text simply cannot sustain, that the story's "accumulated allusions leave no doubt as to Duffy's sexuality."[14] Margot Norris, by contrast, marks the queer reading of "A Painful Case" as an "indeterminate and unverifiable" possibility whose power to "abash the reader in ethically productive ways" lies in the undecidability of Mr Duffy's sexuality. Norris argues that the story arouses readerly expectations of an adultery narrative in order, by frustrating those expectations, to expose the heterosexism of both the adultery narrative and the reader who defaults to it. Such a reader has either missed or declined textual invitations to queer reading and thereby enforced a "compulsory heterosexuality," in Adrienne Rich's phrase; in subsequently reconsidering a queer reading, says Norris, the reader must "take ethical responsibility for now imagining the thoughts, feelings, and anxieties of the possibly homosexual man. . . . the heterosexual reader experiences a thickening of identity and a doubling of vision as different questions pose themselves in an effort to enter a gay subjectivity."[15] The imperative of taking responsibility for the Other is compelling here, but it is pinned to the kind of inflexible, identitarian coordinates Norris otherwise rejects. For this argument not only explicitly posits a heterosexual reader, it also assumes the absolute otherness of queer reading and queer subjectivity for such a straight reader. These assumptions produce several outcomes: first, radical alterity is made to seem a function of sexuality alone. Second, subjectivity (e.g., "gay subjectivity") is conflated with sexuality, ruling out the possibility of a more mobile, multiple, or performative model of sexuality that corresponds only imperfectly with subjectivity. Finally, Norris's reading sets up the straight reader as the lone enforcer of compulsory heterosexuality—an odd result given the story's demonstration of how its possibly homosexual protagonist accedes to compulsory heterosexuality in his actions, confining his dissent to dire and private epigrams.

To Norris's construction of an "abashed" heterosexual reader, one might respond that "A Painful Case" imagines a broader bandwidth of both readers and ethical effects. Norris's reader, in hot pursuit of the adultery narrative, first ignores and only later is ethically chastened by the story's oblique and encrypted references to homosexuality. But those same references would function very differently for the closeted reader, providing the secret password's consolation under a repressive regime, establishing Mr Duffy as a fellow sufferer with whom to feel solidarity or, alternately, as a warning example of the tragic potentials of the closet. One also imagines a reader—Mrs Sinico herself might well have been one—who is alive to the ties between compulsory heterosexuality and patriarchy. However unavailable Mr Duffy's subjectivity-as-gay appears, Mrs Sinico's subjectivity *tout court* is even less accessible, lacking even his moments of unpublished semi-candor. The question of what she wants, thinks, and feels is simply inadmissible to the narrator, and the reader—male or female—who notices this silence or interdiction, instead of being abashed, will begin to consider the political anatomy of a story that consigns both its main female character and its possibly-gay male protagonist to similar fictional closets.

Still another kind of reader seems to be addressed by Mr Duffy's last aphorism; for this reader, the unsettled question of Mr Duffy's sexuality is not just a sign of repression or self-censorship but also an invitation. The aphorism again: "Love between man and man is impossible because there must not be sexual intercourse and friendship between man and woman is impossible because there must be sexual intercourse" (*D* 112). This formulation, which tends to function as the epicenter of queer readings of the story, describes a double-bind—what Colleen Lamos calls "the *pro*scription of homosexuality, side by side with the *pre*scription of heterosexuality." Readings of Duffy as affirmatively homosexual take the epigram to map mutually exclusive modes of desire and subjectivation, concluding that he *is* homosexual—and by the same token *is not* heterosexual—but simply cannot enact his homosexuality. But as Lamos points out, *both* heterosexuality and homosexuality are closed to Duffy, who is stranded between the two: "neither does the disavowal of homosexuality . . . produce a homosexual subject, nor does the disavowal of homosexuality produce a heterosexual subject."[16] One kind of readerly hospitality would attempt to join Duffy in a place of suspended adjudication; it would extend a welcome to him without relying on the mutually exclusive relationship between queer and not-queer, closeted and out, symptomatic and asymptomatic. In a sense, such a hospitality would underwrite the more generatively "queered" reading of the story insofar as it understood the interpretive gesture of "queering" a text, not as a one-time conversion or correction of the text to the fixed status of queer, but as a perpetual opening and reopening of the case: as a vexing of the very concept of a case.

Let us return to Deane's discussion of the story's final sentences, and particularly to his claim that their repetitive style "excludes ethics, by the intensification of repetitive rhythms that betoken morbid self-obsession." Deane's criticism, we should note, is directed less at Duffy than at Joyce; moreover, "A Painful Case" becomes, for Deane, the pattern of Joyce's subsequent fictions, whose incantatory endings betray the critical and political potentials of the texts by aestheticizing them "into a form of writing that has the ambition to be entirely autonomous," self-referential, and therefore exempt from "History."[17] Deane's conclusive dismissal of Joyce's lyrical finales on the model of "A Painful Case" demonstrates how powerfully that story seems to prescribe, in its last paragraph, some act of readerly adjudication in the image of Mr Duffy's decisive aphorisms. But Deane also rather surprisingly dissevers the story's ending from earlier passages that might prepare us to read it more equivocally or multiply. As we have attempted to show, much of what precedes the final lines—the aphoristic profiling, the face-to-face encounter and its relation to politics, the theme of hospitality, the play of name and case—opens the very questions that are, for Deane, so extravagantly foreclosed by the ending. These openings equip us to read the final paragraph as enacting rather than endorsing the closing down of a world. They help us to read that closure as a symptom of Mr Duffy's condition even as they challenge us not to leap from symptom to diagnosis—to a state in which, having drawn conclusions about the Other's pitiable state, we may dispatch his closed case to cold storage. This would be the prospect of radical hospitality opened by the story, for all that its protagonist fails in it: to respond without diagnosis to the symptom of the Other. None of this is to deny "A Painful Case" its profoundly self-regarding energies. They remind us of the way writing—and Joyce's writing in particular—can fix, immobilize, finish off. Joyce's claim that *Dubliners* meant to "betray the soul of that hemiplegia or paralysis which many consider a city" (SL 22) is worthy of Mr Duffy in the way it subjects a whole cityful of painful cases to a terse and scornful diagnosis. But "A Painful Case" does nothing if not recognize and critique this very tendency; it stages the crisis produced by such habits of mind, taking them to the end of the line as if to exhaust them and perhaps to glimpse what lies beyond their terminus. That "beyond" would include "The Dead," whose central theme of hospitality arose, Joyce claimed, from the realization that he had been "unnecessarily harsh" about

Ireland in the other *Dubliners* stories (*SL* 109–10); "A Painful Case," which variously inflicts and flinches at Joycean harshness, may well be the record of that realization. The story asks us to listen, amid its sentencings and arid epigrams, for moments of voice, touch, welcome, and annunciation; in narrating a failed appeal to the ear of the Other, it invites its readers to receive that appeal.

Notes

Living with Joyce: Grand Passion and Small Pleasures

1. Barthes, "Style and its Image," in *Literary Style: A Symposium*, 9.
2. James, Preface to *Roderick Hudson*, in *The Art of the Novel: Critical Prefaces by Henry James*, 5.
3. McMichael, *"Ulysses" and Justice*, 18.
4. Quoted in Budgen, *James Joyce and the Making of "Ulysses,"* 67–68.
5. Barthes, *Camera Lucida*, 93.
6. See Gilbert and Gubar, "Sexual linguistics: gender, language, sexuality," 519.
7. Brophy, *In Transit: An Heroi-Cyclic Novel*, 35.

Chapter 1. The Narrative Norm

1. Budgen, *James Joyce and the Making of "Ulysses,"* 67–68.
2. Wilson, *Axel's Castle*, 217.
3. Goldberg, *The Classical Temper*, 92.
4. See Hayman's *"Ulysses": The Mechanics of Meaning*, especially 75–79, and Burgess's *Joysprick: An Introduction to the Language of James Joyce* for two of the earliest and best discussions of this narrative norm. Discussions of the narrative norm became more common. See, for example, Hugh Kenner's *Joyce's Voices* and French's *The Book as World: James Joyce's "Ulysses."*
5. See, for example, Iser, *The Implied Reader*, 179–233, and Ben D. Klimpel, "The Voices of *Ulysses*," 283–319.
6. See, for example, Erwin K. Steinberg's *The Stream of Consciousness and Beyond in "Ulysses"* for the most extensive treatment of Joyce's use of the stream-of-consciousness technique.
7. Burgess, *Joysprick*, 68.
8. Ibid., 74.
9. Letter, 6 August 1919, *Letters of James Joyce*, 129. However, when I refer to the "initial style" henceforth, I mean specifically the prose style of the third-person narration.
10. Hugh Kenner's ingenuity and prolificacy illustrate the possibilities for characterizing the early narrative style of *Ulysses*. In *The Stoic Comedians: Flaubert, Joyce, and Beckett*, the following narrative sentence is cited as an example of Joyce's characteristic

manipulation of language and his "resolute artistry" (30): "Two shafts of soft daylight fell across the flagged floor from the high barbicans: and at the meeting of their rays a cloud of coalsmoke and fumes of fried grease floated, turning"(*U* 1.315–17). In *Joyce's Voices*, the same marked precision is said to exemplify the "fussiness of setting and decor" of "Edwardian novelese" (68–69). Both descriptions are intriguing, the second moving us, as it does, further away from a view of the early style as normative and nonparodic. The style becomes just another example of a particular kind of rhetoric, despite its temporal primacy in the text. Although the sentence does exhibit stylistic idiosyncrasies, I favor Kenner's first description of it as an example of Joyce's characteristic style, more normative at this point than parodic.

11. See James's Preface to *The Tragic Muse*, reprinted in *The Art of The Novel: Critical Prefaces*, 87: "To put all that is possible of one's idea into a form and compass that will contain and express it only by delicate adjustments and an exquisite chemistry . . . every artist will remember how often that sort of necessity has carried with it its particular inspiration."

12. This sense of excess of labor in the writing appears again in subsequent chapters like "Sirens," "Eumaeus," and "Ithaca," even though different styles are used in each case.

13. See Kenner, *Joyce's Voices*, 69–70.

14. Kermode, "Novels: Recognition and Deception," 117. Kermode's comment, made in reference to Ford's *The Good Soldier*, seems to me to apply much more appropriately to *Ulysses*.

15. Goldberg, *Joyce*, 90.

16. Kenner, "The Rhetoric of Silence," 382–94.

17. Ibid., 383.

18. Meyerhoff, *Time in Literature*, 37.

19. Jameson, "Metacommentary," 13.

20. See Kierkegaard, *The Point of View for My Work as an Author: A Report to History and Related Writings*. The work announces that for the purpose of arriving at "truth," Kierkegaard had lulled his unsuspecting readers into a sense of narrative security in his aesthetic writings, only to subvert this security later in the religious writings.

21. See Goldberg, *Joyce*, 63.

22. Quoted in Budgen, *James Joyce and the Making of "Ulysses,"* 105.

Chapter 2. "Wandering Rocks" and "Sirens": The Breakdown of Narrative

1. 3 September 1920, *Letters of James Joyce*, 145.

2. Kellogg, "Scylla and Charybdis," in *James Joyce's "Ulysses": Critical Essays*, 159.

3. Schechner, *Joyce in Nighttown: A Psychoanalytic Inquiry into "Ulysses,"* 15–49.

4. *The Dublin Diary of Stanislaus Joyce*, 81.

5. See Cope, "Sirens," in *James Joyce's "Ulysses": Critical Essays*, 218.

6. See Clive Hart's chart of the temporal scene of events in this chapter in "Wandering Rocks," in *James Joyce's "Ulysses": Critical Essays*.

7. Stephen considers the problem of the relationship between "an actuality of the pos-

sible as possible" and "infinite possibilities": "Had Pyrrhus not fallen by a beldam's hand in Argos or Julius Caesar not been knifed to death? They are not to be thought away. Time has branded them and fettered they are lodged in the room of infinite possibilities they have ousted. But can those have been possible seeing that they never were? Or was that only possible which came to pass? Weave, weaver of the wind" (*U* 2.48–53).

8. Barthes, *Le Degré zéro de lécriture suivi de nouveaux essais critiques*, 143. The translation is my own.

9. See the volume entitled *Ulysses: "Aeolus," "Lestrygonians," "Scylla and Charybdis," & "Wandering Rocks." A Facsimile of Placards for Episodes 7–10*, in *The James Joyce Archives*.

10. Sultan, "The Sirens at the Ormand Bar: *Ulysses*," 84–85.

11. Kenner, *The Stoic Comedians*, 47.

12. See Gass, "The Medium of Fiction," in *Fiction and the Figures of Life*, 27–28.

13. The narrative itself mimics its own structure: it begins with the word "Begin!" and ends with the word "*Done.*" This mimicry cannot be naturalized according to the conventions that usually govern novel writing and, of course, it emphasizes the constructed nature of the text. In fact, the conclusion of the chapter, Bloom's flatulence, can be regarded as a comic version of a "natural" conclusion, as Bloom is unable to prevent "nature" from taking its course. This too parodies the epiphanies of the early chapters that also end not with a whimper but with a bang.

14. A similar example is one to which I alluded in my discussion of "Aeolus," the descendant of the chiasmus in that chapter: "Miss Kennedy sauntered sadly from bright light, twining a loose hair behind an ear. Sauntering sadly, gold no more, she twisted twined a hair. Sadly she twined in sauntering gold hair behind a curving ear" (*U* 11.81–83).

15. These errors of transcription in the text serve to remind us to what degree "reality" is mediated and at times distorted in the narrative. The following passage plays upon this idea of distortion: "From the saloon a call came, long in dying. That was a tuningfork the tuner had that he forgot that he now struck. A call again. That he now poised that it now throbbed. You hear?" (*U* 11.313–15). The question "You hear?" is worthy of characters in the Anna Livia Plurabelle section of *Finnegans Wake*—the washerwomen who can't hear each other's gossip because the water's running. (In fact, the narrative of "Sirens" has a gossipy quality to it.) It is in *Finnegans Wake* that the kind of local distortions in "Sirens" find their issue. It is not until *Finnegans Wake* that Joyce really explores the idea of the text as a distortion and liberates the aural association of words.

16. Sometimes, this aural liberation produces a kind of "Freudian slip" in the narration. The "Yessex" ("Yes sex") in this sentence is a punning reminder to the reader of what Bloom is trying to forget all day long, but especially at this hour.

17. Richard Ellmann, *Ulysses on the Liffey*, 104–5.

18. It must be noted that Bloom's interior monologue provides an anchor for the reader in the chapter. Even if the narrative no longer displays a stable narrating "self," a palpable sense of the human self is maintained by the interior monologue of the main character. In chapters like "Eumaeus," "Cyclops," and "Ithaca," we lose the sound of the character's inner monologue, which "defamiliarizes" the book even further.

Chapter 3. "Eumaeus": The Way of All Language

1. Letter from Stanislaus to James Joyce, 26 February 1922, in *Letters of James Joyce*, Vol. 3, 58.
2. See Stuart Gilbert, *James Joyce's "Ulysses": A Study*, 30.
3. Bruns, "Eumaeus," in *James Joyce's "Ulysses": Critical Essays*, 368.
4. Iser, *The Implied Reader*, 191.
5. Barthes, *Essais critiques*, 14–15. See *Critical Essays*, trans. Richard Howard, xvii.
6. See Bloom's *The Anxiety of Influence: A Theory of Poetry*.
7. Quoted in Zweig, *The World of Yesterday*; reprinted in Richard Ellmann, *James Joyce*, 410.
8. Hayman, "Language of/as Gesture in Joyce," 221n.
9. I am using Stephen's words metaphorically. As I said in my discussion of "Nausicaa," he refers to material reality in the chapter. But the point is that what is outside the self is always there; it does not depend upon the existence of the self.
10. Quoted in *A Writer's Diary: Being from the Diary of Virginia Woolf*, 49.

Chapter 4. "Ithaca": The Order of Things

1. Quoted in Budgen, *James Joyce and the Making of "Ulysses,"* 258. Joyce did tell Budgen that "Ithaca" was his favorite episode.
2. See the translation of Joyce's letter to Carlo Linati, 21 September 1920, in *Selected Letters of James Joyce*, 270–71.
3. Letter to Budgen, end February 1921, in *Letters of James Joyce*, 159–60. Critics have argued about whether the source of the catechism is the Christian catechism that Joyce recited as a child or the secular catechism that he read in school, such as Mangnall's *Historical and Miscellaneous Questions*. They have argued persuasively for each of these catechisms as the "source" of the form of "Ithaca." See A. Walton Litz; "Ithaca," in *James Joyce's "Ulysses": Critical Essays*, 385–405, and Harry C. Staley, "Joyce's Catechisms," 137–53.
4. Budgen, *James Joyce and the Making of "Ulysses,"* 257.
5. Litz, "Ithaca," 397. Litz goes on to say, however, that in "Ithaca" "Joyce did not renounce his interest in 'the romantic heart of things,' but simply found new means for expressing it." This view of what occurs in "Ithaca" is itself a romanticizing of the text. I will discuss this in more detail shortly.
6. In *Anatomy of Criticism: Four Essays*, Northrop Frye describes the disparity as part of the "novel-anatomy combination": "In the novel-anatomy combination, too, found in the "Ithaca" chapter, the sense of lurking antagonism between the personal and intellectual aspects of the scene accounts for much of its pathos" (314).
7. What significance we are supposed to attribute to this line is another matter. The two main characters have just moved out of obscurity in the direction of light—the Dantesque stars seem to offer resonance and meaning as a symbol. And yet, to call this line symbolic would be to act as if it were in another context. It is more like an allusion to symbol than a functioning symbol in the text. Because the narrative immediately returns

to the language of mathematical calculation, the symbol ("the heaventree") seems to be only one type of "translation" among many possible translations, a way of perceiving that is quickly replaced by another, as it has itself replaced "the apathy of the stars." This is the kind of line every student of *Ulysses* would automatically circle, without having a definite idea of what the phrase actually signifies in the text.

8. An element of comedy is added here if one compares these questions and answers to those in the Christian catechism: the long, convoluted answers to simple questions in "Ithaca" are funny if one remembers the "simple," rotelike answers in the catechism to questions like "What is sin?"

9. Freud, *Jokes and Their Relation to the Unconscious*, 402.

10. See Hayman's discussion of farce in the "Cyclops" chapter in his article "Cyclops," in *James Joyce's "Ulysses": Critical Essays*. In "Cyclops," the exuberant energy of the writing leads to a more farcical performance.

11. Heath, "Structuration of the Novel-Text: Method and Analysis," 75.

12. *The Art of the Novel: Critical Prefaces by Henry James*, 5.

13. "The borough surveyor and waterworks engineer, Mr Spencer Harty, C. E., on the instructions of the waterworks committee, had prohibited the use of municipal water for purposes other than those of consumption (envisaging the possibility of recourse being had to the impotable water of the Grand and Royal canals in 1893) particularly as the South Dublin Guardians, notwithstanding their ration of 15 gallons per day per pauper . . . had been convicted of a wastage of 20,000 gallons per night" (*U* 17.173–80).

14. It is difficult to assign these irrelevant details either empirical or thematic significance, that is, to regard them as salient details of the plot or the theme. The detail is a red herring that leads nowhere in particular; we have no ready method for interpreting it. Roland Barthes, in an essay called "L'effet de réel," has called this kind of detail a sign of "the real"—it exists, he says, for purely referential purposes, to give a sense of facticity to the narrative. It seems to me that the mimetic status of these details is less important than their irrelevance to established categories; they represent both the literary "fact" that resists "recuperation" by our systems of literary criticism and the contingent "fact" that refuses to be assimilated to literary purposes.

15. That is, "What advantages attended shaving by night?" (*U* 17.277); "Why did absence of light disturb him less than presence of noise?" (*U* 17.288).

16. One is reminded of a statement James Boswell was reported to have made about himself, that there are many people who build castles in the air but he was the first to attempt to move into one.

17. The passages on Bloom's dream are reminiscent of Bouvard and Pécuchet's exhaustive efforts to improve their lot, to live out the Utopian bourgeois dream. At some point in reading the three-page description of the dream house, I felt that the observations of Bloom and the narrator were supplemented by Joyce's own desire to be able to use the quaint, faintly archaic vocabulary associated with the English country house, that is, to actually include words like "tumbling rake," "dovecote," "grindstone," et cetera, in the narrative. It is as if in a particularly palpable way, Bloom's desire for a house and Joyce's desire to write these pages were both being expressed.

18. Bloom and Stephen are, to use a line from *Finnegans Wake*, "traduced by their comedy nominator, to the loaferst terms for their aloquent parts" (*FW*, 283). (In fact, the catechism and the "resolution" of the characters into their physical and mathematical equivalents in "Ithaca" anticipate book II, chapter 2, of *Finnegans Wake*.)

19. Kenner, *Dublin's Joyce* 167. Kenner believes, however, that this mind represented in "Ithaca" "epiphanizes" the machinelike mind of the book.

20. Justifiably, one could point to the various structural schemas that Joyce was so fond of dispensing as evidence of his belief in structural organizations. To me, however, the "Ithaca" chapter represents Joyce's basic skepticism about order and schemes of order. It is possible that as a critic of his book he desired to be able to reduce it to the kind of schema he subverted within the writing. But in this case I would prefer to trust Joyce the fiction writer rather than Joyce the letter writer and critic.

21. I am indebted to Betsy Seifter for pointing this out to me.

22. For a list of rhetorical arguments, see Richard Lanham's *A Handlist of Rhetorical Terms: A Guide for Students of English Literature*, 110.

23. Girard, *Deceit, Desire, and the Novel: Self and Other in Literary Structure*, 308.

24. See Kenner, *Dublin's Joyce*, 167.

25. The attractiveness of a final understanding of the text's mysteries can be seen in an essay as recent as M. J. C. Hodgart's "Aeolus," in *James Joyce's "Ulysses": Critical Essays*: "The whole of *Ulysses* is a parable, for him who heareth the word and understandeth it; he indeed beareth fruit" (119).

26. See Budgen, *James Joyce and the Making of "Ulysses*," 15–17.

27. Gass, *On Being Blue: A Philosophical Inquiry*, 31.

28. See Goldman, *The Joyce Paradox: Form and Freedom in His Fiction*, 113–14.

29. See "Myth and Pyrrhonism" in Kenner, *Joyce's Voices*, 39–63.

Chapter 5. Joyce and Feminism

1. Gilbert and Gubar, "Sexual Linguistics," 518.

2. Richard Ellmann, *James Joyce*, revised edition, 549.

3. Scott, *James Joyce*, 127.

4. Stanislaus Joyce, *My Brother's Keeper*, 81.

5. Kristeva, *Powers of Horror*, 208.

6. Bernard Benstock, "Beyond explication: the twice-told tales in *Finnegans Wake*," 105.

7. Derrida, "Plato's Pharmacy," 88.

8. Herr, *Joyce's Anatomy of Culture*, 9.

9. I should add at this point that the genderization of his longing for home is double—for one can speak of it in patriarchal or matriarchal terms—a return, that is, to the Father or to the Mother. Later I will discuss in more detail the search for patriarchal origins.

10. Heath, "Ambiviolences," 53.

11. Bishop, *Joyce's Book of the Dark*, 356.

12. Heath, "Joyce and Language," 144.

13. In an interesting essay, Hélène Cixous looks beyond the quiet surface of "The Sis-

ters" to what she calls "the nervous laughter of writing," a gratuitousness in the language that erupts in the text. This "nervous laughter" might be a precursor of the kind of eruptions that occur in subsequent works by Joyce and suggests that the surface of *Dubliners* is less placid than former analyses of the stories have suggested. See Cixous, "Joyce: The R(use) of Writing."

14. The imagery of lewd Elizabethans *without* its subsequent cancellation appears in *Giacomo Joyce*, an erotic, lyric work which recorded Joyce's obsession with a young female pupil in Trieste. Joyce wrote *Giacomo Joyce* simultaneously with the final chapters of *A Portrait*, but, as Richard Ellmann points out in his introduction to the publication of *Giacomo Joyce* in 1968, Joyce chose not to publish the intensely personal work. Instead he "diffused" the "spirit" of it into other works such as *Exiles, Stephen Hero, A Portrait*, and later *Ulysses* (*GJ* xxii). Perhaps Joyce felt the private diary-like jottings of *Giacomo Joyce* did not effectively veil the quality of his obsession, as if he had confessed not in a foreign language. It is as if he crossed out the false image twice, once when he decided not to publish it and once when he has Stephen disown it.

15. Maud Ellmann, "Polytropic Man: Paternity, Identity and Naming in *The Odyssey* and *A Portrait of the Artist as a Young Man*," 96.

16. See my discussion of the subversion of patriarchal signature in "Paternity, the legal fiction" in Newman and Thornton's *Joyce's "Ulysses": The Larger Perspective*, 89-97.

17. Dinnerstein, 81. This coding of the paternal as invisible and maternal as visible, while consistent with one equation in Western culture between the male and the spiritual and the female and the body, is contrary to the coding in psychoanalytic theory, where the possession of the phallus links the male to the visible and normative and the absence of the phallus links the female to the invisible and the mysterious.

18. See also Jennifer Levine's discussion of this episode in "*Ulysses*," in *The Cambridge Companion to James Joyce*, 131-59.

19. See Senn, "Nausicaa," in Hart and Hayman, 277-311.

20. Power, *Conversations with James Joyce*, 32.

21. McGee, *Paperspace*, 188.

22. See Christine Van Boheemen's excellent discussion of related issues in *The Novel as Family Romance*.

23. Shari Benstock, "Nightletters," 230. Benstock argues that the prevailing reading of women in the *Wake*, focusing as it has on women and voice, has ignored the link between women and writing.

24. See Derrida, *The Postcard: From Socrates to Freud and Beyond*.

25. I would like to thank Robert Caserio, Kathryn Stockton, Barry Weller, and Meg Brady for their very insightful comments on my "compromising letter" on Joyce and women.

Chapter 6. Women Building the Foundation

1. Stein, *Wars I Have Seen*, 3.
2. Solomon, *Eternal Geomater*, ix.
3. *Modern Fiction Studies*, Vol. XV, no. 1.

4. Henke and Unkeless, *Women in Joyce*.

5. See Lodge, *Small World: An Academic Romance*.

6. Norris, 1976; French, 1976; Kristeva, 1980; Cixous, 1972.

7. See *James Joyce: The Augmented Ninth*, for Derrida, "*Ulysses* Gramophone," 27–75, and for Kristeva, "Joyce 'The Gracehoper,'" 167–80.

8. Quoted in "President Portrays Artist at Conference," 2.

9. Boland, "James Joyce: The Mystery of Influence," in *Transcultural Joyce*, 4.

10. Barreca, *Untamed and Unabashed: Essays on Women and Humor in British Literature*.

Chapter 7. "Eumaeus" Redux

1. Lawrence, *The Odyssey of Style in "Ulysses,"* 168.

2. West, "James Joyce: *Ulysses*," 120.

3. There is much talk of labor in the chapter—from Stephen's tipping the unemployed Corley about a job for a "gentleman usher" (*U* 16.158) to the longshoreman's comment on Murphy's tattoo, "[n]eat bit of work" (*U* 16.694), to Bloom's expatiation on the importance of "literary labor" (*U* 16.1153).

4. For a discussion of *Ulysses* as the text that signaled the "eruption" of "everyday" life into literature, see Henri Lefebvre, *Everyday Life in the Modern World*. For a more recent discussion of the changing nature of the "everyday," see Jules David Law, "Simulation, Pluralism, and the Politics of Everyday Life."

5. For an analysis of some of these criticisms, see Jeremy Hawthorn's fine survey of Marxist criticism in his "*Ulysses*, Modernism and Marxist Criticism."

6. Eagleton, *The Ideology of the Aesthetic*, 376. Julia Kristeva in *Revolution in Poetic Language*, like Colin MacCabe in *James Joyce and the Revolution of the Word*, locates Joyce's radicalism in his disruption of symbolic hierarchies, particularly that of male/female.

7. Fredric Jameson and W. J. McCormack have written on *Ulysses* and the "nightmare" of Ireland's colonial history. See Jameson's well-known (but, to my mind, less successful) "*Ulysses* in History" and his more recent "Modernism and Imperialism," as well as McCormack's excellent essay "Nightmares of History: James Joyce and the Phenomenon of Anglo-Irish Literature," in *James Joyce and Modern Literature*.

8. Richard Brown, *James Joyce and Sexuality*, 121.

9. In "The Long Goodbye: *Ulysses* and the End of Liberal Capitalism," Franco Moretti reads *Ulysses* as "a monumental autopsy of an entire social formation," that of British liberal capitalism, 185. *Ulysses*, he says, offers the British ruling class a "hideous caricature of itself and its world" (188). Moretti cites a passage of "Eumaeus" as example, but says no more about the chapter. His interesting essay curiously chooses to ignore Joyce's particularly Irish inflection of class analysis. He therefore reads *Ulysses* too simply as representing the decline of British capitalism rather than as charting colonial Ireland's particular relation to an ideal of productivity it had never really achieved. For in Ireland the petite bourgeoisie struggle for solid bourgeois status and are often threatened by a downward slide into the category of the unemployed. Commenting on the economic

situation in 1922, the year the Irish Free State came into being, Terence Brown remarks: "The economy supported too many unproductive people—the old and young and a considerable professional class; there were few native industries of any size.... The gravest problem, however, was the country's proximity to the United Kingdom with its advanced industrial economy, so that, as Oliver MacDonagh has succinctly stated, 'the Free State . . . was not so much . . . an undeveloped country, as . . . a pocket of underdevelopment in an advanced region'" (T. Brown, *Ireland: A Social and Cultural History: 1922–1979*, 15). For more on the economic and social situation of Dublin at the beginning of the twentieth century, see Mary E. Daly, *Dublin, The Deposed Capital: A Social and Economic History, 1860–1914*.

10. Melchiori, "The Genesis of *Ulysses*," 41.

11. Richard Ellmann, *The Consciousness of James Joyce*, and Dominic Manganiello, *Joyce's Politics*.

12. Richard Ellmann, 82–84. Characteristically, Ellmann subsumes this interest under the banner of Joyce's liberal humanism. For example, Joyce was fascinated with Tolstoy's story "How Much Land Does a Man Need," and called it the finest of all short stories. Ellmann interprets Joyce's attraction in light of Tolstoy's "sympathy for men in their follies" (74), rather than in relation to Tolstoy's ironic treatment of greed. Like Ellmann, Manganiello too quickly assimilates Joyce's fascination with radical political movements into a liberal paradigm, wholly rationalizing his interest in anarchy, for example, as one more expression of his individualism. As McCormack rightly warns, "Joyce's early reading of socialist thinkers should not be seen solely as a personal trait, a sensitive rebel's response to the inadequacies of Irish nationalism. It is intimately part of the emergence of the nexus of political and aesthetic concerns which distinguish the Irish contribution to English modernism" (McCormack, "Nightmares of History: James Joyce and the Phenomenon of Anglo-Irish Literature" 78).

13. Events between the 1904 setting of the novel and 1922 publication only increased the importance of the class and economic issues Joyce evokes in the chapter, events such as class conflicts in Dublin in 1913, the War, and the Russian Revolution. If the Citizen's speeches seem dated in 1922, after the establishment of the Irish Republic, the class and economic issues in "Eumaeus" do not.

14. Interestingly, one of the anarchists in Conrad's novel, Michaelis, is purportedly based on a Fenian anarchist, according to Martin Seymour-Smith in his introduction to the Penguin edition of *The Secret Agent*, 18.

15. Bigazzi, "Joyce and the Italian Press," in Melchiori, ed., *Joyce in Rome: The Genesis of "Ulysses."* 54–55.

16. Fogel, *Coercion to Speak: Conrad's Poetics of Dialogue*, 82.

17. Ulmer, "The Puncept in Grammatology," in Culler, ed., *On Puns: The Foundations of Letters*.

18. In the previous quotation, Bloom goes on to compare the violence undertaken for political convictions with that impelled by "love vendettas"; it is "off the same bat as those love vendettas of the south, have her or swing for her, when the husband frequently . . . inflicted fatal injuries on his adored one" (*U* 16.1060–64). Thus, Bloom's thoughts on political violence are inseparable from the repressed violence he feels to-

ward Molly. In the chapter we see that forms of male solidarity are often linked to male fears about women.

19. Althusser, "Ideology and Ideological State Apparatuses (Notes towards an Investigation)," in *Lenin and Philosophy and Other Essays*, 174.

20. Senn, "'All Kinds of Words Changing Colour': Lexical Clashes in Eumaeus," in *Inductive Scrutinies*, 558.

21. For a different view, see Richard Brown's *James Joyce and Sexuality*. Brown discusses the "new world order," dramatized in *Ulysses*, as it signals both a socialist and feminist apocalypse, in which the prostitute, proletariat, and the artist are linked (123). This view of the "working girl" in *Ulysses* is given play particularly in "Circe." I find Stephen's too-ready appropriation of prostitute as symbol somewhat suspicious.

22. This bourgeois configuration of "points" has an underside, however, like much else in the chapter; another, more violent and opposing discourse exists as well that evokes the "points" of knives reminiscent of Roman history (*U* 16.8i6) and political assassination.

23. One could regard this assertion in light of Marx's fascinating analogy in *Capital* between the father-son relation and the relation between capital and surplus value. "[Capital] differentiates itself as original value from itself as surplus-value; as the father differentiates himself from himself qua the son, yet both are one and of one age: for only by the surplus-value of £10 does the £100 originally advanced become capital, and so soon as this takes place, so soon as the son, and by the son, the father, is begotten, so soon does their difference vanish, and they again become one, £110." Marx, *Selections from Capital, The Marx-Engels Reader*, 335.

24. William Carlos Williams, extract from "A Note on the Recent Work of James Joyce," in *James Joyce: The Critical Heritage*, vol. 2, 1:377–79.

25. Stallybrass and White, *The Politics of Transgression*.

26. Interestingly, Karl Radek in his Marxist critique of *Ulysses* in the thirties described the novel as "a heap of dung, crawling with worms, photographed by a cinema apparatus through a microscope" ("Contemporary World Literature and the Tasks of Proletarian Art," in H. G. Scott, ed., *Problems of Soviet Literature*, 153). This critique of Joyce's cloacal obsession is leveled at the fetishizing of society's dirt in naturalism, which Radek implies is almost pornographic in its unstinting view of the seamy side of society (the microscope alludes to Zola's manifesto for naturalism, which was to put life under a microscope; Radek's description almost comically overdetermines the link among naturalism, dung, and technology).

27. Derek Attridge also comments on the chapter's double entendres that suggest anality, citing the phrase "moving a motion" and "he sat tight" (178). In *Peculiar Language*.

28. One might object that surely it is in nighttown that the displaced content of carnival surfaces in the novel. But I would contend that in "Circe," unlike "Eumaeus," these "bottom" issues are displaced onto a more "private" psychological arena. As White claims, the carnivalesque did not disappear from culture but was displaced onto the bourgeois discourses of psychoanalysis and art—"that which had been excluded at the level of

communal practice returned at the level of subjective articulation, as both phobia and fascination.... It is more than accidental that the major foci of carnival pleasure—food, dirt, and mess, sex and extreme body movements—find their neurasthenic, unstable, and mimicked counterparts in the discourse of hysteria" (163). White locates pantomime as the technique by which these dramas are enacted in the psyche (White, "Hysteria and the End of Carnival: Festivity and Bourgeois Neurosis," in *The Violence of Representation: Literature and the History of Violence*).

Now, without going into an analysis of "Circe," I would merely say that this notion of the displacement of carnival onto fantasy through pantomimic repetition wonderfully describes the nighttown chapter. Although it is possible to relate the use of fetish in the chapter to social production, seeing it as commodity fetishism, as Moretti has done, still the chapter seems most concerned with evoking libidinous psychic mechanisms through pantomimic exaggerations. The expressionist drama externalizes the inner dramas previously only glimpsed in the text. In "Eumaeus," dirt, mess, anality return in a different guise, in the social body of the "bottom" tenth of Dubliners.

29. Wittgenstein, *Philosophical Investigations*. G. E. M. Anscombe, 199.
30. Staten, *Wittgenstein and Derrida*, 89.
31. Culler, "The Call of the Phoneme: Introduction," in *On Puns*, 4.
32. Derrida's invocation of the "gift/Gift" can be traced back through his important essay on Bataille, "From Restricted to General Economy: A Hegelianism without Reserve," in *Writing and Difference*. Extending Bataille's idea of a general economy without reserve into a "general writing," Derrida emphasizes Bataille's notion of the "sliding" or twisting of language. Summarizing Bataille, Derrida says that "what must be found, no less than the word, is the point, *the place in a pattern* at which a word drawn from the old language will start, by virtue of having been placed there and by virtue of having received such an impulsion, to slide and to make the entire discourse slide. A certain strategic twist must be imprinted upon language; and this strategic twist, with a violent and sliding, furtive movement must inflect the old corpus in order to relate its syntax and its lexicon to major silence" (264).

What is at stake here is a radical revision of the notion of use, utility, productivity. Indeed, my discussion of waste and anality, as elements in Joyce's chapter that represent the eruption of excess into the discourse of productivity, could be related to Bataille's notion of expenditure (itself based on Mauss's discussion of gift exchange in primitive societies; see Georges Bataille, "The Notion of Expenditure"). However, I find Bataille's linking of extravagant wealth to the idea of *dépense* not wholly applicable to Joyce's focus in "Eumaeus" on the banality of the everyday within capitalism. Bataille's suggestive analyses seem to me to falter at the point of his discussion of capitalism. Perhaps closer in spirit to Joyce's treatment of the "non-productive" in "Eumaeus" is Baudrillard's critique of the "tenor of value" and the "mirror of production" in both capitalism and Marxism. Also taking off from Bataille, Baudrillard critiques the notion of productivity and use and points to the "play" that is left out of both bourgeois and Marxist discourse. The "productive *Eros*" in both, he says, "represses all the alternative qualities of meaning and exchange in symbolic discharge towards process of production, accumulation, and appropriation." This Baudrillard calls "submit[ting] . . . to the destiny of political economy and the terrorism of value" (Baudrillard, "The Mirror of Production," in *Selected Writings,* 113).

33. Derrida, "*Ulysses* Gramophone," 31.

Chapter 8. Legal Fiction or Pulp Fiction in "Lestrygonians"

1. In Kant's *Anthropology,* as cited in Derrida, "Economimesis," 23.
2. See Laplanche and Pontalis, *The Language of Psycho-analysis,* 206.
3. See Freud, *Totem and Taboo,* in *The Complete Psychological Works,* 13:1–162. Two other key writings in which Freud develops the concept further are "Mourning and Melancholia," in *Complete Psychological Works* 14:237–60, in which he speaks of incorporation as the subject identifying in the oral mode with the lost object, and *Group Psychology and the Analysis of the Ego,* in *Complete Psychological Works,* 18:67–143, in which he discusses the phenomena in more social terms related to a group identification with a powerful leader, based on an emotional common quality.
4. Derrida, "'Eating Well,'" 113.
5. Kristeva, "Joyce 'The Gracehoper,'" 168.
6. See Henry Staten's excellent chapter "How the Spirit (Almost) Became Flesh: The Gospel of John" in *Eros in Mourning: Homer to Lacan,* 47–70. See also Staten's essay "The Decomposition of *Ulysses,*" 380–92.
7. For a general "Feminist-Vegetarian Critical Theory" (which, however, wholly ignores the realm of the religious), consult Carol J. Adams, *The Sexual Politics of Meat.* See also Tucker's helpful study, *Stephen and Bloom at Life's Feast.*
8. Richard Ellmann, *Ulysses on the Liffey* appendix.
9. One is reminded of the image of generative return from the dead corpse to the living crops in the phrase "the cropse of our seedfather" in *Finnegans Wake* (*FW* 55.8).
10. Earlier, less charged moments anticipate this perception, for example at the very beginning of "Lestrygonians," when Bloom momentarily confuses his name with the "Blood of the Lamb": "Bloo. . . . Me? No. / Blood of the Lamb" (8.08–9). In "Aeolus," Bloom recalls with equanimity a Jewish account of the food chain, the chant *Chad Gadya* (One Kid) that closes the Passover seder: "And then the angel of deaths kills the butcher and he kills the ox and the dog kills the cat. Sounds a bit silly till you come to look into it well. Justice it means but it's everybody eating everyone else. That's what life is after all" (7.211–14). As Don Gifford puts it, "the kid [eaten by the cat], bottommost and most injured of all, is, of course, the people of Israel" (*"Ulysses" Annotated,* 133). The chant ends with God slaying the angel of death, avenging the victimization of the Jews.
11. See Rice's *Cannibal Joyce,* which appeared after the writing of this essay.
12. Nolan, *James Joyce and Nationalism,* 81.
13. Jameson, "*Ulysses* in History," 131.
14. Kristeva, *Powers of Horror,* 3–4, 109.
15. McMichael, "*Ulysses*" and Justice, 179–80, 181.
16. Gifford, *"Ulysses" Annotated,* 601.

17. Compare Bloom's thoughts earlier in the day about Milly: "Milly too. Young kisses: the first. . . . Lips kissed, kissing, kissed. Full gluey woman's lips" (*U* 4.444–50).
18. Budgen, *James Joyce and the Making of "Ulysses,"* 106.
19. This image resembles Kristeva's description of those devotees of the abject who look for the "desirable and terrifying, nourishing and murderous, fascinating and abject inside of the maternal body" (*Powers of Horror*, 54).
20. Kristeva, "Joyce 'The Gracehoper,'" 178.

Chapter 9. "Twenty Pockets Arent Enough For Their Lies"

1. The photograph is reproduced in Richard Ellmann, *James Joyce*, rev. ed., plate VIII.
2. This sleight of hand, what Marx called the capitalist "trick" of commodity fetishism, mystifies the connection between labor and capital. I will discuss fetishism in more detail below.
3. Pietz, "Fetishism and Materialism: The Limits of Theory in Marx," in *Fetishism as Cultural Discourse*, 131.
4. Apter, Introduction, in *Fetishism as Cultural Discourse*, 2.
5. Apter, 4.
6. After writing this essay and delivering it as a talk at the Joyce Symposium in Rome, I became aware of Peter Sims's fine article entitled "A Pocket Guide to *Ulysses*," *James Joyce Quarterly* 26: 239–58.
7. Flugel, *The Psychology of Clothes*, 72.
8. Flugel, 83. See Vincent Pecora's description of the persistence of an archaic *oikos*, or "noble household," in modern literature and philosophy, which includes a discussion of Bloom's household property, specifically, his potato. Pecora concentrates on the way in which a certain tradition of thought from Durkheim to Mauss viewed fetishism, with its nostalgic magic, as potentially liberating "things deadened by rationality, profit [and] utility" (Pecora, *Households of the Soul*, 47).
9. Hollander, *Sex and Suits*, 55.
10. Wicke, *Advertising Fictions*, 128.
11. Pietz attributes this view of the fetish as an expression of subjectivity to Hegel, whose view countered the more "objective" view of the fetish from Kant: "In contrast to Kant, Hegel emphasized the importance of random association and contingency in fetishism, which he viewed as the first spiritual expression of human subjectivity per se, in the form of arbitrary caprice and particular desire, projected and objectified as power in some (any) material object" (124, n.14).
12. "I distributed them equally among my four pockets, and sucked them turn and turn about. This raised a problem which I first solved in the following way. I had say sixteen stones, four in each of my four pockets these being the two pockets of my trousers and the two pockets of my greatcoat. Taking a stone from the right pocket of my greatcoat and putting it in my mouth, I replaced it in the right pocket of my greatcoat by a stone from the right pocket of my trousers, which I replaced by a stone from the left pocket of my trousers, which I replaced by a stone from the left pocket of my greatcoat,

which I replaced by the stone which was in my mouth, as soon as I had finished sucking it. Thus there were still four stones in each of my four pockets, but not quite the same stones" (Beckett, *Molloy*, 69). In this ritual performance, Molloy appears as a wildly exaggerated incarnation of Bloom's punctiliousness and obsessiveness.

13. Sims says that in "Circe" Bloom's pockets "play an important role as sources of comfort and prophylactic protection.... The potato, soap, and condom form a trinity of hygienic talismans, each addressing a different requirement of the phallus' protection" (245). My point is that in "Circe" Bloom's pockets are turned inside out in a risky gesture of exposure.

14. Hugh Kenner, *The Stoic Comedians*, 105.

Chapter 10. Bloom in Circulation: Who's He When He's Not at Home?

1. Barta, *Bely, Joyce, and Döblin*, xiii. See also Wirth-Nesher, *City Codes*, for a general discussion of space and movement in the urban novel.

2. Benjamin, *Charles Baudelaire*.

3. Benjamin, "On Some Motifs in Baudelaire," in *Illuminations*, 172. For a fine discussion of Benjamin's treatment of Baudelaire, see Susan Buck-Morss, *The Dialectics of Seeing*.

4. Gleber, 4. See especially chapter 1, "Walking Texts: Toward a Theory of Literary Flanerie" (3–21) and chapter 3, "Passages of Flanerie: Kracauer and Benjamin" (43–60). See also Benjamin's *The Arcades Project*.

5. On the Benjamin/Joyce panels, Luke Gibbons spoke of flanerie in "'Met him pike hoses': Joyce, 1798 and Modern Memory," and Patrick McGee delivered "Communist Flânerie, or Joyce's Boredom." Enda Duffy presented "The Coach to Venice: Dreaming Cities, Sleeping Streets." Duffy's book *The Subaltern "Ulysses"* includes a long chapter entitled "Traffic Accidents: The Modernist Flaneur and Postcolonial Culture" (53–92).

6. See Golsan, "The Beholder as *Flâneur*."

7. Certeau, *The Practice of Everyday Life*, xix. Further references will be cited parenthetically in the text.

8. Nicholson, *The "Ulysses" Guide*, vii.

9. Benjamin, *Charles Baudelaire*, 46.

10. Budgen, 68.

11. For a fuller discussion of this language and its ideological nuances, see "'Eumaeus' Redux," chapter 7.

12. Stewart, *On Longing*, 116. Further references will be cited parenthetically in the text.

13. Rodstein, "Back to 1904." Rodstein demonstrates that Joyce's representation of nationalism, particularly in "Cyclops," is "structured within an intricate time scheme in which the very different political landscape of 1904 plays against the tumultuous events of the decade in which *Ulysses* was written" (146).

14. See Hickey and Hickey, *Faithful Departed*, xv.

15. Patricia Hutchins; David Pierce; Frank Delaney.

16. The first International James Joyce Symposium was held in Dublin in 1967, and for a number of years it was limited to cities where Joyce had actually lived.

17. In *Bloomsway*, Fennell gives an "evocation of contemporary Dublin" in which he follows the itinerary of Leopold Bloom.

18. The succession of Bloomsdays has generated a host of souvenirs for the tribe known as Joyceans—photographs, objects, programs, T-shirts—souvenirs that objectify desire. There is something nostalgic in these Joycean rituals that is simultaneously countered by annual (or more frequent) attempts to produce something new. Both the nostalgia and scholarly ambition were apparent in the 2004 International James Joyce Symposium in Dublin, which commemorated the one-hundred-year anniversary of the fictional day in *Ulysses*.

19. Seidel, *Epic Geography*.

Chapter 11. Close Encounters

1. Frank, "Spatial Form in Modern Literature," 3–62.

2. Luhmann, *Theories of Distinction*, 100. Further references will be cited parenthetically in the text.

3. G. Spencer Brown, *Laws of Form*, v.

4. Rasch, "Introduction: The Self-Positing Society," in Luhmann, *Theories of Distinction*, 21.

5. James, Preface to *Roderick Hudson*, in *The Art of the Novel: Critical Prefaces*, 5.

6. See Derrida, *Of Hospitality: Anne Dufourmantelle Invites Jacques Derrida to Respond*, 25: "Absolute hospitality should break with the law of hospitality as right or duty, with the 'pact' of hospitality. To put it in different terms, absolute hospitality requires that I open up my home and that I give not only to the foreigner . . . but to the absolute, unknown, anonymous other, and that I *give place* to them." Further references will be cited parenthetically in the text as *Hospitality*.

7. Derrida, *Of Grammatology*.

8. Derrida, "Before the Law," in *Acts of Literature*. Further references will be cited parenthetically in the text as "Law."

9. Jameson, "Modernism and Imperialism," in *Nationalism, Colonialism, and Literature*, 50–51. Further references will be cited parenthetically in the text.

10. Like Jameson, Harold Bloom, in "The Breaking of Form," shows how the attempted exclusion of the other can signify as a formal absence. Unlike Jameson, whose Marxist interest focuses on collective identities rather than on individual figures, Bloom looks at the way individual poets engage in Oedipal struggles with their precursors: "The defensive measures of the poetic self against the fantasized precursor can be witnessed in operation only by the study of a difference . . . [that] depends upon our awareness not so much of presences as of absences, of *what is missing in the poem because it had to be excluded*" (15). His anxiety of influence is described as "an openness that *must* in time scar the narcissism of the poet *qua* poet" (17).

11. More recent work on Joyce engages the relation between his semicolonial status and the formal deformations in his texts. See Christine Van Boheemen-Saaf, in *Joyce,*

Derrida, Lacan, and the Trauma of History, who argues that it is precisely Joyce's "peculiar placement" as Irish colonial subject that inaugurates the scarring of his text (52). See also Enda Duffy's recent essay, "Disappearing Dublin: *Ulysses,* Postcoloniality, and the Politics of Space." Completely reversing Jameson's reading of the possibility of totality in *Ulysses,* Duffy sees the missing details in the text as a sign of the potential for resistance:

> Reading modern works, critics tend to consider the unsaid a negative entity: the secret the text pushes into its unconscious. This is appropriate for texts that bolster existing hegemonic powers. When, however, a subaltern text is in question, then the unsaid may exist as the unarticulated possibility of a utopia ... this eloquent subaltern unsaid marks, therefore, the trace of *ressentiment,* where the abject refuses to acknowledge the monuments, and scars, of the master's dominance. (54)

12. Forster, *A Passage to India.* Further references will be cited parenthetically to this edition.

13. Forster, *Howards End,* 187.

14. See Said, *Beginnings: Intention and Method,* 138.

15. Suleri, *The Rhetoric of English India,* 145. Further references will be cited parenthetically in the text.

16. Forster, *A Room with a View* and *Where Angels Fear to Tread.*

17. Mohanty, "Us and Them: On the Philosophical Bases of Political Criticism," 13. This distinction underpins the logocentrism of Western metaphysics. In his 1929–1930 lectures on the nature of metaphysics, Martin Heidegger explores the ethical limits of inclusion and questions the difference between the human, the animal, and the stone. He concludes that only man has the capacity for "world-making" and excludes both the animal and the stone from *Dasein*'s openness of being. See part 2 of Heidegger's *The Fundamental Concepts of Metaphysics: World, Finitude, Solitude.*

18. See Forster, "The Other Boat" and "The Life to Come," in *The Life to Come, and Other Stories.*

19. Forster is quoted in Stallybrass, Introduction to Forster, *The Life to Come, and Other Stories* (xiv). Further references to Stallybrass's Introduction will be cited parenthetically in the text as "Introduction."

20. Mark C. Taylor, "Infinity: Emmanuel Levinas," 204. Further references will be cited parenthetically in the text.

21. For fascinating readings of the "queering" of Forster's texts, see the essays collected in Martini and Piggford, eds., *Queer Forster.* See, especially, Tamera Dorland, "'Contrary to the Prevailing Current': Homoeroticism and the Voice of Maternal Law in 'The Other Boat.'"

22. The word "queer," meaning explicitly homosexual, is an American coinage of the 1920s. In Irish parlance, the word signaled peculiarity, strangeness, and eccentricity even in Joyce's day—see the *Oxford English Dictionary.* Also see Valente's edited collection, *Quare Joyce.*

23. See J. Hillis Miller's discussion in "The Critic as Host," 20.

24. Rabaté, *James Joyce and the Politics of Egoism*, 167. Further references will be cited parenthetically in the text.

25. Norris, "A Walk on the Wild(e) Side: The Doubled Reading of 'An Encounter,'" *Quare Joyce*.

26. Deane, "Dead Ends: Joyce's Finest Moments," 25. Further references will be cited parenthetically in the text.

27. It is not, therefore, equivalent to the closed lyric circle envisioned by Stephen Dedalus in *A Portrait of the Artist as a Young Man*, "the form wherein the artist presents his image in immediate relation to himself" (*P* 214). Although it is outside the scope of this essay, one could discuss Stephen's typology of forms, lyrical, epic, and dramatic, in terms of the geometries of inclusion and exclusion and hospitality that I have been charting in this essay. The now-famous definition of the dramatic form, wherein "the artist, like the God of the creation, remains within or behind or beyond or above his handiwork, invisible, refined out of existence, indifferent, paring his fingernails" (*P* 215) is a definition fraught with the paradoxes of form-making that plagued Bertram Russell in his attempts to exclude the paradox of omniscience from his logical program—for a discussion of these paradoxes, and their treatment by cyberneticists and set theorists, see Rasch's introduction to Luhmann's *Theories of Distinction*, particularly 15–19.

28. See Stuart Gilbert, *James Joyce's "Ulysses": A Study*, 30.

Chapter 12. Joyce in Transit

1. James Joyce, *Ulysses: The Corrected Text*, 9.147–49.
2. DiBattista, "The bogey of realism in John McGahern's *Amongst Women*," 21.
3. Bassnett-McGuire, *Translation Studies*, 55.
4. Derrida, "Envois," in *The Postcard: From Socrates to Freud and Beyond*, 52.
5. Moretti, "The Long Goodbye: *Ulysses* and the End of Liberal Capitalism," 185. See also Richard Ellmann, *James Joyce*; Hugh Kenner, *Ulysses* and *Joyce's Voices*.
6. See Bhabha, "How Newness Enters the World: Postmodern Space, Postcolonial Times and the Trials of Cultural Translation," in *The Location of Culture*, 223.
7. Jameson, "Modernism and Imperialism," 60.
8. Kiberd, *Inventing Ireland: The Literature of the Modern Nation*, 344.
9. See Boland, "James Joyce: The Mystery of Influence," *Transcultural Joyce*, 13.
10. Boland, "James Joyce," 14.
11. Brophy, *In Transit: An Heroi-Cyclic Novel*, 143. Further references are cited parenthetically in the text.
12. Newman, "Brigid Brophy," in *Dictionary of Literary Biography*, 14: 137–38.
13. Deleuze and Guattari, *Anti-Oedipus: Capitalism and Schizophrenia*; Kristeva, *Desire in Language: A Semiotic Approach to Literature and Art*.
14. Ortiz, *Cuban Counterpoint: Tobacco and Sugar*, 102.
15. Mutilation of the herms was the crime for which Alcibiades was deprived of command of the Athenian expedition to Sicily during the Peloponnesian War.
16. Norman Brown, *Love's Body*, 50.
17. Dock, "An Interview with Brigid Brophy," 159.

18. Brophy, *Prancing Novelist*, 81.
19. Brophy, *Don't Never Forget: Collected Views and Reviews*, 245.
20. Ibid., 243.

Chapter 13. Reopening "A Painful Case"

1. The two numbers of *Critical Inquiry* dedicated to the case as genre appeared after this essay was completed. Rather than revise our piece into a direct engagement with these already influential numbers, we have let the points of contact remain serendipitous. The present essay might be read, then, as a kind of inadvertent supplement to those eighteen essays. See *Critical Inquiry* 33 (Summer 2007) and 34 (Autumn 2007), particularly special issue editor Lauren Berlant's introductory essays to each number. We also missed the chance to benefit from Cóilín Owens's *James Joyce's Painful Case*, a book-length study of the story we address.

2. Kershner, *Joyce, Bakhtin, & Popular Culture: Chronicles of Disorder*, 111.

3. Kershner also observes Duffy's elision from these sentences and links it to the character's spectrality: "We cannot fail to notice that in the description of his most intimate activity Duffy is not present. He haunts the syntax of the sentences like a passive ghost, never appearing even as pronoun. Like a déclassé Deity, he is the absent cause of his own creation" (112).

4. The apple that "might have been left" and forgotten in Duffy's desk has been much remarked on. R. B. Kershner connects it to an anecdote about the German dramatist Schiller, whose wife told Goethe that her husband could not write without the odor produced by a drawer full of rotting apples. Roberta Jackson reads Joyce's allusion to the Schiller anecdote as signaling Duffy's homosexuality on the grounds that German culture functioned at the time *Dubliners* was written as both a terminological source and a shibboleth for same-sex desire. For Colleen Lamos, the rotting apple "testifies to Duffy's constrained appetite in general." It is also worth noting, apropos of the weird elision of agency in the sentence, that the narrator's uncertainties as to the exact source of the "faint fragrance" and to the very existence of a rotting apple that "might have been left" depart from the omniscient point of view that otherwise characterizes the narrative. See Kershner, "Mr. Duffy's Apple," in *James Joyce Quarterly* 29: 406; Roberta Jackson, "The Open Closet in *Dubliners*: James Duffy's Painful Case," in *James Joyce Quarterly* 37: 93; Lamos, "Duffy's Subjectivation: The Psychic Life of 'A Painful Case,'" in *European Joyce Studies 10: Masculinities in Joyce/Postcolonial Constructions*, 62.

5. In this way, the ethics of the writer as instrumentalist and master are implicitly introduced. Joyce always boasted of the use he could make of the cases he discovered around him, and it is a commonplace of Joyce lore that his friends worried what he would make of them in his fiction.

6. Levinas, *Ethics and Infinity: Conversations with Philippe Nemo*, 85–87.

7. In "Having to Answer," an unpublished essay on the law of the "second person" in "A Painful Case," James McMichael says: "For me, Duffy has to be touched by Mrs Sinico's insistently particular need before he can as much as begin to identify the political oppressions operating within himself ... [I]t is my view that on the way toward all third

persons who are collectively the stuff of any first person's political world, there can be no detour around the second person."

8. See Jana Giles, "The Craft of 'A Painful Case': A Study of the Revisions," 209; see also *James Joyce Archive* 4, 133.

9. The passage, commonly associated with the Eucharist, is from I Corinthians 5:7–8: "For even Christ our Passover is sacrificed for us: therefore let us keep the feast, not with old leaven, neither with the leaven of malice and wickedness; but with the unleavened bread of sincerity and truth." We are grateful to Vicki Mahaffey for hearing this echo and drawing it to our attention.

10. The constellation of city–hospitality–outcast in "A Painful Case" makes Sophocles' *Oedipus at Colonus* one of its unrecognized intertexts. See Derrida's discussion of the play in *Of Hospitality*. For Derrida on cities of refuge, see the first essay in his *On Cosmopolitanism and Forgiveness*.

11. Redmond, *Home Rule: Speeches of John Redmond, M.P.*, page number unknown.

12. Leonard, *Reading "Dubliners" Again: A Lacanian Perspective*; the descriptor "self-congratulatory" in relation to Duffy's realizations is Leonard's (227).

13. Deane, "Dead Ends: Joyce's Finest Moments," in *Semicolonial Joyce*, 25.

14. Jackson, 95.

15. Norris, *Suspicious Readings of "Dubliners"* 169, 170, 168. Heterosexuality in Rich's discussion is "compulsory" in the sense of being conceptually and ideologically presumptive—that is, beyond question, taken for granted—and not in the sense of being compelled through the use of brute force, although Rich touches on situations in which the latter is also true. See Adrienne Rich, "Compulsory Heterosexuality and Lesbian Experience," 631–60.

16. Lamos, 66; original emphasis.

17. Deane, 34, 35.

Bibliography

Adams, Carol J. *The Sexual Politics of Meat*. New York: Continuum, 1990.
Althusser, Louis. "Ideology and Ideological State Apparatuses (Notes towards an Investigation)." *Lenin and Philosophy and Other Essays*. Trans. B. Brewster. London: New Left Books, 1971.
Apter, Emily. Introduction. Apter and Pietz 1–9.
Apter, Emily, and William Pietz, eds. *Fetishism as Cultural Discourse*. Ithaca, N.Y.: Cornell University Press, 1993.
Attridge, Derek, ed. *The Cambridge Companion to James Joyce*. Cambridge, England: Cambridge University Press, 1990.
Attridge, Derek. *Peculiar Language: Literature as Difference From the Renaissance to James Joyce*. Ithaca, N.Y.: Cornell University Press, 1988.
Attridge, Derek, and Daniel Ferrer, eds. *Post-Structuralist Joyce: Essays from the French*. Cambridge: Cambridge University Press, 1984.
Attridge, Derek, and Marjorie Howes, eds. *Semicolonial Joyce*. Cambridge: Cambridge University Press, 2000.
Barreca, Regina. *Untamed and Unabashed: Essays on Women and Humor in British Literature*. Detroit: Wayne State University Press, 1994.
Barta, Peter I. *Bely, Joyce, and Döblin: Peripatetics in the City Novel*. Gainesville: University Press of Florida, 1996.
Barthes, Roland. *Camera Lucida: Reflections on Photography*. Trans. Richard Howard. New York: Hill and Wang, 1981.
———. *Critical Essays*. Trans. Richard Howard. Evanston, Ill.: Northwestern University Press, 1972.
———. *Le Degré zéro de lécriture suivi de nouveaux essais critiques*. Paris: Seuil, 1972.
———. "L'effet de réel." *Communications* 11 (1968): 84–89.
———. *Essais critiques*. Paris: Seuil, 1964.
———. "Style and its Image." *Literary Style: A Symposium*. Ed. Seymour Chatman. New York: Oxford University Press, 1971. 3–10.
Bassnett-McGuire, Susan. *Translation Studies*. London: Methuen, 1980.
Bataille, Georges. "The Notion of Expenditure." *Visions of Excess: Selected Writings, 1927–1939*. Trans. Allan Stoeckl, Carl R. Lovitt, and Donald M. Leslie, Jr. Ed. Allan Stoeckl. Minneapolis: University of Minnesota Press, 1985.
Baudrillard, Jean. "The Mirror of Production." *Selected Writings*. Stanford, Calif.: Stanford University Press, 1988. 98–118.

Beckett, Samuel. *Three Novels by Samuel Beckett: "Molloy," "Malone Dies," "The Unnamable."* New York: Grove Press, 1955.

Benjamin, Walter. *The Arcades Project.* Trans. Howard Eiland and Kevin McLaughlin. Cambridge, Mass.: Belknap, 1999.

———. *Charles Baudelaire: A Lyric Poet in the Era of High Capitalism.* Trans. Harry Zohn. London: Verso, 1983.

———. *Illuminations.* Trans. Harry Zohn. Ed. Hannah Arendt. New York: Schocken Books, 1969.

Benstock, Bernard. "Beyond explication: the twice-told tales in *Finnegans Wake.*" *Joyce: The Centennial Symposium.* Ed. Morris Beja et al. Urbana: University of Illinois Press, 1986. 95–108.

Benstock, Shari. "Nightletters: woman's writing in the *Wake.*" *Critical Essays on James Joyce.* Ed. Bernard Benstock. Boston: G. K. Hall, 1985. 221–33.

Berlant, Lauren. Introduction. *Critical Inquiry* 33 (Summer 2007).

———. Introduction. *Critical Inquiry* 34 (Autumn 2007).

Bhabha, Homi K. "How Newness Enters the World: Postmodern Space, Postcolonial Times and the Trials of Cultural Translation." *The Location of Culture.* London: Routledge, 1994. 212–35.

Bigazzi, Carla. "Joyce and the Italian Press." Melchiori 52–66.

Bishop, John. *Joyce's Book of the Dark: "Finnegans Wake."* Madison: University of Wisconsin Press, 1986.

Bloom, Harold. *The Anxiety of Influence: A Theory of Poetry.* New York: Oxford University Press, 1973.

———. "The Breaking of Form." *Deconstruction and Criticism.* Ed. Harold Bloom. New York: Continuum Publishers, 1979. 1–37.

Boland, Eavan. "James Joyce: The Mystery of Influence." *Transcultural Joyce.* Ed. Karen R. Lawrence. New York: Cambridge University Press, 1998. 11–20.

Brophy, Brigid. *Don't Never Forget: Collected Views and Reviews.* New York: Holt, Rinehart and Winston, 1966.

———. *In Transit: An Heroi-Cyclic Novel.* 1969. New York: G. P. Putnam's Sons, 1970.

———. *Prancing Novelist: A Defence of Fiction in the Form of a Critical Biography in Praise of Ronald Firbank.* London: Macmillan, 1973.

Brown, G. Spencer. *Laws of Form.* New York: Julian Press, 1972.

Brown, Norman O. *Love's Body.* New York: Random House, 1966.

Brown, Richard. *James Joyce and Sexuality.* Cambridge: Cambridge University Press, 1985.

Brown, Terence. *Ireland: A Social and Cultural History: 1922–1979.* London: Fontana, 1981.

Bruns, Gerald L. "Eumaeus." Hart and Hayman 363–83.

Buck-Morss, Susan. *The Dialectics of Seeing: Walter Benjamin and the Arcades Project.* Cambridge, Mass.: The MIT Press, 1995.

Budgen, Frank. *James Joyce and the Making of "Ulysses."* Bloomington: Indiana University Press, 1960.

Burgess, Anthony. *Joysprick: An Introduction to the Language of James Joyce*. London: Andre Deutsch, 1973.
Certeau, Michel de. *The Practice of Everyday Life*. Trans. Steven Rendall. Berkeley: University of California Press, 1984.
Cixous, Hélène. *The Exile of James Joyce*. New York: David Lewis, 1972.
———. "Joyce: The R(use) of Writing." Attridge and Ferrer 15–30.
Cope, Jackson. "Sirens." Hart and Hayman 217–42.
Culler, Jonathan. "The Call of the Phoneme: Introduction." Culler 1–16.
Culler, Jonathan, ed. *On Puns: The Foundations of Letters*. Oxford: Basil Blackwell, 1988.
Daly, Mary E. *Dublin, The Deposed Capital: A Social and Economic History, 1860–1914*. Cork, Ireland: Cork University Press, 1984.
Deane, Seamus. "Dead Ends: Joyce's Finest Moments." Attridge and Howes 21–36.
Delaney, Frank. *James Joyce's Odyssey: A Guide to the Dublin of "Ulysses."* London: Hodder and Stoughton, 1981.
Deleuze, Gilles, and Felix Guattari. *Anti-Oedipus: Capitalism and Schizophrenia*. Trans. Robert Hurley, Mark Seem, and Helen R. Lane. Minneapolis: University of Minnesota Press, 1981.
Derrida, Jacques. "Before the Law." *Acts of Literature*. Ed. Derek Attridge. New York: Routledge Publishers, 1992. 181–220.
———. "'Eating Well,' or the Calculation of the Subject: An Interview with Jacques Derrida." *Who Comes after the Subject?* Ed. Eduardo Cadava, Peter Connor, and Jean-Luc Nancy. New York: Routledge, 1991. 96–119.
———. "Economimesis." *Diacritics* 11 (Summer 1981).
———. "From Restricted to General Economy: A Hegelianism without Reserve." *Writing and Difference*, 251–77.
———. *Of Grammatology*. Baltimore: Johns Hopkins University Press, 1976.
———. *Of Hospitality: Anne Dufourmantelle Invites Jacques Derrida to Respond*. Trans. Rachel Bowlby. Stanford, Calif.: Stanford University Press, 2000.
———. *On Cosmopolitanism and Forgiveness*. Trans. Mark Dooley and Michael Hughes. London: Routledge, 2001.
———. "Plato's Pharmacy." *Dissemination*. Trans. Barbara Johnson. Chicago: University of Chicago Press, 1981. 61–172.
———. *The Postcard: From Socrates to Freud and Beyond*. Trans. Alan Bass. Chicago: University of Chicago Press, 1987.
———. "Two Words for Joyce." Attridge and Ferrer 145–59.
———. "*Ulysses* Gramophone: Hear Say Yes in Joyce." *James Joyce: The Augmented Ninth*. Ed. Bernard Benstock. Syracuse, N.Y.: Syracuse University Press, 1988. 27–75.
———. *Writing and Difference*. Trans. Alan Bass. Chicago: University of Chicago Press, 1978.
DiBattista, Maria. "The bogey of realism in John McGahern's *Amongst Women*." *Transcultural Joyce*. Ed. Karen R. Lawrence. Cambridge: Cambridge University Press, 1998. 21–36.

Dinnerstein, Dorothy. *The Mermaid and the Minotaur*. New York: Harper and Row, 1963.

Dock, Leslie. "An Interview with Brigid Brophy." *Contemporary Literature* 17 (Spring 1976): 151–70.

Dorland, Tamera. "'Contrary to the Prevailing Current': Homoeroticism and the Voice of Maternal Law in 'The Other Boat.'" Martini and Piggford 193–219.

Duffy, Enda. "The Coach to Venice: Dreaming Cities, Sleeping Streets." 17th International James Joyce Symposium. Goldsmiths College, University of London. June 2000.

———. "Disappearing Dublin: *Ulysses*, Postcoloniality, and the Politics of Space." Attridge and Howes 37–57.

———. *The Subaltern "Ulysses."* Minneapolis: University of Minnesota Press, 1994.

Eagleton, Terry. *The Ideology of the Aesthetic*. Oxford: Basil Blackwell, 1990.

Eagleton, Terry, Fredric Jameson, and Edward Said. *Nationalism, Colonialism, and Literature*. Ed. Seamus Deane. Minneapolis: University of Minnesota Press, 1990.

Ellmann, Maud. "Polytropic man: paternity, identity and naming in *The Odyssey* and *A Portrait of the Artist as a Young Man*." MacCabe, *James Joyce: New Perspectives* 73–104.

Ellmann, Richard. *The Consciousness of James Joyce*. New York: Oxford University Press, 1977.

———. *James Joyce*. New York: Oxford University Press, 1959.

———. *James Joyce*. 1959. Rev. ed. New York: Oxford University Press, 1982.

———. *Ulysses on the Liffey*. Oxford: Oxford University Press, 1972.

"Feminist Joyceans Demand More Say." *Boston Globe*, June 13, 1983.

Fennell, Desmond. *Bloomsway: A Day in the Life of Dublin*. Dublin: Poolbeg Press, 1990.

Flugel, J. C. *The Psychology of Clothes*. New York: International Universities Press, 1930.

Fogel, Aaron. *Coercion to Speak: Conrad's Poetics of Dialogue*. Cambridge, Mass.: Harvard University Press, 1985.

Forster, E. M. *Howards End*. New York: Random House, 1921.

———. *The Life to Come, and Other Stories*. New York: W. W. Norton, 1972.

———. *A Passage to India*. San Diego: Harcourt Brace Jovanovich, 1924.

———. *A Room with a View*. London: Edward Arnold, 1908.

———. *Where Angels Fear to Tread*. London: Edward Arnold, 1905.

Frank, Joseph. "Spatial Form in Modern Literature." *Sewanee Review* 53 (1945). Rev. and rpt. in *The Widening Gyre: Crisis and Mastery in Modern Literature*. Bloomington: Indiana University Press, 1963. 3–62.

French, Marilyn. *The Book as World: James Joyce's "Ulysses."* Cambridge, Mass.: Harvard University Press, 1976.

———. *The Women's Room*. New York: Summit Books, 1977.

Freud, Sigmund. *Group Psychology and the Analysis of the Ego. The Complete Psychological Works*. Trans. James Strachey. London: Hogarth Press, 1953–1974. 18:67–143.

———. *Jokes and Their Relation to the Unconscious*. Trans. James Strachey. 1905. Reprinted in *Theories of Comedy*. Ed. Paul Lauter. New York: Doubleday & Company, 1964.

———. "Mourning and Melancholia." *The Complete Psychological Works*. Trans. James Strachey. London: Hogarth Press, 1953–1974. 14: 237–60.
———. *Totem and Taboo*. *The Complete Psychological Works*. Trans. James Strachey. London: Hogarth Press, 1953–1974. 13: 1–162.
Frye, Northrop. *Anatomy of Criticism: Four Essays*. Princeton, N.J.: Princeton University Press, 1957.
Gass, William, H. "The Medium of Fiction." *Fiction and the Figures of Life*. New York: Alfred A. Knopf, 1970.
———. *On Being Blue: A Philosophical Inquiry*. Boston: David R. Godine, 1975.
Gibbons, Luke. "'Met him pike hoses': Joyce, 1798 and Modern Memory." 17th International James Joyce Symposium. Goldsmiths College, University of London. June 2000.
Gifford, Don, with Robert J. Seidman. *"Ulysses" Annotated: Notes for James Joyce's "Ulysses."* Rev. Edition. Berkeley: University of California Press, 1988.
Gilbert, Sandra M., and Susan Gubar. "Sexual linguistics: gender, language, sexuality." *New Literary History* 16 (1985): 515–43.
Gilbert, Stuart. *James Joyce's "Ulysses": A Study*. New York: Vintage Books, 1955.
Giles, Jana. "The Craft of 'A Painful Case': A Study of the Revisions." *New Perspectives on Dubliners*. European Joyce Studies 7. Amsterdam: Rodopi, 1997.
Girard, René. *Deceit, Desire, and the Novel: Self and Other in Literary Structure*. Trans. Yvonne Freccero. Baltimore: Johns Hopkins University Press, 1965.
Gleber, Anke. *The Art of Taking a Walk: Flanerie, Literature, and Film in Weimar Culture*. Princeton, N.J.: Princeton University Press, 1999.
Goldberg, S. L. *The Classical Temper: A Study of James Joyce's "Ulysses."* London: Chatto and Windus, 1961.
———. *Joyce*. 1962. Rpt. ed. New York: Capricorn Books, 1972.
Goldman, Arnold. *The Joyce Paradox: Form and Freedom in His Fiction*. London: Routledge & Kegan Paul, 1966.
Golsan, Katherine. "The Beholder as *Flâneur*: Structures of Perception in Baudelaire and Manet." *French Forum* 21.2 (May 1996): 165–86.
Hart, Clive. "Wandering Rocks." Hart and Hayman 181–216.
Hart, Clive, and David Hayman, eds. *James Joyce's "Ulysses": Critical Essays*. Berkeley: University of California Press, 1974.
Hawthorn, Jeremy. "*Ulysses*, Modernism and Marxist Criticism." *James Joyce and Modern Literature*. Ed. W. J. McCormack and Alistair Stead. London: Routledge, 1982. 112–25.
Hayman, David. "Cyclops." Hart and Hayman 243–75.
———. "Language of/as Gesture in Joyce." *"Ulysses"; cinquante ans après: franco-anglais sur le chef-d'oeuvre de James Joyce*. Ed. Louis Bonnerot. Paris: Didier, 1974.
———. *"Ulysses": The Mechanics of Meaning*. Englewood Cliffs, N.J.: Prentice-Hall, 1970.
Heath, Stephen. "Ambiviolences: notes for reading Joyce." Attridge and Ferrer 31–68.
———. "Joyce and language." MacCabe, *James Joyce: New Perspectives* 129–48.

———. "Structuration of the Novel-Text: Method and Analysis." *Signs of the Times: Introductory Readings in Textual Semiotics.* Cambridge, U.K.: Granta, 1971.
Heidegger, Martin. *The Fundamental Concepts of Metaphysics: World, Finitude, Solitude.* Trans. William McNeill and Nicholas Walker. Bloomington: Indiana University Press, 1995.
Henke, Suzette, and Elaine Unkeless, eds. *Women in Joyce.* Urbana: University of Illinois Press, 1982.
Herr, Cheryl. *Joyce's Anatomy of Culture.* Urbana: University of Illinois Press, 1986.
Hickey, Kieran, and Des Hickey. *Faithful Departed: The Dublin of James Joyce's "Ulysses."* Dublin: Ward River Press, 1982.
Hodgart, M. J. C. "Aeolus." Hart and Hayman 115–30.
Hollander, Anne. *Sex and Suits.* New York: Alfred A. Knopf, 1994.
Hutchins, Patricia. *James Joyce's Dublin.* London: The Grey Walls Press, 1950.
Iser, Wolfgang. *The Implied Reader: Patterns of Communication in Prose Fiction from Bunyan to Beckett.* Baltimore: Johns Hopkins University Press, 1974.
Jackson, Roberta. "The Open Closet in *Dubliners*: James Duffy's Painful Case." *James Joyce Quarterly* 37 (Fall 1999/Winter 2000): 83–97.
James, Henry. *The Art of the Novel: Critical Prefaces by Henry James.* New York: Charles Scribner's Sons, 1962.
———. Preface to *Roderick Hudson*. James.
———. Preface to *The Tragic Muse*. James.
Jameson, Fredric. "Metacommentary." *PMLA* 86 (Jan. 1971): 13.
———. "Modernism and Imperialism." *Nationalism, Colonialism, and Literature.* Ed. Seamus Deane. Minneapolis: University of Minnesota Press, 1996. 44–66.
———. "*Ulysses* in History." McCormack and Stead 126–41.
Joyce, James. *Dubliners*. Ed. Robert Scholes in consultation with Richard Ellmann. New York: Viking Press, 1967.
———. *Finnegans Wake.* New York: Viking Press, 1939.
———. *Giacomo Joyce.* Ed. Richard Ellmann. New York: Viking Press, 1968.
———. *James Joyce Archives.* Ed. Michael Grodin et al. New York: Garland Publishing, 1977–1979.
———. *Letters of James Joyce.* Vol. 1, ed. Stuart Gilbert, 1957. Vols. 2 and 3. Ed. Richard Ellmann. New York: Viking Press, 1966.
———. *A Portrait of the Artist as a Young Man.* Ed. Chester G. Anderson. New York: Viking Press, 1964.
———. *Selected Letters of James Joyce.* Ed. Richard Ellmann. New York: Viking Press, 1975.
———. *Stephen Hero.* Ed. John J. Slocum and Herbert Cahoon. New York: New Directions, 1963.
———. *"Ulysses": The Corrected Text.* Ed. Hans Walter Gabler with Wolfhard Steppe and Claus Melchior. New York: Random House, Vintage, 1986.
Joyce, Stanislaus. *The Dublin Diary of Stanislaus Joyce.* Ed. George Harris Healey. London: Faber and Faber, 1962.

———. *My Brother's Keeper: James Joyce's Early Years*. Ed. Richard Ellmann. London: Faber, 1958.
Kellogg, Robert. "Scylla and Charybdis." Hart and Hayman 147–79.
Kenner, Hugh. *Dublin's Joyce*. 1956. Rpt. Boston: Beacon Press, 1962.
———. *Joyce's Voices*. Berkeley: University of California Press, 1978.
———. "The Rhetoric of Silence." *James Joyce Quarterly* 14 (Summer 1977): 382–94.
———. *The Stoic Comedians: Flaubert, Joyce, and Beckett*. Berkeley: University of California Press, 1962.
———. *Ulysses*. Baltimore: Johns Hopkins University Press, 1987.
Kermode, Frank. "Novels: Recognition and Deception." *Critical Inquiry* 1 (Sept. 1974): 103–22.
Kershner, R. B. *Joyce, Bakhtin, & Popular Culture: Chronicles of Disorder*. Chapel Hill: University of North Carolina Press, 1989.
———. "Mr. Duffy's Apple." *James Joyce Quarterly* 29 (Winter 1992).
Kiberd, Declan. *Inventing Ireland: The Literature of the Modern Nation*. Cambridge, Mass.: Harvard University Press, 1995.
Kierkegaard, Søren. *The Point of View for My Work as an Author: A Report to History and Related Writings*. Trans. Walter Lowrie. Ed. Benjamin Nelson. New York: Harper & Brothers, 1962.
Klimpel, Ben D. "The Voices of *Ulysses*," *Style* 9 (Summer 1975): 283–319.
Kristeva, Julia. *Desire in Language: A Semiotic Approach to Literature and Art*. Ed. Leon S. Roudiez. Trans. Thomas Gora, Alice Jardine, and Leon S. Roudiez. New York: Columbia University Press, 1980.
———. "Joyce 'The Gracehoper' or the Return of Orpheus." *James Joyce: The Augmented Ninth*. Ed. Bernard Benstock. Syracuse, N.Y.: Syracuse University Press, 1988. 167–80.
———. *Powers of Horror: An Essay on Abjection*. Trans. Leon S. Roudiez. New York: Columbia University Press, 1982.
———. *Revolution in Poetic Language*. Trans. Margaret Waller. New York: Columbia University Press, 1984.
Lamos, Colleen. "Duffy's Subjectivation: The Psychic Life of 'A Painful Case.'" *Masculinities in Joyce/Postcolonial Constructions*. European Joyce Studies 10. Ed. Christine Van Boheemen-Saaf and Colleen Lamos. Amsterdam: Rodopi, 2001. 59–71.
Lanham, Richard. *A Handlist of Rhetorical Terms: A Guide for Students of English Literature*. Berkeley: University of California Press, 1969.
Laplanche, J., and J. B. Pontalis. *The Language of Psycho-analysis*. Trans. Donald Nicholson-Smith. New York: W. W. Norton, 1973.
Law, Jules David. "Simulation, Pluralism, and the Politics of Everyday Life." *Coping With Joyce: Essays from the Copenhagen Symposium*. Ed. Morris Beja and Shari Benstock. Columbus: Ohio State University Press, 1989. 195–205.
Lawrence, Karen R. "'Beggaring Description': Politics and Style in Joyce's 'Eumaeus.'" *Modern Fiction Studies* 38 (1992): 355–76.
———. "Close Encounters." *James Joyce Quarterly* 41 (Fall 2003/Winter 2004): 127–42.

———. "*In Transit*: From James Joyce to Brigid Brophy." Lawrence, *Transcultural Joyce* 37–45.
———. *The Odyssey of Style in "Ulysses."* Princeton, N.J.: Princeton University Press, 1981.
———. "Paternity, the legal fiction." *Joyce's "Ulysses": The Larger Perspective*. Ed. Robert Newman and Weldon Thornton. Newark: University of Delaware Press, 1987. 89–97. Rpt. in *James Joyce: The Augmented Ninth*. Ed. Bernard Benstock. Syracuse, N.Y.: Syracuse University Press, 1988. 233–243.
———. *Transcultural Joyce*. Cambridge: Cambridge University Press, 1998.
———. "'Twenty Pockets Arent Enough For Their Lies': Pocketed Objects as Props of Bloom's Masculinity in *Ulysses*." *Masculinities in Joyce: Postcolonial Constructions*. Ed. Christine van Boheeman-Saaf and Colleen Lamos. Amsterdam: Rodopi, 2001. 163–76.
Lefebvre, Henri. *Everyday Life in the Modern World*. Trans. Sacha Rabinovitch. London: Allen Lane, 1971.
Leonard, Garry. *Reading "Dubliners" Again: A Lacanian Perspective*. Syracuse, N.Y.: Syracuse University Press, 1993.
Levinas, Emmanuel. *Ethics and Infinity: Conversations with Philippe Nemo*. Trans. Richard A. Cohen. Pittsburgh: Duquesne University Press, 1985.
Levine, Jennifer. "*Ulysses*." *The Cambridge Companion to James Joyce*. Ed. Derek Attridge. 131–59.
Litz, A. Walton. "Ithaca." Hart and Hayman 385–405.
Lodge, David. *Small World: An Academic Romance*. London: Secker & Warburg, 1984.
Luhmann, Niklas. *Theories of Distinction: Redescribing the Descriptions of Modernity*. Ed. and intro. William Rasch. Trans. Elliott Schreiber, Joseph O'Neil, Kerstin Behnke, and William Whobrey. Stanford, Calif.: Stanford University Press, 2002.
MacCabe, Colin. *James Joyce and the Revolution of the Word*. New York: Barnes & Noble Books, 1979.
———, ed. *James Joyce: New Perspectives*. Brighton: Harvester, 1982.
Manganiello, Dominic. *Joyce's Politics*. London: Routledge, 1980.
Martini, Robert K., and George Piggford, eds. *Queer Forster*. Chicago: University of Chicago Press, 1997.
Marx, Karl. *Selections from "Capital," The Marx-Engels Reader*. Ed. Robert C. Tucker. New York: W. W. Norton, 1978.
McCormack, W. J. "Nightmares of History: James Joyce and the Phenomenon of Anglo-Irish Literature." McCormack and Stead 77–107.
McCormack, W. J., and Alistair Stead, eds. *James Joyce and Modern Literature*. Routledge, 1982.
McGee, Patrick. "Communist *Flânerie*, or Joyce's Boredom." 17th International James Joyce Symposium. Goldsmiths College, University of London. June 2000.
———. *Paperspace: Style as Ideology in Joyce's "Ulysses."* Lincoln: University of Nebraska Press, 1988.
McMichael, James. "Having to Answer." Unpublished essay.
———. *"Ulysses" and Justice*. Princeton, N.J.: Princeton University Press, 1991.

Melchiori, Giorgio. "The Genesis of *Ulysses*." Melchiori 37–50.
———, ed. *Joyce in Rome: The Genesis of "Ulysses."* Rome: Bulzoni, 1984.
Meyerhoff, Hans. *Time in Literature*. Berkeley: University of California Press, 1955.
Miller, J. Hillis. "The Critic as Host." *Deconstruction and Criticism*. Ed. Harold Bloom. New York: Continuum Publishers, 1979. 177–95.
Modern Fiction Studies. Special Issue: James Joyce. Vol. XV. No. 1 (Spring 1969).
Mohanty, S. P. "Us and Them: On The Philosophical Bases of Political Criticism." *Yale Journal of Criticism* 2 (Spring 1989).
Moretti, Franco. "The Long Goodbye: *Ulysses* and the End of Liberal Capitalism." *Signs Taken for Wonders: Essays in the Sociology of Literary Forms*. Trans. Susan Fischer, David Forgacs and David Miller. London: Verso, 1983.
Newman, S. J. "Brigid Brophy.." Vol. 14. *Dictionary of Literary Biography*. Ed. Jay L. Halio. Detroit: Bruccoli Clark Book, 1983. 137–38.
Nicholson, Robert. *The "Ulysses" Guide: Tours Through Joyce's Dublin*. London: Metheun, 1988.
Nolan, Emer. *James Joyce and Nationalism*. New York: Routledge, 1995.
Norris, Margot. *The Decentered Universe of "Finnegans Wake": A Structuralist Analysis*. Baltimore: Johns Hopkins University Press, 1976.
———. *Suspicious Readings of "Dubliners."* Philadelphia: University of Pennsylvania Press, 2003.
———. "A Walk on the Wild(e) Side: The Doubled Reading of 'An Encounter.'" Valente 19–34.
Ortiz, Fernando. *Cuban Counterpoint: Tobacco and Sugar*. Trans. Harriet de Onis. New York: Alfred A. Knopf, 1947.
Pecora, Vincent P. *Households of the Soul*. Baltimore: Johns Hopkins University Press, 1997.
Pierce, David. *James Joyce's Ireland*. New Haven, Conn.: Yale University Press, 1992.
Pietz, William. "Fetishism and Materialism: The Limits of Theory in Marx." Apter and Pietz 119–51.
Power, Arthur. *Conversations with James Joyce*. Ed. Clive Hart. London: Millington, 1974.
"President Portrays Artist at Conference." *Irish Times*, June 16, 1992. 2.
Rabaté, Jean-Michel. *James Joyce and the Politics of Egoism*. Cambridge: Cambridge University Press, 2001.
Radek, Karl. "Contemporary World Literature and the Tasks of Proletarian Art." *Problems of Soviet Literature*. Ed. H. G. Scott. Moscow: Co-operative Publishing Society of Foreign Workers in the USSR, 1935. 73–182.
Rasch, William. "Introduction: The Self-Positing Society." Luhmann, *Theories of Distinction*. 1–28.
Redmond, John Edward. *Home Rule: Speeches of John Redmond, M.P.* London: T. Fisher Unwin, 1910. Page number unknown.
Rice, Thomas Jackson. *Cannibal Joyce*. Miami: University Press of Florida, 2008.
Rich, Adrienne. "Compulsory Heterosexuality and Lesbian Experience." *Signs: Journal of Women in Culture and Society* 5 (Summer 1980): 631–60.

Rodstein, Susan de Sola. "Back to 1904: Joyce, Ireland, and Nationalism." *Joyce: Feminism/Post/Colonialism*. Ed. Ellen Carol Jones. Amsterdam: Rodopi, 1998. 145–86.
Said, Edward W. *Beginnings: Intention and Method*. New York: Basic Books, 1975.
Schechner, Mark. *Joyce in Nighttown: A Psychoanalytic Inquiry into "Ulysses."* Berkeley: University of California Press, 1974.
Scott, Bonnie Kime. *James Joyce*. Feminist Readings Series. Brighton: Harvester, 1987.
Seidel, Michael. *Epic Geography: James Joyce's "Ulysses."* Princeton, N.J.: Princeton University Press, 1976.
Senn, Fritz. "'All Kinds of Words Changing Colour': Lexical Clashes in 'Eumaeus.'" *Inductive Scrutinies*. Ed. Christine O'Neill. Dublin: The Lilliput Press, 1994. 156–75.
———. "Nausicaa." Hart and Hayman 277–311.
Seymour-Smith, Martin. Introduction. *The Secret Agent*. By Joseph Conrad. Harmondsworth, Middlesex: Penguin, 1984. 1–36.
Sims, Peter. "A Pocket Guide to *Ulysses*." *James Joyce Quarterly* 26 (Winter 1989): 239–58.
Solomon, Margaret C. *Eternal Geomater: The Sexual Universe of "Finnegans Wake."* Carbondale: Southern Illinois University Press, 1969.
Staley, Harry C. "Joyce's Catechisms." *James Joyce Quarterly* 6 (Winter 1968): 137–153.
Stallybrass, Peter, and Allon White. *The Politics of Transgression*. Ithaca, N.Y.: Cornell University Press, 1986.
Staten, Henry. "The Decomposition of *Ulysses*." *PMLA* (May 1997): 380–92.
———. *Eros in Mourning: Homer to Lacan*. Baltimore: Johns Hopkins University Press, 1995.
———. *Wittgenstein and Derrida*. Lincoln: University of Nebraska Press, 1984.
Stein, Gertrude. *Wars I Have Seen*. New York: Random House, 1945.
Steinberg, Erwin K. *The Stream of Consciousness and Beyond in "Ulysses."* Pittsburgh: University of Pittsburgh Press, 1973.
Stewart, Susan. *On Longing: Narratives of the Miniature, the Gigantic, the Souvenir, the Collection*. Durham, N.C.: Duke University Press, 1993.
Suleri, Sara. *The Rhetoric of English India*. Chicago: University of Chicago Press, 1992.
Sultan, Stanley. "The Sirens at the Ormand Bar: *Ulysses*." *Kansas City Review* 26 (Winter 1959): 83–92.
Taylor, Mark C. "Infinity: Emmanuel Levinas," *Altarity*. Chicago: University of Chicago Press, 1987.
Tindall, William York. *James Joyce: His Way of Interpreting the Modern World*. New York: Charles Scribner's Sons, 1950.
Tucker, Lindsey. *Stephen and Bloom at Life's Feast: Alimentary Symbolism and the Creative Process in James Joyce's "Ulysses."* Columbus: Ohio State University Press, 1984.
Ulmer, Gregory. "The Puncept in Grammatology." Culler 164–89.
Valente, Joseph, ed. *Quare Joyce*. Ann Arbor: University of Michigan Press, 1998.
Van Boheemen, Christine. *The Novel as Family Romance: Language, Gender, and Authority from Fielding to Joyce*. Ithaca, N.Y.: Cornell University Press, 1987.
Van Boheemen-Saaf, Christine. *Joyce, Derrida, Lacan, and the Trauma of History: Reading, Narrative, and Postcolonialism*. Cambridge: Cambridge University Press, 1999.

West, Alick. "James Joyce: *Ulysses.*" *Crisis and Criticism and Selected Literary Essays.* London: Lawrence & Wishart, 1975.

White, Allon. "Hysteria and the End of Carnival: Festivity and Bourgeois Neurosis." *The Violence of Representation: Literature and the History of Violence.* Ed. Nancy Armstrong and Leonard Tennenhouse. London: Routledge, 1989. 157–70.

Wicke, Jennifer. *Advertising Fictions: Literature, Advertisement, and Social Reading.* New York: Columbia University Press, 1988.

Williams, William Carlos. "A Note on the Recent Work of James Joyce." *Transition* 8 (November 1927). Rpt. in *James Joyce: The Critical Heritage.* Ed. Robert H. Deming. Vol. 2. New York: Barnes, 1970. 1: 377–9.

Wilson, Edmund. *Axel's Castle: A Study in the Imaginative Literature of 1870–1930.* New York: Charles Scribner's Sons, 1959.

Wirth-Nesher, Hana. *City Codes: Reading the Modern Urban Novel.* Cambridge: Cambridge University Press, 1996.

Wittgenstein, Ludwig. *Philosophical Investigations.* Trans. G. E. M. Anscombe. New York: Harper, 1969.

Woolf, Virginia. *A Writer's Diary: Being from the Diary of Virginia Woolf.* Ed. Leonard Woolf. New York: Harcourt, Brace and Company, 1953.

Zweig, Stefan. *The World of Yesterday.* New York: The Viking Press, 1943.

Index

Alcibiades, 219n15
Althusser, Louis, 99; on social interpellation, 108, 109
amulets. *See* fetishism
anamnesis, 168, 169
annunciation, apocalyptic, 116
Aphrodite, birth of, 179
Apter, Emily, 136; *Fetishism as Cultural Discourse*, 133–34
"Araby," women characters of, 79
Aristotle, 3; definition of plot, 33
L'Asino (weekly), 103, 105, 114
Attridge, Derek, 212n27
Augustine, St.: "On Christian Doctrine," 66
Avanti! (socialist daily), 103

Barreca, Regina, 95
Barthes, Roland: on citational process, 2; on Flaubert, 33; on language, 47–48; on the real, 207n14. Works: *Camera Lucida*, 4; *Essais critiques*, 47–48
Bass Ale, trademark of, 84
Bassnett-McGuire, Susan, 169
Bataille, Georges, 115; on general economy, 213n32
Baudelaire, Charles: flaneur figures of, 140, 142
Baudrillard, Jean: on productivity, 213n32
Beckett, Samuel: *Molloy*, 138, 215n12
Beja, Murray, 90, 93, 95
Benjamin, Walter: on Baudelaire, 140; on urban life, 143–44
Benstock, Bernard, 90, 95; on role of narrator, 75
Benstock, Shari, 94; on *Finnegans Wake*, 209n23; "Nightletters," 87
Berlant, Lauren, 220n1
Bhabha, Homi: *The Location of Culture*, 170

binarism: cultural, 75; in "Ithaca," 62–63; in Joyce's works, 78
Bishop, John: *Joyce's Book of the Dark*, 77
Bloom, Harold, 48; "The Breaking of Form," 217n10
Bloomsday (June 16th), 149; 100th anniversary of, 4; nostalgia in, 217n18
Boland, Eavan, 94–95; on literary influence, 179
Booth, Wayne, 49
Bosinelli, Rosa Maria, 94
Boswell, James, 207n16
Bowen, Elizabeth, 91
Brophy, Brigid: debt to Joyce, 7–8, 173, 176–78; great novel list of, 179
—*In Transit*, 171–79; circulation metaphors of, 173–74; gender identity in, 174–75, 178; law of the father in, 173; parentage metaphor in, 178; parody of castration in, 176; patriarchy in, 171; post-1968 sensibility of, 172; postmodernism of, 172; protagonist of, 174–75, 177; transculturality of, 176
Brown, Norman O., 176
Brown, Richard, 102; *James Joyce and Sexuality*, 212n21
Brown, Terence, 104, 211n9
Browne, Thomas, 63
Bruns, Gerald, 45, 46
Budgen, Frank, 3, 4, 16, 53, 130; on "Ithaca," 54, 56; *James Joyce and the Making of "Ulysses,"* 148
Burgess, Anthony, 17
burlesque, literary technique of, 58

capitalism: the everyday in, 213n32; in Joyce's works, 170, 210n9; surplus value in, 212n23
carno-phallogocentrism, 121, 131

"case": etymologies of, 184, 195; as genre, 220n1
catechism, in "Ithaca," 53–54, 55, 59–63, 65–66, 207n8
Catholicism, Joyce's, 122
Certeau, Michel de, 151; *The Practice of Everyday Life*, 142
Cervantes, Miguel de: *Don Quixote*, 1
Chad Gadya (Passover chant), 214n6
characters, Joyce's: adaptability of style to, 17; linguistic labels of, 31; women, 71–72, 73, 76–78, 88, 91
Church, Margaret, 91, 92
circulation, phallogocentric theories of, 176
cities: colonial, 144–45; flaneurs in, 146; as locus of hospitality, 193–94; in modernist novel, 140; of refuge, 221n10; textual reading of, 142, 145, 146; walking of, 142–46
Cixous, Hélène, 91, 208n13; *The Exile of James Joyce*, 91
class: in construction of subjectivity, 5; effect of colonialism on, 103; divisions in, 110; in Eumaeus, 103, 106, 107, 112, 117, 211n13; interclass identification, 105, 106, 110; in Irish discourse, 104; Irish professional, 211n9; Joyce's analysis of, 210n9; in "A Painful Case," 190, 197; role of gender in, 109
"Clay": free indirect discourse in, 20; women characters of, 79
clichés: as classification system, 49; in "Eumaeus," 2, 44, 45, 46, 48–50, 51–52, 56, 117; Joyce's use of, 50, 51–52; use in narrative, 52
Clongowes Wood College, Joyce at, 72
closure: aesthetic function of, 184; difficulties of, 64
clothing, masculine image of, 135. See also pockets
colonialism: and bureaucracy, 185; cities of, 144–45; in Dublin, 102–3, 156, 185, 194; effect on Irish artists, 102; exclusion under, 155; flaneurs in, 146–47; friendship in, 158, 165; homoeroticism in, 159; hospitality in, 194; other in, 156; relationship of modernism to, 171; in *Ulysses*, 156
colonizers, and colonized, 170
comedy: Freud on, 58; in "Ithaca," 57, 58–59, 63, 207n8; language of, 44; in "Telemachus," 39; in *Ulysses*, 21, 24

commodities, Marx on, 134
the commonplace: discourse of, 99; in "Eumaeus," 43, 99, 112
Conrad, Joseph: beast of burden motif of, 105, 106; *The Secret Agent*, 105–6, 211n14
Cope, Jackson, 29
Cormac (Irish king), 122, 125
corpse: in *Finnegans Wake*, 214n9; in "Hades," 128; in Jewish belief, 126; Kristeva on, 126, 127; in "Lestrygonians," 122–23, 124, 125, 127
"Counterparts," women characters of, 79
creation: creating consciousness and, 27; parodies of, 20
Culler, Jonathan, 116
culture, Western: Hermes myth in, 175; repressed feminine in, 74
Curran, C. P., 132

Dante, *Divine Comedy*, 57
Davitt, Michael, 107
"The Dead": gnomon in, 161; hospitality in, 160, 164–65, 183, 200; inclusion and exclusion in, 156; lyricism of, 57, 166; other in, 164; politics in, 183; women characters of, 79, 80
the dead, voices of, 168
Deane, Seamus, 170; "Dead Ends," 165–66; on "A Painful Case," 196–97, 200
deconstruction: Joyce as precursor of, 75; in Joyce studies, 4–5
defense mechanisms, in Joyce's works, 6
Deleuze, Gilles: *Anti-Oedipus*, 172
Derrida, Jacques: on carno-phallogocentrism, 121; on cities of refuge, 221n10; debt to Joyce, 75, 116–17; on "Eumaeus," 117; on *Finnegans Wake*, 5; on gifts, 213n32; on hospitality, 154–55, 165; on the inaccessible, 161; on inheritance, 169; on modernist fiction, 94; on *Oedipus at Colonus*, 221n10; on postcards, 86, 89. Works: "Before the Law," 161; *Of Grammatology*, 155; *On Hospitality*, 165, 217n6; "*Ulysses* Gramophone," 93, 94
desire: discourse of, 104; displacement of, 138, 139; female, 85–86; in *Finnegans Wake*, 86, 87; investment in objects, 134, 139; magical investments of, 133; as personal phenomenon, 75

DiBattista, Maria, 168
dietary exclusions, Jewish, 128, 129
Dinnerstein, Dorothy: *The Mermaid and the Minotaur*, 83
disclosure, in Joyce's style, 74
disguise, in Joyce's works, 28, 74
displacement, 48; of desire, 138, 139; humiliations of, 142; Joyce's use of, 52
distinction: creation of, 153–54; in liberal humanism, 157, 158
Döblin, Alfred: *Berlin Alexanderplatz*, 141
dreams, Joyce's, 71, 72–73, 74, 81, 87, 88–89
Dublin: class conflict in, 211n12; collective hunger of, 123; colonialism in, 102–3, 156, 185, 194; hospitality of, 193–94; journalese of, 43; Joyce's portraits of, 3–4, 15–16, 22, 29, 148, 163, 200; masculine community of, 125, 126; material objects of, 133; place names of, 150; sanitation work in, 113; social class in, 101, 111, 113–15; underclass of, 79, 112, 147, 213n28
Dubliners: characters of, 11; exclusionary devices in, 165; feminist scholarship on, 91; hospitality in, 7; meaning of characters' lives in, 16; picture of Dublin in, 200; submerged population of, 49
Duffy, Enda, 216n5; "Disappearing Dublin," 218n11; on flanerie, 141, 147
Dufourmantelle, Anne, 160, 164–65

Eagleton, Terry, 170; *Ideology of the Aesthetic*, 101, 102
Edward VII (king of Great Britain), coronation of, 194
Eliot, T. S., 52
Elizabethan imagery, Joyce's, 81, 209n14
Ellmann, Maud, 81–82
Ellmann, Richard, 76, 132, 169; on *Giacomo Joyce*, 209n14; on Joyce's humanism, 211n12. Works: *The Consciousness of James Joyce*, 103; *Ulysses on the Liffey*, 40, 73
"An Encounter," 163
epic literature, 1
epiphany: in *Portrait of the Artist*, 40, 80; readers' desire for, 67
Eucharist: in Joyce's works, 6, 121–23, 221n9; in "Lestrygonians," 125–26, 127, 130, 131; oral ritual of, 122

"Eveline," 9; decision making in, 10; women characters of, 79
exclusion: under colonialism, 155; in *Dubliners*, 165; in friendship, 157; in modernist texts, 153–56

face-to-face encounters: ethics of, 189; in "A Painful Case," 189, 191, 200
fatherhood: in *Finnegans Wake*, 5, 179; invisibility of, 83; in *Portrait of the Artist*, 5, 81–82. *See also* patriarchy
father-son relationships: in Freud, 121; Marx on, 212n23; in *Ulysses*, 125
femininity, props of, 139
feminism: in American academy, 93; Joyce and, 71–73; studies of Joyce, viii, 4, 5, 6, 73, 90–96
Fennell, Desmond: *Bloomsway*, 149, 217n17
fermentation: in "Lestrygonians," 129, 130; sexual origin of, 130
Ferrero, Guglielmo, 103
fetishes: associated with women, 138; in commodity culture, 138; as expression of subjectivity, 215n11; as phallic substitutions, 136–37, 138–39; in pockets, 134; potatoes as, 134, 144; textual objects as, 137. *See also* props
fetishism, 133–34; commodity, 213n28, 215n2; liberating aspects of, 215n8; random associations in, 215n11
fiction: closure in, 184; in legal thought, 155; modernist, 94; women as, 77. *See also* novels; texts
fiction, Joyce's: binarism in, 78; capitalism in, 170, 210n9; clichés in, 50, 51–52; conception of significance in, 15; defense mechanisms in, 6; digression in, 16; disguise in, 28, 74; displacement in, 52; Eucharist in, 6, 121–23, 221n9; feminine libido in, 74; filial rebellion in, 78, 79; flanerie in, 141, 142, 145–47; hospitality in, 151–52, 159–66; inventio in, 63–64; nostalgia in, 141; origin in, 76; patriarchy in, 6, 74; postcolonialism in, 95; race in, 95
Finnegans Wake: accusing women in, 71–72; Anna Livia Plurabelle section, 205n15; Bass Ale trademark in, 84; clichés of, 50; desire in, 86, 87; fatherhood in, 5, 179; feminist scholarship on, 91; "Ithaca" and, 208n18;

Finnegans Wake—continued
longing for origin in, 76; male fear in, 75; narrative voice of, 75; other in, 5, 74; paradoxes in, 162; political reading of, 101; women in, 73, 77, 78, 87, 209n23; writing in, 74
Firbank, Ronald, 178–79
flanerie, 216n5; aesthetics of perception in, 141–42; in Baudelaire, 140, 142; in Joyce's works, 141, 142, 145–47; nostalgia in, 141, 150
flaneurs: colonial, 146–47; as subaltern subjects, 141
Flaubert, Gustave: language of, 48; *Madame Bovary*, 49; received ideas in, 99; sentences of, 33
Fleischmann, Marthe, 86–87, 89
Flotow, Friedrich von: *Martha*, 72
Flugel, J. C.: *The Psychology of Clothes*, 134, 135
Fogarty, Anne, 96
Fogel, Aaron, 105, 106
Ford, Ford Madox: *The Good Soldier*, 21, 204n14
Forster, E. M., 152; homosexuality of, 159; other in, 157; queering of texts of, 218n21. Works: *Howard's End*, 156, 157; "The Life to Come," 159; "The Other Boat," 159; *A Room with a View*, 157; *Where Angels Fear to Tread*, 157
—*A Passage to India*, 156–59; the extraordinary in, 157; form in, 156; homoeroticism in, 159; hospitality in, 157; inclusion and exclusion in, 157–58; liberal framework of, 165
Foucault, Michel: *The Order of Things*, 63
Frank, Joseph, 153
French, Marilyn: *The Book as World*, 92
Freud, Sigmund: on comedy, 58; on constitution of self, 121; father-son relationships in, 121; on orality, 214n3; *Totem and Taboo*, 121
friendship: colonial, 158, 165; exclusion in, 157; male-female, 191, 192, 199. *See also* hospitality
Frye, Northrop, 206n6

Gabler, Hans, 92
Gass, William, 67
ghosts, resubstantiation of, 168
Giacomo Joyce, 209n14
Gibbon, Edward, 84
Gibbons, Luke, 141, 216n5
Gifford, Don, 214n10

Gilbert, Sandra, viii, 71; on patrolingualism, 84–85
Gilbert, Stuart, 15, 44
Girard, René, 64
Glasheen, Adaline, 90, 91
Gleber, Anke: *The Art of Taking a Walk*, 140, 147
Goldberg, S. L., 22, 68; on artists' awareness, 26
Goldman, Arnold, 91; *The Joyce Paradox*, 67–68
Gorman, Herbert, 72
Guattari, Felix: *Anti-Oedipus*, 172
Gubar, Susan, viii, 71; on patrolingualism, 85

hailing: in *Ulysses*, 108, 146; and vocation, 108
Hauptmann, Gerhart: *Michael Kramer*, 186
Hawthorn, Jeremy, 210n5
Hayman, David, 207n10; "Language of/as Gesture in Joyce," 50
Heath, Stephen, 59; "Ambiviolences," 77; "Joyce and language," 78
Hegel, Georg Wilhelm Friedrich: on fetishes, 215n11
Heidegger, Martin, 218n17
Heilbrun, Carolyn, 91
Henke, Suzette, 92; *Women in Joyce*, 91
Hermes, myth of, 175
herms, mutilation of, 178, 219n15
Herr, Cheryl: *Joyce's Anatomy of Culture*, 75–76
heterosexuality: compulsory, 198, 199, 221n15; patriarchy and, 199
Hodgart, M. J. C.: "Aeolus," 208n25
Hollander, Anne: *Sex and Suits*, 135
Homer, *Odyssey*, 1, 123, 142, 144
homoeroticism: in colonialism, 159; medicalization of, 198
homosexuality: Forster's, 159; in "A Painful Case," 220n4
hospitality: absolute, 154, 217n6; across borders, 169; as boundary, 152; in colonialism, 194; in *The Dead*, 160, 164–65, 183, 200; Derrida on, 154–55, 165; discourses of, 154; of Dublin, 193–94; in *Dubliners*, 7; between East and West, 156; in Greek culture, 7, 164; in Joyce's works, 151–52, 159–66; in opening of self, 5–6; to others, 5, 151–52, 185, 217n6; in "A Painful Case," 8, 185, 192, 193–94, 200; in *A Passage to India*, 157; and politics, 153;

radical, 157, 185; regulation of society, 153; sacred, 162–63; sovereignty in, 164; in *Ulysses*, 163, 166–67; unconditional, 165
humanism, liberal: distinction in, 157, 158; Joyce's, 211n12; limits of, 159, 164
hysteria, the carnivalesque and, 213n28

icons, cultural: Joyce as, 170; transmission of, 169
identification: erotic, 123, 130; in Eucharist, 121–22, 123; fluidity of, 6, 93, 131; Freud on, 121; through incorporation, 131; inter-class, 103, 106; Irish with English, 112; in Joyce's fiction, 5; male, 109; through orality, 123, 124, 131; with other, 6, 94, 107; psychoanalytic concept of, 121; rituals of, 7; socio-economic, 100; of women characters, 93
inclusion: ethical limits of, 218n17; forms of, 153; Hindu, 157–58; in literary genres, 156; in modernist texts, 153–56
ingestion, and formation of self, 120–21, 123
inheritance, of texts, 169
International James Joyce Foundation, 90; bylaws of, 94; women's influence in, 93–94; women trustees of, 94, 96
International James Joyce Symposia, 4; Dublin (1967), 90, 217n16; Dublin (2000), 7, 141; Dublin (2004), 1, 217n18; Frankfurt (1984), 93–94; Monaco (1990), 6; Provincetown (1983), 92–93; Rome (1998), 7; Seville (1994), 95; Trieste (2002), 7; Women's Caucus of, 92, 93, 94–95; Zurich (1979), 91
inventio (rhetoric), Joyce's use of, 63–64
Ireland: colonial, 100, 102–3, 172–73, 210n7, 211n9; economy of, 211n9; expatriation from, 173; imagined community of, 166; nationalism in, 103, 216n13; petite bourgeoisie of, 112–13, 210n9; political divisions in, 100; transculturality in, 171
Irigaray, Luce, 176
Irish Free State, 211n9, 211n13
Iser, Wolfgang, 47

Jackson, Roberta, 220n4
James, Henry: on delicacy of narrative, 20, 204n11; on depiction of relations, 60, 154; *Prefaces*, 26; on preparation, 26; on writing of novels, 3

Jameson, Fredric, 170; on colonial Ireland, 210n7; on father-son relationships, 125; "Modernism and Imperialism," 155–56; on psychological novels, 25
Jolas, Maria, 91
Joyce, James: artistic beliefs of, 26; attacks on literary style, 53; belief in structural organizations, 208n20; beliefs on art, 74; Catholicism of, 122; cloacal obsession of, 212n26; at Clongowes Wood College, 72; correspondence with women, 6, 88–89; as cultural icon, 170; Curran's photograph of, 132; defining of modernism, 170; depiction of friends, 220n5; Derrida's debt to, 75; dream book of, 76–77; dreams of women, 71, 72–73, 74, 81, 87, 88–89; Elizabethan imagery of, 81, 209n14; and feminism, 71–73; feminist studies of, viii, 4, 5, 6, 73, 90–96; interest in socialism, 103–4, 211n12; interest in syndicalism, 103, 104; interest in Tolstoy, 211n12; as internationalist, 169; and Irish nationalism, 103, 216n13; as Irish writer, 170, 171; liberal humanism of, 211n12; library of, 103, 105; literary forms of, 26; longing for home, 76, 208n9; and Marthe Fleischmann, 86–87, 89; Marxist studies of, 5, 100, 210n5, 212n26; meaning of women for, 89; misogyny charges against, 71, 91; Pater's influence on, 52; patriarchal discourse of, 6, 74; political readings of, 101; as precursor of deconstruction, 75; psychoanalytic interpretations of, 5; radicalism of, 210n6; radical modernism of, 170; in Rome, 105, 114; semi-colonial status of, 156, 217n11; skepticism about language, 47; skepticism about order, 76; strategies of disguise, 28; structural approaches to, 2; symbolic approaches to, 2; symmetries in, viii; transcultural position of, 171, 173, 177, 179; translations of, 168–69; in Trieste, 103, 105, 177
Joyce, Stanislaus, 185; on "Eumaeus," 43; on Joyce's style, 28, 74
Joyce, Stephen, 96
Joyce Centre (Dublin), 1
Joyce studies: critical preoccupations of, 4; deconstruction in, 4–5; feminist, viii, 4, 5, 6, 73, 90–96. *See also* International James Joyce Symposia

Kafka, Franz: "Before the Law," 155
Kant, Immanuel: on moral law, 155; on objective sight, 120; on "subjective" senses, 120
Kellogg, Robert, 28
Kenner, Hugh, 91, 169; on "Ithaca," 64; on sound notation, 35–36; on use of adverbs, 21. Works: *Dublin's Joyce*, 68, 73; *Joyce's Voices*, 204n10; "The Rhetoric of Silence," 24; *The Stoic Comedians*, 35–36, 203n10
Kermode, Frank, 21, 204n14
Kershner, R. B., 186, 220nn3–4
Kiberd, Declan, 170
Kierkegaard, Søren: narrative subversion by, 26, 204n20
Kristeva, Julia, 131; on the abject, 215n19; on death, 126, 127; on Eucharist symbolism, 6; on Joyce's radicalism, 210n6; on patriarchal discourse, 74; view of *écriture féminine*, 94; on women's body, 85. Works: *Desire in Language*, 92, 172; *James Joyce: The Augmented Ninth*, 121–23; "Joyce 'The Gracehoper,'" 93

Lacan, Jacques, 94
ladies' magazines, Victorian, 2, 86
Lamos, Colleen, 199, 220n4
language: Barthes on, 47–48; citationality of, 78; of comedy, 44; erotic potential of, 78; errancy of, 85; errors of transmission in, 38; female, 76–77, 83; Joyce's skepticism about, 47; limitations of, 48, 50; material potential of, 78; as patterned sound, 39; reality and, 41, 46–47, 48; relationship to music, 35, 41; separation from origins, 177; Wittgenstein on, 115
Laplanche, Jean, 121
law: cases in, 184; of the father, 163, 173; moral, 155; as place, 161
Lawrence, Karen R.: *The Odyssey of Style*, 2, 5, 6; presidency of International Joyce Foundation, 95
Leonard, Garry, 196, 197
Lestrygonians, Homeric, 120
Levinas, Emmanuel, 162; alterity in, 159; on face-to-face encounters, 189
libido, feminine: in Joyce's works, 74
Lilith, 84

The Little Review: "Wandering Rocks" in, 34
Litz, A. Walton, 55, 206n5
Lodge, David: *Small World*, 91–92
logocentricism, of Western metaphysics, 218n17
Luhmann, Niklas: *Theories of Distinction*, 153–54
Lukács, György, 94
Lyotard, Jean-François, 172

Manganiello, Dominic, 107, 211n12; *Joyce's Politics*, 103
Mangnall, Richmal: *Historical and Miscellaneous Questions*, 206n3
Marengo, Carla, 94
Marx, Karl: on commodities, 134; on father-son relations, 212n23
Marxism: critique of *Ulysses*, 100, 210n5, 212n26
masculinity: in clothing, 135; construction of, 5, 87, 137; props for, 133, 139; in public sphere, 136; solidarity in, 110, 212n18
the maternal: as visible, 83, 209n14
maternity, fiction of, 82
Mauss, Marcel, 213n32
McCormack, W. J., 210n7, 211n12
McGee, Patrick, 141; *Paperspace*, 87
McMichael, James: on "A Painful Case," 220n7; *"Ulysses" and Justice*, 3, 126–27
Melchisedek, rite of, 129
Melville, Herman: "Bartleby, the Scrivener," 21
Modern Fiction Studies: special Joyce issue, 91
modernism: in fiction, 94; inclusion and exclusion in, 153–56; interior narrative in, 120; international, 170, 177; Joyce's, 170; political implications of, 101; and postcolonialism, 171; postmodernism's debt to, 172; radical, 170; relationship to colonialism, 171
modernity: in city walking, 146; in flanerie, 140
Mohanty, S. P., 158
Monaghan, Kenneth, 1
Moretti, Franco, 170, 210n9, 213n28; on the bourgeois, 114
"A Mother," female development in, 79
music, relationship to language, 35, 41

narrative: as adjunct of character, 17, 18; interior, 120; the non-narratable and, 59; relevance of details in, 33; symbolic geography of, 156; use of clichés in, 52; in Western philosophy, 155. *See also specific titles*
narrators, unreliable, 21
nationalism, Irish: Joyce's view of, 103, 216n13
Newman, S. J.: *Dictionary of Literary Biography*, 171–72
Nolan, Emer, 125, 170
Norris, Margot, 96, 198; *The Decentered Universe of "Finnegans Wake,"* 92
nostalgia: in Bloomsday celebrations, 217n18; in city walking, 143–44, 150; in flanerie, 141, 150; Homeric, 141, 142; Joyce's use of, 141; in *Ulysses*, 142, 148–49
novels: beauty of style in, 53; cities in, 140; conventional tools of, 20; interpretation strategies of, 26; laws of composition, 36–37; limitations of, 22; modernist, 94, 140; nineteenth-century, 156; psychological, 25; symbolic patterns of, 153. *See also* fiction; texts

O'Connor, Frank, 79
Odysseus, 15, 177; *metis* of, 145; moly of, 134
omniscience, paradox of, 219n27
origin: in Joyce's works, 76; Platonic vocabulary of, 169
Ortiz, Fernando, 172
other: attention to, 190; circumscribing of, 151; in colonialism, 156; in "The Dead," 164; demands of, 189; in "Eumaeus," 167; exclusion of, 217n10; in *Finnegans Wake*, 5; in Forster's fiction, 157; hospitality to, 5, 151–52, 185, 217n6; identification with, 94; incorporation into subject, 121; judgment of, 191–92; male fear of, 75; in "A Painful Case," 8, 9, 190–92, 193, 200, 201; as subject, 189; in *Ulysses*, 151, 166; woman as, 6, 73
Owens, Cóilín: *James Joyce's Painful Case*, 220n1

"A Painful Case," 165–66; as adultery narrative, 197–98; agency in, 186–87, 220n4; aphorisms in, 187, 191, 199, 200; civic life in, 193, 194; direct discourse in, 8–9, 188; ethics in, 189–90, 198–99; Eucharist allusion in, 221n9; face-to-face encounter in, 189, 191, 200; female development in, 79; gaze in, 188–89, 193; generative scholarship on, 183; hearing in, 8–9; homosexuality in, 220n4; hospitality in, 8, 185, 192, 193–94, 200; manuscript of, 192; medico-legal settings of, 197; other in, 8, 9, 190–92, 193, 200, 201; the peripheral in, 193; the political in, 189–90; queer reading of, 198–99, 220n4; readers of, 198–99; self-alienation in, 191; self-portraiture in, 9, 187, 195; self-reflexivity of, 184; senses of "case" in, 186, 187, 195, 197; social geography of, 193; urban infrastructure of, 185; working classes in, 190, 197
Pater, Walter, 35; influence on Joyce, 52; on music, 40
the paternal: as invisible, 209n14
patriarchy: and heterosexuality, 199; ideology of, 76; Irish, 171; in Joyce's works, 6, 74; legal fictions of, 84; in "Oxen of the Sun," 83, 84; rebellion against, 79; in *Ulysses*, 71; undermining of, 84
Patrick, Saint, 177
patrolingualism, 84–85
Pecora, Vincent, 215n8
Penelope, ALP on, 73
phallogocentrism: carno-, 121, 131; in circulation, 176
phallus: fetish substitutions for, 136–37, 138–39; interiorization of, 121; possession of, 209n17; as prop, 139; as transcendental signifier, 175
Pietz, William, 215n11; *Fetishism as Cultural Discourse*, 133–34
Plato: on anamnesis, 168
plot, relevance in, 61
pockets: in Beckett's *Molloy*, 138; in commodity culture, 137; and consciousness, 138; in construction of masculinity, 87; fetishes in, 134; and interior monologues, 135; props in, 133; in public-private exchanges, 136; in rationalizing of desire, 136; sexual differentiation of, 138; in *Ulysses*, 133, 134–35, 145, 216n13
poetry: absences in, 217n10; divine inspiration of, 168–69

politics: in "The Dead," 183; in "Eumaeus," 101–5; hospitality and, 153; as ideology, 103; in "A Painful Case," 189–90; radical, 101, 104–5; retrogressive, 101; socialist, 104; style and, 166

A Portrait of the Artist as a Young Man: denotative style in, 17; epiphany on the beach in, 40, 80; fatherhood in, 5, 81–82; female desire in, 85; flanerie in, 141; narrative voice of, 18; representation of mind in, 22; self-representation in, 219n27; "Telemachiad" and, 15; women characters of, 78, 80–82

postcolonialism: flanerie in, 141; in Joyce's works, 95; modernism and, 171

postcolonial theory, 169

postmodernism: debt to modernism, 172; decentering of, 177; master narratives of, 172; political implications of, 101

post-structuralism, on inheritance of texts, 169

potato: as fetish object, 134, 144

Power, Arthur, 86

power, cultural inscriptions of, 79

power, women's: male anxieties over, 75

productivity, bourgeois ethic of, 99–101, 111–13, 213n32

props: of femininity, 139; gendered, 139; magic powers of, 133; of masculinity, 133, 139. *See also* fetishes

psychoanalysis: bourgeois discourses of, 212n28; concept of identification, 121; fetish objects in, 134; in interpretation of Joyce, 5

puns, essence and accident in, 116

"queer," in Irish parlance, 218n22
queering, of texts, 199–200, 218n21, 220n4
Quinn, John, 27

Rabaté, Jean-Michel, 164; *Joyce and the Politics of Egoism*, 163
race, in Joyce's works, 95
Radek, Karl, 212n26
rationality: in *Ulysses*, 111, 113, 147; value of, 111
readers: deciphering of symbols, 67; desire for epiphany, 67; expectations for *Ulysses*, 26; ideal, 66
reality: defamiliarized, 29; divisibility of, 59–60; and language, 41, 46–47, 48; narrative statements concerning, 39; unmediated, 46

rebellion, filial: in Joyce's works, 78, 79
Redmond, John Edward, 194
relationships: father-son, 121, 125, 212n23; infinite, 60, 62
reproduction: economy of, 117; and textual production, 84
resistance, types of, 101
rhetoric, classical topoi of, 63–64, 208n22
Rich, Adrienne, 198, 221n15
Robinson, Mary, 94
Rodstein, Susan de Sola, 148; on nationalism, 216n13
Rome, Joyce in, 105, 114
Royal Society, prose of, 53
Rushdie, Salman: radical modernism of, 170
Russell, Bertram: on form-making, 219n27

Said, Edward: on nineteenth-century novel, 156
Saint-Amour, Paul, viii, 8
Sassoon, Siegfried, 159
Schechner, Mark: *Joyce in Nighttown*, 28
Scott, Bonnie, 92, 93, 94; *James Joyce*, 73
Seidel, Michael: *Epic Geography*, 150
self: expression in writing, 74; formation through ingestion, 120–21, 123; opening through hospitality, 5–6; in stream of consciousness, 25; struggle with precursors, 217n10
Senn, Fritz, 90, 91, 92, 109; on "Eumaeus," 110; "Nausicaa," 85
sentences: of "Eumaeus," 44; expandability of, 33; Flaubert's, 33; of "Sirens," 37–38; of "Wandering Rocks," 31–32, 33–34
sexuality, women's: control of, 109
Shakespeare, William: Stephen's theory of, 27, 28, 73–74, 83
simony, in Joyce's short stories, 163, 164
Sims, Peter, 216n13; "A Pocket Guide to *Ulysses*," 215n6
"The Sisters": Dublin in, 163; gnomon in, 162; hospitality in, 160, 162–63; inclusion and exclusion in, 156; language of, 209n13; law in, 161; law of the father in, 163; women characters of, 79, 80; women's body in, 85
socialism, Joyce's interest in, 103–4, 211n12

society: interpellation of subjects in, 108; received locutions of, 45
sodomy, in Joyce's short stories, 163, 164
Solomon, Margaret, 91, 92; *Eternal Geometer*, 90
Sophocles, *Oedipus at Colonus*, 221n10
souvenirs, 148; as calendar, 149
Spencer Brown, G.: *Laws of Form*, 153
Sprat, Thomas, 53
Staley, Tom, 90
Stallybrass, Peter: *The Politics of Transgression*, 113, 114
Staten, Henry, 115–16, 214n6
Stein, Gertrude: *Wars I Have Seen*, 90
Steinberg, Erwin K., 21
Stephen Hero: flanerie in, 141, 142; socialist concerns of, 104; women characters of, 80–82
Stewart, Susan, 147, 150; on souvenirs, 148–49
Straumann, Henrich, 86, 89
stream of consciousness, 203n6; self in, 25; in Telemachiad, 16, 17, 22, 60; travesty of, 46
style, literary: Joyce's attacks on, 53; and politics, 166
subjectivity: in commodity exchange, 137; fetishes as expression of, 215n11; women's, 87
subjects: colonial, 158; incorporation of other into, 121; interpellating of, 108; others as, 189
Suleri, Sara, 158, 159; *The Rhetoric of English India*, 156
Sullivan, John, 72
Sultan, Stanley, 34
Svevo, Italo: *Confessions of Zeno*, 58
Swift, Jonathan: *Gulliver's Travels*, 59
syndicalism, Joyce's interest in, 103, 104

Taylor, Mark C., 159, 162
texts: afterlife of, 168; authors' ordering of, 65; constructed nature of, 205n13; as distortion, 205n15; fetishizing of, 137; ideal readers of, 66; inheritance of, 169; queering of, 199–200, 218n21, 220n4; as rhetorical exercises, 36; subaltern, 218n11; as transubstantiations, 131. *See also* fiction; novels
texts, modernist: absences in, 155–56; inclusion and exclusion in, 153–56; metropolitan, 155; production of meaning in, 154

Tindall, William York: *James Joyce*, 73
Tolstoy, Leo: "How Much Land Does a Man Need?," 211n12
transculturation: in Ireland, 171; in Joyce's works, 171, 173, 177, 179; literary, 168
Trieste, Joyce in, 103, 105, 177
"Two Gallants," women characters of, 79

Ulmer, Gregory, 116; on puncepts, 105
Ulysses: accusing women in, 71–72; aesthetic of comprehensiveness in, 15–16; allegorical levels of, 15; back-dating of, 148; Bloom chapters of, 22–25; Bloom's subjectivity in, 5, 6, 127; citational language of, 3; colonialism in, 156; comedy in, 21, 24; completeness in, 16; construction of self in, 25; data inventories in, 139; decorum of, 18–19; displacement in, 48, 142; empirical world of, 18, 24; epic aspects of, 1, 2, 3; epithets in, 31; fatherhood in, 5; father-son relationships in, 125; feminist apocalypse in, 212n21; fetish objects in, 133, 134–35; First World social reality of, 170; hailing of subjects in, 108; halfway point of, 27; historical realism in, 3–4; hospitality in, 163, 166–67; infinite possibilities in, 205n7; initial style of, 18; Linati scheme of, 123, 166; linguistic connections in, 65; literary criticism in, 28–29; longing for origin in, 76; Marxist critique of, 100, 210n5, 212n26; metempsychosis of, 168; modernity of, 140; narrative changes in, 2; narrative mimicry in, 21, 22; narrative norm of, 2, 15, 17, 19, 26, 203n4; narrator-character relationship in, 23–24; new world order in, 212n21; nostalgia in, 142, 148–49; *nostos* section of, 99; omissions in, 24; orality in, 121; other in, 151, 166; patriarchal language of, 71; pockets references in, 133, 134–35, 145, 216n13; political readings of, 101; possibilities of meaning in, 66–67; production of meaning in, 20; readers' expectations of, 26; rhetorical masks of, 28; significance of date of, 149; socialist apocalypse in, 212n21; sound notation in, 35–36; as souvenir of Dublin, 148–49; Third World aspects of, 170; totality in, 218n11; transculturation in, 168; voyeurism in, 143; walking in, 140, 141, 142–46, 149–50

Ulysses—continued

—"Aeolus": chiasmus in, 205n14; conversation in, 44; headings of, 2, 27, 33, 40, 43–44, 45, 53; narrative of, 35, 44; order in, 30; potentiality in, 33; rhetorical figures of, 40, 44; sound in, 35; style of, 2; the subliterary in, 52

—"Calypso": Bloom's interiority in, 119–20; commodity culture in, viii; domestic ritual in, 57; eating in, 124, 166; sound in, 35

—"Circe": Bloom's pockets in, 216n13; "bottom" issues in, 114, 212n28; cultural imagination in, 109; pickpockets in, 138; psychic potentiality in, 34; psychic space of, 100; women characters of, 71–72, 212n21; women's body in, 85

—"Cyclops," 86; clichés of, 50; Dublin idiom in, 45, 46; farce in, 207n10; mimicry in, 22; narrative of, 18, 46; nationalism in, 216n13; parodies in, 49

—"Eumaeus": beast of burden motif in, 105–6; the bourgeois in, 109, 110, 112–15, 117, 147; bourgeois productivity in, 99–101, 111–13, 213n32; class discourse in, 103, 106, 107, 112, 211n13; classical allusion in, 43; clichés of, 2, 44, 45, 46, 48–50, 51–52, 56, 117; commonplaces of, 43, 99, 112; cultural imagination in, 109; cultural voice of, 99; destruction of literature in, 52; discourse of desire in, 104; discourse of points in, 110–11, 212n22; double entendres in, 114, 212n27; economic issues in, 6, 102, 111, 115, 147, 211n13; euphemism in, 46; the everyday in, 117, 213n32; excess of labor in, 204n12; future orientation in, 116; labor in, 100, 210n3; labor of language in, 101–2; language of, 42–44; linguistic memory in, 44, 49; literary style of, 42–47, 48–52; male solidarity in, 110, 212n18; Marx in, 102, 104; material reality in, 206n9; narrative of, 34, 42, 44–45, 99; other in, 167; the pedestrian in, 110–11, 116, 117; political readings of, 101–2; potentiality in, 34; precision in, 42; radical politics of, 104–5; rationality in, 111, 113, 147; received ideas in, 6, 99; recognition scene of, 50–51; self-mockery in, 49; sentences of, 44; social space in, 100–101; socio-political discourses of, 103–4, 106–8, 118; song of sirens in, 109–10; stream-of-consciousness travesty in, 46; waste in, 114–15, 213n28, 213n32

—"Hades": food in, 124, 128; narrator-character sympathy in, 23; stream of consciousness in, 25

—"Ithaca," 9; avoidance mechanisms in, 55; binarism in, 62–63; Bloom's dream in, 61, 207n17; catalogue of facts in, 53–54, 56, 58, 66–67; catechism in, 53–54, 55, 59–63, 65–66, 207n8; classification system of, 64; cognitive events of, 60; coldness of, 54, 56, 57, 67; comedy in, 57, 58–59, 63, 207n8; comparison in, 62, 65; defamiliarization in, 59; emotional leveling in, 54; excess of labor in, 58, 204n12; and *Finnegans Wake*, 208n18; the hypothetical in, 61–62; indeterminacy in, 61; intellectualizing in, 56; inventio in, 63–64; inventory in, 135, 144; lateral imagination in, 55, 60, 62; lyrical passages of, 56–57; modes of knowledge in, 63; narrative displacement in, 55; narrative of, 53, 54–55, 59–63, 66; narrator's mind in, 63, 208n19; novel-anatomy combination in, 206n6; potentiality in, 33; potential meanings in, 67; relationships in, 62–65; rhetorical topoi of, 63, 64; risk in, vii; rite of Melchisedek in, 129; romanticizing of text in, 206n5; scientific language in, 52, 54, 63, 207n7; skepticism about order in, 208n20

—"Lestrygonians": Bloom's interiority in, 130; Bloom's subjectivity in, 127; cannibalism in, 122–23, 124–25, 127; character development in, 27; elegiac tone of, 131; Eucharist in, 125–26, 127, 130, 131; fermentation in, 129, 130; food chain in, 124; food-sex relationship in, 126–30; ingestion in, 120–21, 129–30; metatextuality of, 131; nostalgia in, 143; orality in, 6, 121, 123, 124; peristalsis in, 123; walking in, 149–50

—"Lotus-Eaters": conclusion of, 119; stream of consciousness in, 46

—"Nausicaa": female desire in, 85–86; free indirect discourse in, 86; male gaze in, 86; narrative of, 18, 39; style of, 2; submerged population of, 49; voyeurism in, 86, 120; women's body in, 86; women walkers in, 147

—"Nestor": maternal images in, 82–83; potentiality in, 33

—"Oxen of the Sun": literary criticism in, 28–29; mimicry in, 22; narrative of, 46; pastiche in, 52; patriarchy in, 83, 84; post-creation in, 83; potentiality in, 34; womb symbolism of, 84
—"Penelope": female representation in, vii; women's subjectivity in, 87
—"Proteus": character in, 25; empirical world in, 24; narrative of, 16, 17; stream of consciousness in, 22; symbols in, 67; the visible in, 120
—"Scylla and Charybdis": artistic creation in, 73–74, 83; character development in, 27–28; literary criticism in, 27; narrative of, 28; narrator-character sympathy in, 23–24; paternity in, 74, 83
—"Sirens": empirical reality in, 41; escape from plot in, 40–41; excess of labor in, 39, 204n12; indirect discourse of, 39; interior monologue of, 37, 205n18; mediated reality in, 205n15; musical analysis in, 34; narrative of, 34–41, 205n13, 205n15; overture of, 34, 35–36; potentiality in, 34; as rhetorical exercise, 36; rhetorical figures of, 40–41; sentences of, 37–38; sound in, 35–36, 38–39; stylistic technique in, 29; words comprising, 36–37
—"Telemachiad": denotative norm of, 22; free indirect discourse in, 18, 19; interior monologue in, 18; narrative of, 16–17, 22; narrator-character relationship in, 23; poetic language of, 17–18; and *Portrait of the Artist*, 15; representation of mind in, 22; stream of consciousness in, 16, 17, 22, 60
—"Telemachus": adverb use in, vii, 21; comedy in, 39; excess of labor in, 20; mimicry in, 21, 22; naive narrator of, 19, 20, 21; narrative of, vii, 19–21
—"Wandering Rocks": accidental connections in, 30; categories of potentiality in, 33, 34; *Dubliners* in, 101; fact accumulation in, 29, 31–32; hailing in, 108, 146; inventory in, 31; narrative memory in, 30; narrative of, 29–34, 35, 58; paratactic imagination in, 29; sentence structure of, 31–32, 33–34; time and space in, 30; verbal repetition in, 30–31; walking in, 146–47
Unkeless, Elaine: *Women in Joyce*, 91
utterance, performric, 116

Van Boheemen-Saaf, Christine, 94
violence, political, 106–7, 211n18
Virgil, *Aeneid*, 1
voyeurism, 86, 120, 143

A Wake Newsletter, 90
walking: in cities, 142–46; nostalgia in, 143–44, 150; rhetoric of, 146; in *Ulysses*, 140, 141, 142–46, 149–50; by women, 147
West, Alick, 100
West, Rebecca, 91
White, Allon: on the carnivalesque, 212n28; *The Politics of Transgression*, 113, 114
Wicke, Jennifer, 136
Wilde, Oscar: influence on Firbank, 178–79; *The Soul of Man under Socialism*, 103
Williams, William Carlos: on Joyce's language, 112–13
Wilson, Edmund: *Axel's Castle*, 16
Wittgenstein, Ludwig: on ordinary language, 115
women: absence of, 109; bodily power of, 84; commodification of, 109; cultural construction of, 76, 78; and cultural production, 84; in "The Dead," 79, 80; disruptive metaphor of, 76; fetishes associated with, 138; as fiction, 77; in *Finnegans Wake*, 73, 77, 78, 87, 209n23; as illegitimacy figures, 74; Joyce's attitude toward, 71, 88; Joyce's correspondence with, 6, 88–89; Joyce's dreams of, 71, 72–73, 74, 81, 87, 88–89; male representation of, vii, 73, 87; meaning for Joyce, 89; as muse of representation, 80; as nature, 78; as nightmare, 75; as other, 6, 73; in *Portrait of the Artist*, 78, 80–82; power of, 75; procreative power of, 83; secret language of, 76–77, 83; sexuality of, 109; subjectivity of, 87; as Truth of Nature, 77; walking by, 147
women writers, Irish: Joyce and, 171
Woolf, Virginia: *Mrs. Dalloway*, 141
writing: anxiety about, 48; dual nature of, 74; as expression of self, 74; as feminine, 78; iterability of, 120

Yeats, William Butler, 113

Zola, Emile: naturalism of, 212n26
Zurich James Joyce Foundation, 91

Karen R. Lawrence served as president of the International James Joyce Foundation, 1991–1996. She has written or edited five books on literature and has published widely on James Joyce. Her books include *The Odyssey of Style in Ulysses*; *Penelope Voyages: Women and Travel in the British Literary Tradition*; *Transcultural Joyce*; *Decolonizing Tradition: New Views of Twentieth-Century "British" Literary Canons*; and *Techniques for Living: Fiction and Theory in the Work of Christine Brooke-Rose*.

In 2007, Karen Lawrence became the tenth president of Sarah Lawrence College.

THE FLORIDA JAMES JOYCE SERIES
Edited by Sebastian D. G. Knowles

The Autobiographical Novel of Co-Consciousness: Goncharov, Woolf, and Joyce, by Galya Diment (1994)
Bloom's Old Sweet Song: Essays on Joyce and Music, by Zack Bowen (1995)
Joyce's Iritis and the Irritated Text: The Dis-lexic Ulysses, by Roy Gottfried (1995)
Joyce, Milton, and the Theory of Influence, by Patrick Colm Hogan (1995)
Reauthorizing Joyce, by Vicki Mahaffey (paperback edition, 1995)
Shaw and Joyce: "The Last Word in Stolentelling," by Martha Fodaski Black (1995)
Bely, Joyce, and Döblin: Peripatetics in the City Novel, by Peter I. Barta (1996)
Jocoserious Joyce: The Fate of Folly in Ulysses, by Robert H. Bell (paperback edition, 1996)
Joyce and Popular Culture, edited by R. B. Kershner (1996)
Joyce and the Jews: Culture and Texts, by Ira B. Nadel (paperback edition, 1996)
Narrative Design in Finnegans Wake: *The Wake Lock Picked*, by Harry Burrell (1996)
Gender in Joyce, edited by Jolanta W. Wawrzycka and Marlena G. Corcoran (1997)
Latin and Roman Culture in Joyce, by R. J. Schork (1997)
Reading Joyce Politically, by Trevor L. Williams (1997)
Advertising and Commodity Culture in Joyce, by Garry Leonard (1998)
Greek and Hellenic Culture in Joyce, by R. J. Schork (1998)
Joyce, Joyceans, and the Rhetoric of Citation, by Eloise Knowlton (1998)
Joyce's Music and Noise: Theme and Variation in His Writings, by Jack W. Weaver (1998)
Reading Derrida Reading Joyce, by Alan Roughley (1999)
Joyce through the Ages: A Nonlinear View, edited by Michael Patrick Gillespie (1999)
Chaos Theory and James Joyce's Everyman, by Peter Francis Mackey (1999)
Joyce's Comic Portrait, by Roy Gottfried (2000)
Joyce and Hagiography: Saints Above!, by R. J. Schork (2000)
Voices and Values in Joyce's Ulysses, by Weldon Thornton (2000)
The Dublin Helix: The Life of Language in Joyce's Ulysses, by Sebastian D. G. Knowles (2001)
Joyce Beyond Marx: History and Desire in Ulysses *and* Finnegans Wake, by Patrick McGee (2001)
Joyce's Metamorphosis, by Stanley Sultan (2001)
Joycean Temporalities: Debts, Promises, and Countersignatures, by Tony Thwaites (2001)
Joyce and the Victorians, by Tracey Teets Schwarze (2002)
Joyce's Ulysses *as National Epic: Epic Mimesis and the Political History of the Nation State*, by Andras Ungar (2002)
James Joyce's "Fraudstuff," by Kimberly J. Devlin (2002)
Rite of Passage in the Narratives of Dante and Joyce, by Jennifer Margaret Fraser (2002)
Joyce and the Scene of Modernity, by David Spurr (2002)
Joyce and the Early Freudians: A Synchronic Dialogue of Texts, by Jean Kimball (2003)
Twenty-first Joyce, edited by Ellen Carol Jones and Morris Beja (2004)
Joyce on the Threshold, edited by Anne Fogarty and Timothy Martin (2005)
Wake Rites: The Ancient Irish Rituals of Finnegans Wake, by George Cinclair Gibson (2005)
Ulysses *in Critical Perspective*, edited by Michael Patrick Gillespie and A. Nicholas Fargnoli (2006)
Joyce and the Narrative Structure of Incest, by Jen Shelton (2006)
Joyce, Ireland, Britain, edited by Andrew Gibson and Len Platt (2006)
Joyce in Trieste: An Album of Risky Readings, edited by Sebastian D. G. Knowles, Geert Lernout, and John McCourt (2007)

Joyce's Rare View: The Nature of Things in Finnegans Wake, by Richard Beckman (2007)
Joyce's Misbelief, by Roy Gottfried (2007)
James Joyce's Painful Case, by Cóilín Owens (2008)
Cannibal Joyce, by Thomas Jackson Rice (2008)
Manuscript Genetics, Joyce's Know-How, Beckett's Nohow, by Dirk Van Hulle (2008)
Catholic Nostalgia in Joyce and Company, by Mary Lowe-Evans (2008)
A Guide through Finnegans Wake, by Edmund Lloyd Epstein (2009)
Bloomsday 100: Essays on Ulysses, edited by Morris Beja and Anne Fogarty (2009)
Joyce, Medicine, and Modernity, by Vike Martina Plock (2010)
Who's Afraid of James Joyce?, by Karen R. Lawrence (2010; first paperback edition, 2012)
Ulysses *in Focus: Genetic, Textual, and Personal Views*, by Michael Groden (2010; first paperback edition, 2012)
Foundational Essays in James Joyce Studies, edited by Michael Patrick Gillespie (2011)
Empire and Pilgrimage in Conrad and Joyce, by Agata Szczeszak-Brewer (2011)
The Poetry of James Joyce Reconsidered, edited by Marc C. Conner (2012)
The German Joyce, by Robert K. Weninger (2012)
Joyce and Militarism, by Greg Winston (2012)
Renascent Joyce, edited by Daniel Ferrer, Sam Slote, and André Topia (2013)
Before Daybreak: "After the Race" and the Origins of Joyce's Art, by Cóilín Owens (2013)

www.ingramcontent.com/pod-product-compliance
Lightning Source LLC
Chambersburg PA
CBHW022110150426
43195CB00008B/349